A Full Life

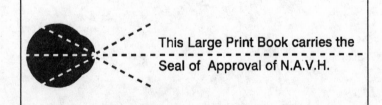

This Large Print Book carries the
Seal of Approval of N.A.V.H.

A FULL LIFE

REFLECTIONS AT NINETY

JIMMY CARTER

THORNDIKE PRESS
A part of Gale, Cengage Learning

GALE
CENGAGE Learning

Farmington Hills, Mich • San Francisco • New York • Waterville, Maine
Meriden, Conn • Mason, Ohio • Chicago

Thorndike Press, a part of Gale, Cengage Learning.

ALL RIGHTS RESERVED
Thorndike Press® Large Print Popular and Narrative Nonfiction.
The text of this Large Print edition is unabridged.
Other aspects of the book may vary from the original edition.
Set in 16 pt. Plantin.

LIBRARY OF CONGRESS CATALOGING-IN-PUBLICATION DATA

Carter, Jimmy, 1924-
    A full life : reflections at ninety / by Jimmy Carter. — Large print edition.
      pages cm — (Thorndike press large print popular and narrative nonfiction)
    ISBN 978-1-4104-8202-0 (hardcover) — ISBN 1-4104-8202-2 (hardcover)
    1. Carter, Jimmy, 1924- 2. Presidents—United States—Biography. 3. United States—Politics and government—1977-1981. I. Title.
E873.A3 2015b
973.926092—dc23
[B]   2015019544

Published in 2015 by arrangement with Simon & Schuster, Inc.

Printed in the United States of America
1 2 3 4 5 6 7 19 18 17 16 15

To Rosalynn, who has
kept my life full of love

CONTENTS

INTRODUCTION

Reaching my ninetieth birthday is a good time to look back on moments that changed my life and reflect on some of the memories that are especially important to me. Some of these events affected me profoundly or taught me lessons, large and small. Others are amusing, and some make me contemplate who I was at that time. There are some that I enjoyed and savor, and others that I wish had never happened or that I could change.

I spent four of my ninety years in the White House, and they were, of course, the pinnacle of my political life. Those years, though, do not dominate my chain of memories, and there was never an orderly or planned path to get there during my early life. At each step in my career, I made somewhat peremptory decisions about the next one.

I had no idea of returning home during

the eleven years when I served in the navy, or of running for political office while I was farming and expanding my business. I ran for Congress and then shifted to governor to fill a competitive urge, and then really enjoyed making decisions as a top government executive. I saw the presidency as a way to accomplish specific goals that I considered important, decided four years in advance to be elected, and my entire family joined in the all-out campaign.

With hard work and favorable circumstances, I was chosen, and I relished the challenges and opportunities to make important decisions as president. I always tried to address the issues forthrightly. I wanted another term, but seemed to be plagued with a series of misfortunes when the time for reelection came. I look back on those four years with peace and satisfaction, knowing that I did my best and had some notable accomplishments. Vice President Mondale summarized our administration by saying, "We told the truth, we obeyed the law, we kept the peace." I would add, "We championed human rights."

Teaching, writing, and helping The Carter Center evolve during more recent times seem to constitute the high points in my life. I don't think I have changed much in this entire process, but I have learned some helpful lessons, and they are the primary subject of this book.

I have written a number of books about some of my experiences, including my boyhood on a farm, my religious beliefs, my outdoor adventures, our time in the White House, and major projects of The Carter Center during the past thirty-four years. I still receive between fifteen hundred and three thousand letters each month, varying according to how controversial my latest statements or writings have been, but there are always a number of them from readers of these earlier books who wish to share their similar experiences with me. There is a list of these books on page iii of the original Simon & Schuster edition for readers who desire to pursue any of these subjects more deeply. I have also commented in op-eds and published speeches on a number of important political issues, especially in an attempt to bring peace in the Middle East and to promote human rights. Many of them are posted on the website www.carter center.org.

Some of the more personal and intimate events of my life are covered here for the first time, including my years on battleships and submarines, my seventeen years as a farmer involved in local community affairs, my reasons for entering politics and eventually running for president, the campaigns themselves, some of the unpublicized things that happened to me or my family during our years in the White House, special people, my relationships with other presidents, and how Rosalynn and I have spent our more private times since the Washington years.

CHAPTER ONE:
ARCHERY AND THE RACE ISSUE

MY FAMILY

My life has been shaped inevitably by the experiences and decisions of my forefathers, and I have learned a lot about my family history. My mother was Bessie Lillian Gordy, and I knew all her intimate relatives and many of her distant cousins. We would sometimes drive after church services to Richland, her hometown, to have dinner with her close-knit family, where the table conversation often led to an explosion of emotions and angry departures. My father was James Earl Carter, and I never knew even his close cousins who lived in the county seat just nine miles from our home in Plains. It seemed that the Carters were not interested in each other.

During my first year as president, leaders of the Church of Jesus Christ of Latter-day Saints came to the White House and presented me with a genealogical study of my Carter family. The information went back thirteen generations, to the early 1600s, and included birth, death, and marriage records, land deeds, and data from some of the early courthouse proceedings that involved legal disputes. I put it all in a big box and sent it to our home in Plains. After leaving the White House I bought my first computer and entered the Mormon research data when I was sent the first edition of a software program called Family Tree Maker. My wife Rosalynn's family always had three reunions each year (there would have been four if two Smiths hadn't married each other), so in 1998 I decided to have a reunion of the direct descendants of my great-great-grandfather Wiley Carter, on what would have been his two hundredth birthday. More than 950 people came, and I corrected mistakes in my family records and brought them up to date. More recently, I gave the data to our son Jeffrey, and he has published a much more definitive study, *Ancestors of Jimmy and Rosalynn Carter,* focusing on our time in America.

These were rough pioneer days as immigrants struggled for existence or preeminence, and even our more recent family history was, to a surprising degree, shaped by violence. Wiley Carter (1798–

1864) was deputized in a sheriff's posse in Wilkes County when he shot and killed a man named Usry. There was a routine one-day trial, and the sheriff testified, "Usry was evidently preparing to shoot Carter. The two men were cursing each other and both raised their guns about the same time and fired. Usry was killed." Wiley was found not guilty of murder because the victim was armed and threatening. However, it was known that there had been a long history of ill will between the two men, and after the trial a lot of resentment was stirred up in the community by Usry's family and friends. After Wiley's wife, Ann, delivered her eleventh child and died, Wiley remarried and moved to a farm about ten miles north of where the town of Plains is located. He had traded for the land with an original owner, who won it in a lottery that was held in 1833, after Indians had been forced to leave West Georgia in the late 1820s. Wiley's second wife had another son, who moved to Texas.

Wiley's fourth son, Littleberry Walker Carter (1829–1873), was my great-grandfather. He served with two of his brothers as artillerymen in the Confederate army. They fought in twenty-one battles and finally left the service in Florida, a month after Lee surrendered at Appomattox. He then bought and operated a farm just west of Americus that later became Souther Field (now Jimmy Carter Regional Airport), where Charles Lindbergh made his first solo flight. He was killed "in an argument over the proceeds of a flying jenny [merry-go-round]" in 1873, as recorded in the county newspaper.

Known as Billy, his son and my grandfather William Archibald Carter (1858–1903) moved in 1888 about fifty miles south to a rural community known as Rowena, where he was a farmer, operated two sawmills and a winery, and owned a cotton gin. He was small but tough. One time when he was harvesting sugarcane, his machete was deflected into his thigh, inflicting a deep gash. Billy used his belt to stop the flow of blood, sent to the house for a needle and thread, sewed up the wound, and resumed work. He was shot and killed in a fight with a man named Will Taliaferro, in an altercation over a desk stolen by Taliaferro from Billy's cotton gin. After his property was sold, Billy's family moved back to Plains and purchased a farm in nearby Webster County in 1904, which my father, Earl Carter, became responsible for operating as a teenager. I can only imagine the

16

multiple skills needed to perform all the duties of my ancestors, and it may be that my inclination to pursue new ideas and to design and create things in my woodshop is inherited from them.

My mother, Lillian Gordy, left her job as a postal clerk in Richland and moved eighteen miles to Plains (population about five hundred) in 1920 to become a registered nurse. She married Earl when she finished her training, in 1923. I was born in October 1924, and our family lived in a house on South Bond Street with Edgar and Allie Smith as next-door neighbors. Edgar was the only automobile mechanic in the community, and directly across the street from his shop my father owned and operated a small general store after completing military service as a first lieutenant in World War I. The Smiths' daughter Rosalynn was born in August 1927, and my mother later told me that I was taken to the house next door and peeked into the cradle to see the newest baby on the street. Our families were very close, and Rosalynn's younger sister was named for Mama, who nursed Rosalynn's father during his terminal illness with leukemia. Daddy became a full-time farmer in 1928, when I was four years old. I was raised on a farm he bought about two and a half miles west of Plains in the rural community known as Archery.

ARCHERY

My boyhood home in Archery was a Sears, Roebuck house that had been built six years before our family occupied it. At that time the Sears catalogue offered homes of several sizes, with three basic options: (1) all the components of a complete house and the tools needed to construct it, loaded into a single railroad boxcar with plans and instructions; (2) everything needed for a house except the lumber; and (3) just the plans and instructions, practically free but requiring doors, windows, hardware, and other parts that were sold by Sears. We learned later that our home was one of the second options, since genetic testing showed that its wooden frame and siding had come from trees harvested on the farm.

There was no running water, electricity, or insulation, and the only heat sources besides the kitchen stove were some open fireplaces, all fueled by wood and used just when badly needed. We relieved ourselves in "slop jars" during the night and emptied them in an outdoor toilet when it was daylight. It was the only privy on the farm; other families just used the bushes for

My boyhood home in Archery was a Sears, Roebuck house that had been built six years before our family occupied it in 1928. There were about two hundred people who lived in the unincorporated community of Archery.

concealment. We drew water from a well in the backyard until 1935, when Daddy had a windmill installed and ran a pipe from its tank into our kitchen and bathroom. He made a shower bath by punching holes in the bottom of a galvanized bucket hanging over a concrete floor, and the used water ran through a pipe onto the ground outside. It was especially cold in winter, but more convenient than a galvanized bathtub.

19

Electricity reached some farms near us in 1939, and after a year or so Daddy prevailed on the local cooperative to extend the lines to our home.

My room was on the northeast corner, far from any stove or fireplace, so my most vivid and unpleasant memories are of cold weather. I remember shivering at night even under blankets, and my bare toes curling up when I stepped out of bed onto the cold floor and made a dash for my parents' room and the warmth of some still-glowing embers in their fireplace. Strangely, I don't really recall the discomfort of the hot summer days of South Georgia. This house and the outbuildings are now owned by the National Park Service, and the historic site is preserved as it was in 1937.

Our family meals when Mama was on nursing duty were prepared by one of the African-American women who lived on the farm, and my two sisters related quite intimately to them. Neither my sisters nor my mother ever did field work. When not in school, I spent every spare moment during workdays around the barn area and in the fields — with my father whenever possible. I was especially close to Jack and Rachel Clark, who lived in the house nearest ours. Jack was in charge of all the livestock, the

I was especially close to Jack and Rachel Clark, who lived in the house nearest ours. Except for my parents, Rachel Clark was the person closest to me.

equipment, and operation of the barn and its environs. He rang the big farm bell every morning at an hour before daylight and was responsible for milking the cows. Jack worked closely with Daddy in assigning different workers to their tasks.

Daddy had multiple talents, and he devoted many of them to becoming as self-sufficient as possible on the farm. He was reluctant to pay anyone else to do jobs that he could learn to do himself, so he became a competent forester, farmer, herdsman, blacksmith, carpenter, and shoemaker. I guess he was still a merchant at heart, and he refined as many of our raw products into retail items as possible. I had to leave home for school sometimes before daybreak, but in the afternoons I helped Jack milk eight cows. We always had plenty of sweet milk, buttermilk, cream, and butter in our house. Some of the excess milk was made into chocolate and vanilla drinks, put in eight-ounce bottles with waxed cardboard tops, and placed in iceboxes in grocery stores and filling stations within a five-mile circle around Plains. Daddy picked up the unsold drinks every Monday and we fed them to our hogs. Other milk was run through a separator on our back porch, and the pure cream was marketed through the Suwanee store in town. We called the remaining skim milk "blue john" and fed it to the hogs. (Now, that's all we drink.) Wool sheared from our sheep was swapped for blankets that we sold in our farm commissary, and we picked the down from the breasts of about fifty geese and exchanged it for pillows and comforters. The geese also helped by eating worms and other insects from our cotton plants. Each year we converted about twenty-five acres of sugarcane into syrup that Daddy marketed with a "Plains Maid" label, and sometimes he did the same thing with catsup made from homegrown tomatoes. We slaughtered about twenty hogs a few times each year on the coldest days, and Daddy made sausage and rubbed the hams, shoulders, and side meat with preservative spices, then cured the meat in the smokehouse behind our home before selling it in our store.

He also believed that everything and everyone on the farm should somehow "earn its keep," even including my Shetland pony.

Always a Reckoning

There always seemed to be need
for reckoning in early days.
What came in equaled what went out
like oscillating ocean waves.
On the farm, our wages matched
the work we did in woods and fields,
how many acres plowed and hoed,
how much syrup was distilled,
how many pounds of cotton picked,
how much cordwood cut and stacked.
All things had to balance out.
I had a pony then that lacked
a way to work and pay her way,
except that every year or two
Lady had a colt we sold,

but still for less than what was due
to buy the fodder, hay, and corn
she ate at times she couldn't be
on pasture. Neither feed nor colts
meant all that much that I could see,
but still there was a thing about
a creature staying on our place
that none of us could eat or plow,
did not give eggs, or even chase
a fox or rabbit, that was sure
to rile my father. We all knew
that Lady's giving me a ride
paid some on her debt, in lieu
of other ways — but there would be
sometimes I didn't get around
to riding in my off-work hours.
And I was sure, when Daddy frowned
at some mistake I might've made, he
would be asking when he could,
"How long since you rode Lady?"

There were about two hundred people
who lived in the unincorporated community
of Archery, and except for the Seaboard
Airline Railroad section foreman, Mr.
Ernest Watson, we were the only white family. The boys with whom I worked or played
were African-American, and we learned how
to make our own toys. Our favorite was a
thick steel hoop from a wooden keg, ten to

twelve inches in diameter. We rolled our hoops for miles, even hours at a time, propelling them with a strong, stiff wire that had a loop on one end to provide a hand-hold and a V-shaped notch on the other to fit behind the hoop. We would have felt undressed without our rubber-banded flips, or slingshots, and a supply of small round rocks in our pockets for ammunition. Other projectiles were also important to us, and they could have been deadly weapons. One of the easiest to make and most enjoyable was a kind of dart made from a large corncob, four or five inches long, with a needle-sharpened nail inserted into the pith of one end and two chicken feathers in the other that were set at precise angles to give the thrown weapon the correct amount of spin before it embedded in a tree or a target on the side of a building.

We used the same sharpened points on dog-fennel spears, and were surprised at how far we could throw them with the help of spear throwers called "atlatls," which we devised after reading about them in *Boys' Life* magazine or one of our Indian books. We haunted Daddy's shop for days as we improved on our basic design of rubber guns. After cutting out shapes of long-barreled pistols, we mounted spring clothespins, wrapped them with rubber bands to increase their grip, and then stretched a cross section of inner tube strips around the end of each barrel. A squeeze on the clothespin released the loop of inner tube as a projectile. We ultimately devised repeaters that would shoot as many as a dozen rubber bands. We would fight wars until everyone on one side or the other had been "killed" by being hit. We also made popgun barrels by removing the pith from the centers of American elder limbs and used green chinaberries as projectiles. We learned to make kites and competed in designing and flying the smallest one.

When not working, my black playmates and I spent as much time as possible in the woods hunting and fishing, or just exploring. The repair shop and two filling stations in town were good places to search for wheels of different sizes that were being discarded. We used them with homemade wooden bodies to devise wagons and two-wheeled carts. Most of these were pulled or pushed by us, but we made one with two shafts that we hitched to our largest billy goat.

Daddy soon evolved a way for me to create an attractive product and take it to market. With no tractors on the farm and no need for fossil fuels except kerosene for lamps and lanterns, we planted corn as the primary source of fuel and energy, and produced cotton and peanuts as cash crops. It happened that peanuts began to ripen soon after school days ended each summer, and beginning when I was five years old I would go out into the nearby fields each afternoon and pull up the plants, shake the dirt from around the nuts, and haul a load to our yard in a little wagon. There I picked about ten pounds of the more mature peanuts off the vines, washed them thoroughly, and put them in a large pot of salty water to soak overnight. Early in the morning I boiled them for a half hour or so, tasting them for proper saltiness, and then divided them into about twenty paper bags of a half pound each. For Saturdays, when Plains was filled with shoppers from the surrounding farms, I prepared twice as many.

After breakfast, I would walk down the railroad tracks to town, a distance of about two miles, with my boiled peanuts in a wicker basket. I stayed in Plains until all the peanuts were sold, and usually this was done before dinnertime. At five cents a bag, my earnings were a dollar a day, as much as a grown and skilled laborer earned in the fields. I had about ten dependable customers, and would go from store to store up and down our only street to find shoppers, traveling salesmen, and other transients to buy the additional peanuts. My only expenses were the bags and the salt. I kept a careful notebook record of my sales and deposited earnings in my uncle Alton Carter's mercantile store, which served as the town's bank.

A few years later, when cotton reached its lowest price in history (five cents a pound), Daddy suggested that I use my savings to buy five bales, of five hundred pounds each. These were kept in one of our storehouses on the farm, and I sold them for eighteen cents a pound when the market recovered. With this income I bought five houses from the deceased undertaker's estate and rented two for $2.00 each, two for $5.00, and one for $2.50, for a total of $16.50 per month. Whether I worked or not, my houses were earning fifty-five cents a day! Each month I rode my bicycle from house to house until I finally cornered every renter. They always seemed to be elusive unless a windowpane was missing, the roof leaked, a door didn't close properly, or one of the steps was broken. These were all repairs that I could do myself. After I left home for college, my father struggled to collect the rent for a few months before deciding it was best to sell the houses.

Daddy was a strict disciplinarian, but he resorted to physical punishment only rarely. I still remember vividly the five times that he whipped me, with either his belt or a switch from a wild peach tree in the yard. In every case, the process was like an orderly trial, with a full understanding between him and me about what I had done wrong, his explanation of the reason for the penalty, and my promise not to repeat my misbehavior. If I had any feelings of resentment, they were soon put aside. I never considered disobeying an order or even a request from Daddy. I loved and admired him, and one of my preeminent goals in life was to earn his approbation. I learned to expect his criticisms, always constructive, but his accolades were rare.

My most memorable criticism from my father occurred when I was about ten years old. While trying to kill one of our white leghorn broilers for supper, I struck down, and a sharp stem of stiff weed stuck between the bones of my right wrist. Dr. Bowman Wise attempted unsuccessfully to probe for it, and my wrist began to swell during the next week and was increasingly painful when I bent it. One day after a noonday break, I was lying across a stool reading a book, when Daddy came through the room and I heard him say to Mama, "I reckon that boy's enjoying his books while the rest of us go to the field." I got up in a few minutes, went into the backyard, and used my belt to tie the palm of my hand, fingers up, tightly onto a fence post. Then I raised my arm, bending my wrist more and more until the pus-enclosed piece of stick popped out of the sore. Mama wrapped it in a bandage, and I ran to the field to be with my daddy.

Much later, I wrote a poem that expressed my feelings:

I Wanted to Share My Father's World

This is a pain I mostly hide,
but ties of blood, or seed, endure,
and even now I feel inside
the hunger for his outstretched hand,
a man's embrace to take me in,
the need for just a word of praise.
I despised the discipline
he used to shape what I should be,
not owning up that he might feel
his own pain when he punished me.
I didn't show my need to him,
since his response to an appeal
would not have meant as much to me,
or been as real.

30

From those rare times when we did cross
the bridge between us, the pure joy
survives. I never put aside
the past resentments of the boy
until, with my own sons, I shared
his final hours, and came to see
what he'd become, or always was —
the father who will never cease to be
alive in me.

As a farm boy and later as an engineer, warehouseman, and farmer, I have had normal duties that required work with my hands, but even in my earlier days I enjoyed those experiences enough to extend them into a voluntary stage, as a hobby. I don't know that any of my forefathers shared my fascination with building furniture or painting pictures, but they had to become competent in performing the tasks required in clearing land, building and furnishing homes, and providing and maintaining vehicles and tools required in earning a living.

I was the only boy in the family until my brother, Billy, came when I was twelve years old, so my father concentrated a lot of his attention on me. Whenever possible I followed him around, and wanted to emulate everything he did. This created a wonderful

CARTER

Daddy had multiple talents, and he devoted many of them to becoming as self-sufficient as possible on the farm. He was reluctant to pay anyone else to do jobs that he could learn to do himself, so he became a competent forester, farmer, herdsman, blacksmith, carpenter, and shoemaker.

partnership for letting me learn, as a kind of apprentice, some of the skills of a craftsman. One of my earliest memories was hurrying behind Daddy on the path from our house to the blacksmith shop. The small building is still there, and I recall vividly that Daddy would sometimes let me turn the handle on the forge blower as the coals became increasingly hot and the inserted iron changed color slowly from cherry red toward white until it met Daddy's expectations and could be moved to the adjacent anvil for shaping. This was my first real job, when I was about five years old. He would explain to me patiently the rudiments of the entire process. Later, when able, I would hold the item on the anvil with the tongs while he beat on it with a sledgehammer before dousing it in water or oil to obtain the correct hardness and toughness. When I became big enough, I performed entire blacksmithing tasks by myself.

I always assumed that Daddy had known the rudiments of carpentering from his earlier days and, helped by Jack Clark, learned to perform the routine tasks of a blacksmith. This included shaping and sharpening steel plow points, rejoining pieces of broken equipment, shoeing horses and mules, and even installing steel rims on the wooden wheels of our wagons and buggies. This last task required expanding the entire rim with heat, then quickly putting it in place and letting it shrink into a tight fit as it cooled. The anvil, bolted to a heavy base of a hickory stump, was in the center of the shop, and a waist-high workbench almost completely surrounded the dirt floor. On the bench and hanging on the walls were the woodworking tools — saws, hammers, squares, braces and bits, levels, pry bars, tapes, and folding rules. We kept our hand tools just inside the door, and there was a large drill press standing against the wall that was used for boring either wood or steel. Only much later, when we received electricity on our farm, did Daddy install a horizontal lathe. A few feet from the shop was a large grinding wheel mounted in front of something like a tractor seat, so that pushing the pedals spun the grinder toward the operator. The corrosive wheel was immersed in part of an old rubber tire filled with water to keep it cool. This was the device that was most frequently in use, as anyone on the place could bring axes, hoes, knives, and other cutting tools to be honed. The plow points were made of much thicker metal and were sharpened in the forge and on the anvil. We kept pieces of scrap iron outside, around the shop.

A lot of our work on the farm was with wood, and the small jobs could be handled inside the shop, like making handles for hammers, axes, hoes, shovels, and rakes, and repairing wagon tongues, singletrees, and wooden parts of the plows we used for preparing land and cultivation. We also made our own wheelbarrows. Larger wood projects were supported on two or three sawhorses outside, or preferably at the building site. There was always a waiting list for building new hog farrowing pens or storage sheds for cotton seed, fertilizer, and equipment, or repairing fences and the homes or other buildings on the farm. This kind of work was done on days when fields were too wet to work, in the dormant winter months, or during "lay-by" time (after the crops were too big to plow and before harvest).

The shop was a fascinating place, where our family's shoes were also repaired. I remember an array of metal shoe lasts of different sizes, shaped to match the feet of Daddy, Mama, my two sisters, and me. We had a supply of leather of different thicknesses that could be cut to replace worn-out soles with little wooden pegs, nails, and glue or sometimes to repair the upper body of the shoe using stitches of strong twine. As I grew older and stronger, I learned to weld and cut metal with a torch and do most of the ironworking and cobbler chores, and was proud of my grown-up responsibilities, but it was the woodworking tools that really appealed to me. I relished the repair of houses, barns, and storage places, and was eager to help when new farrowing pens were built for our sows and pigs.

Daddy had a pickup truck, which I learned

A lot of our work on the farm was with wood, and the small jobs could be handled inside the shop. It was a fascinating place, where our family's shoes were also repaired.

to drive as soon as I could see over the dashboard, and was sometimes trusted to haul seed or fertilizer to the fields. I was permitted to drive it to proms and church parties in Plains when I was twelve years old. A friend and I rescued a wrecked and abandoned Model T Ford, and we removed the entire body and affixed a wooden seat to the main frame. The automobile repairman (Rosalynn's father) in Plains helped us get the engine running, and we used our stripped-down vehicle for off-the-road excursions.

My primary duties on the farm were all related to work in the field. When chopping cotton or hoeing weeds, all of us moved at a common pace up and down the rows, and adults received the same wages, a dollar a day. My normal pay as a small boy was twenty-five cents, which doubled when I was strong enough to carry two-gallon buckets of water from a nearby spring to the "hands" in the field. At harvesttime there was something of a competition, as workers were paid on the basis of measured achievement: how many pounds of cotton were picked from the stalk or how many peanuts were stacked on poles after being pulled from the ground and the dirt shaken off. Regardless of age, all workers could move at their own pace. There was an inevitable daily competition, in which Rachel Clark always excelled.

Plowing mules was different. Only a few of the more dependable men were trusted to handle the draft animals and equipment, even including the rudimentary breaking of land at the beginning of each season. The ultimate achievement was in cultivating the precious crops after they began to grow. There was a lot of skill and strength involved in the precise control of plow blades as they skimmed by the tender plants, loosening the soil for increased growth and, more important, controlling the weeds and grass that could choke out the crop and prevent its bearing fruit. There was a proper way to train and control the draft animals so they could do their job and remain in good physical and mental condition. In the often stifling heat, it was easy for them to become overworked, which could cause permanent loss of vigor or even a quick death. Mules usually had the good sense to refuse to walk as they approached this danger point of heat exhaustion, but horses, at least in this case, had much less intelligence about self-protection.

As I grew up, one of my natural ambitions was to escape from the company of other children and women in just hoeing, picking cotton, and shaking peanuts and to graduate to the exalted status of a skilled plowman who could cultivate a crop. I have to admit that, before leaving the farm for college and the navy at the age of sixteen, I never fully reached this goal — as judged by my father. My first effort at plowing was in preparing the land in our large garden plot, between our house and the workshop. This was in the wintertime, using one very docile mule named Emma, and under the supervision of Jack Clark. It was difficult to guide Emma properly, with the reins and my weak verbal orders, and the small turning plow made an erratic path through the soil — both horizontally and vertically. At least I couldn't do any real damage, and I learned with the mistakes.

By the time I was twelve years old I was permitted to break land in the field, even using two mules with the deeper turning plows. This was one of the most boring and challenging duties that I had as a boy, but to me it was a great achievement. In a field of several acres, the first furrow — often begun before sunrise — was around the often odd-shaped periphery of the field, as close to the surrounding forests, fences, or hedgerows as possible. Clinging to the unpredictably plunging handles of the plow and struggling to guide the mules with verbal commands and the rope lines to the bridle bits was a constant challenge for my small frame and weak voice. The gait of the mules was more suited to the long steps of an adult, and sometimes I had to trot to stay up with the plow. Loud cries of "gee" and "haw" were of some help as verbal directions for my leaders to move to the right or left.

Encompassing several acres, each long circumference would advance a little less than a foot toward the center of the field. At first it would seem that this goal would never be reached, but, although slow, progress was steady and gratifying. My mind was relatively unfocused, so I was often free for idle thoughts. A well-sharpened and balanced steel blade cutting through the soil seemed like a perfect instrument. Both physically and psychologically, I had to be in tune with the mules, accommodating their idiosyncrasies and hoping that I could prevail in most of the inevitable disagreements. There had to be a proper environment for success, involving the current weather and the effects of previous rainfall and sunshine on the soil. The comfort level was very high when all the factors were compatible. With my limited school mathematics, I would sometimes try to compute how many miles I would have to walk before completing this task and moving on to the next chore assigned by my father. Later, I would check my estimate by noting the time required and assuming that the mules and I walked an average of two miles per hour, adjusted for turning corners and brief rest periods. A day's plowing was between twenty-two and twenty-five miles. Invariably, the drudgery was overcome by looking back at the end of a day and seeing how much cropland had been prepared for planting. I enjoyed a sense of accomplishment and self-satisfaction, knowing that I had done all that was humanly possible, even as a boy, and had left behind me the visible proof of my work.

I still have similar emotions while working in my woodshop. Periods of drudgery that come with the repetitive use of chisel, drawknife, spokeshave, plane, rasp, scraper, sandpaper, or paintbrush fade into relative insignificance when I can examine the final result of my labor. The excitement of an original design, the meticulous detail of precise measurements, accommodation of the characteristics of the chosen wood, the heft and beauty of the hand tools — some of them ancient in design — are all positive aspects of crafting a piece of furniture. I like to see what I have conceived, what I have made. The pleasure has not faded as the years have passed; in fact, my diminishing physical strength has eliminated some of the formerly competing hobbies and made woodworking and painting even more precious to me.

All of us school classmates who were farm boys became members of the Future Farmers of America when we reached the eighth grade, and one of our responsibilities was to improve the skills we had needed and learned on the farm. For the finer aspects of woodworking, such as making furniture, the school shop was much more spacious and better equipped than the one we had at home, with instruction books, a small planing mill, a wood lathe, and glue. We had tests on identifying the various trees in our local forests and on the characteristics of their wood. We also learned how to cruise timber to estimate the value of the trees in a particular tract of land. In school I learned how to make relatively simple chairs, tables, and cabinets. My most challenging project, on which I received my final grade, was a scale model of the White House!

Of more practical use was the ability to

construct barns, small homes, sheds, and storage bins of different sizes. We learned how to make plans and cost estimates, and we competed with other FFA boys at the local, congressional district, and state levels with quite complex carpentering tasks. One that I remember was cutting a rafter from a two-by-six or two-by-eight board that would fit on the slanted dormer portion of a cottage roof. There was an intimate and almost constant interrelationship between what we were learning in school and what we were doing on the farm — and between my father and my ag teacher. When I had a project of raising a young calf to a grown steer, Daddy let me design and build, with as little help as possible, a shed on the back of our smokehouse. This included, of course, the feeding trough, a swinging door, and a wooden window.

THE ISSUE OF RACE

As a child, I never thought about social or legal distinctions between our white family and the African-American families that surrounded us in Archery. I knew, of course, that our house was larger than theirs, that my father gave the orders on the farm, and that we had an automobile or pickup truck while our neighbors walked or rode in a wagon or on a mule. I assumed that these advantages accrued to us because Daddy worked harder and was fortunate in owning the land on which we lived. I took for granted that having separate schools and churches was just a matter of custom, and when I went to St. Mark AME Church in Archery I could see spirit, sincerity, and fervor in their worship services that we lacked at our church in Plains. I didn't realize that only white people could vote in an election or serve on a jury, and in those days I never heard anyone comment about these legal differences.

My concept of racial discrimination was confused by the dominating presence in our rural community of a distinguished black man, who was the richest and most sophisticated person I knew. Bishop William Decker Johnson owned and operated what was considered to be an excellent school for black children across the railroad track from St. Mark AME Church, and I remember that at Christmastime he always had a nice gift for every child who attended the church or school. His charge was all the African Methodist Episcopal churches in five Northern states, and there was a lead article in our county newspaper whenever he came home to spend a few days in Archery.

Bishop Johnson always rode in the backseat of a large black Cadillac or Packard, with his chauffeur driving, and there was a well-known photograph of him in Paris, with the Eiffel Tower in the background. For me and many others he was the epitome of prestige and success.

It was not the custom for a black person to come to the front door of a white family's home, and when Bishop Johnson wanted to speak with my father he conformed to the mores of the time without acknowledging any difference in status. His chauffeur would come to our house and determine that Daddy was there, then go back and bring the bishop to the front yard. He would blow the horn, and my father would go outside to talk to his guest, either through the car window or with both standing under a large magnolia tree. My mother paid little attention to these distinctions, and she was impervious to criticism because of her independent temperament; also, as a registered nurse, she was a member of the exalted medical community. The bishop's son, Alvan, was a student at Harvard University and Mama's friend. When Alvan returned home on vacation he would come to our front door and knock, and my mother would welcome him for a conversation in our living room or on the front porch. If Daddy was at home at the time, he would quietly leave the house and go to the barn or workshop until Alvan left. I never knew my parents to discuss the issue, at least within earshot of us children.

When I was six years old I went to Plains High School in town, where about 250 white students attended grades one through eleven. Our school, although small, won honors as one of the best in the state because of our outstanding superintendent, Miss Julia Coleman. She encouraged all of us to write themes, learn about classical music and art, read a long list of books, debate, and act in stage plays. Every day began with a half hour of chapel services, where we heard announcements, sang hymns, recited Holy Scripture, and listened to a brief religious homily. A small bus picked me and later my two sisters up in front of our house and took us to and from school. It had been wrecked in its earlier life, and the narrow body sat at a distinct angle from the main frame. Some of the students derided it as the "cracker box," which it resembled, but we were proud of the free ride each day. I made new friendships with my white classmates, of course, but I still felt more at home in Archery with my black friends, with whom I spent my late afternoons and school vacation times. There were never any rankings among us except those derived from who caught the biggest fish, picked the most cotton, had performed better in the last baseball game, or prevailed in a wrestling match or footrace.

I recall vividly a seemingly minor incident that has profoundly affected the rest of my life. When I was about fourteen years old, I had been working with two friends in a field north of our house and barn. As we approached what we called the "pasture gate," they stepped back to let me go through the opening ahead of them. I was surprised, and immediately thought they must be playing a trick on me, with perhaps a trip wire near the ground on which I would stumble. It was at about this same time that I had begun to play varsity basketball, attend weekend parties in Plains, and become interested in girlfriends. I never mentioned this to anyone at the time, but as the years passed I surmised that this first indication of the unearned deference of my black playmates toward me was the result of a cautionary word from their parents that the time had come to conform to the racial distinctions that were strictly observed among adults.

Much later, I wrote a poem after visiting Archery:

The Pasture Gate

This empty house three miles from town
was where I lived. Here I was back,
and found most homes around were gone.
The folks who stayed here now were black,
like Johnny and A.D., my friends.
As boys we worked in Daddy's fields,
hunted rabbits, squirrels, and quail,
caught and cooked catfish and eels,
searched the land for arrowheads,
tried to fly the smallest kite,
steered barrel hoops with strands of wire,
and wrestled hard. At times we'd fight,
without a thought who might be boss,
who was smartest or the best;
the leader for a few brief hours
was who had won the last contest.
But then — we were fourteen or so —
as we approached the pasture gate,
they went to open it, and then
stood back. This made me hesitate,
sure it must have been a joke,
a trip wire, maybe, they had planned.
I reckon they had to obey
their parents' prompting. Or command.
We only saw it vaguely then,

but we were transformed at that place.
A silent line was drawn between
friend and friend, race and race.

Mama was a full-time nurse during my early childhood, at first employed by Wise Sanitarium for bedside duty with patients, and she was paid a regular salary of four dollars a day for twelve-hour duty. My parents were living in an upstairs apartment early in their marriage in what is now a bed-and-breakfast, and their former room has a plaque on the door reading THE CONCEPTION ROOM. Dr. Sam Wise was the chief surgeon, and my mother had become his assistant. As she approached delivery time, Dr. Sam suggested that they move to a ground-floor apartment so she wouldn't have to climb stairs, and there happened to be an empty room across from the operating room when it was time for her first child. I was the first president born in a hospital.

After we moved to Archery and our daddy's farm income improved, Mama began serving increasingly as a private nurse — almost a doctor — in the homes of her patients. It was relatively easy work if the patient was the father or one of the children, but if the mother was incapacitated the nurse was expected to be responsible for the household affairs, sometimes helped by a female relative. Mama worked almost exclusively among our black neighbors in Archery. The prescribed payment was six dollars for twenty-hour duty, so her normal routine was to come home at ten o'clock at night, take a shower and wash her uniforms, leave us children a note outlining our duties for the next day, and go back on duty at two in the morning. We children would see her only during the intervals when she was changing from one patient to another. Her pay was spasmodic during those Great Depression days, usually in the form of chickens, eggs, pigs, or perhaps work around our house and yard by members of the family. It was a time of hardship and sharing, and she never let ability to pay be a factor in whom she served. Mama would take vacations on occasion, especially during lay-by time in the early summer, when she and Daddy would travel to big league baseball cities, and during November, when she gathered a group of helpers and harvested and sold all the pecans from trees on our land. Nuts on lower limbs could be knocked down with a long bamboo pole, and someone had to climb to higher branches to knock or shake the nuts to the ground. From her income she bought my sisters' clothes and met their other needs.

Except for my parents, Rachel Clark was the person closest to me. Whenever possible I worked side by side with her in the fields and tried to emulate her extraordinary speed and dexterity. She could pick more cotton and shake and stack more peanuts than anyone else in the Archery community. When field work was not available, she would take me fishing with her in the nearby creeks, and during these excursions she gave me gentle lectures about wildlife and my proper relationship with God and with other people. She had the aura of a queen, but was gentle and modest, and always sought ways to be helpful to others. As often as possible, I spent the night in the Clarks' home, where I slept on a pallet on the floor. Rachel moved it close to the fireplace on cold nights.

One of our favorite people during my high school years was a pretty teenage black girl named Annie Mae Hollis. She was very close to my two sisters, and they spent a lot of time together. She stayed on with my family after I left for college, and later had a job with a wealthy couple who owned Chasen's restaurant in Hollywood. Throughout her life, she remained in touch with us, and

My mother, Lillian Gordy, left her job as a postal clerk in Richland and moved eighteen miles to Plains (population about five hundred) in 1920 to become a registered nurse. She married Earl when she finished her training, in 1923. I was born in October 1924. This painting shows her at age seventy, as a Peace Corps Volunteer in India.

she returned to Plains in 1953, when she heard that my father was ill.

Even when I was a child, my mother was known within our community for her refusal to accept any restraints on her treatment of black citizens as equals. My sister Gloria would report that there were critical remarks made by some of the other women, but Mama laughed them off as inconsequential. We children just assumed that registered nurses were different, but I believe it is accurate to say that all four of us siblings tended to share this attitude toward our black neighbors. My father always treated his African-American customers and employees with meticulous fairness and respect, but he believed completely that the two races should be segregated. Like all other men that I knew in and around Plains, he accepted this as a premise ordained by Bible scriptures and confirmed by a century of Jim Crow laws that were reversed a year after his death with the Supreme Court ruling that racially segregated schools were no longer legal.

Daddy was deeply involved in local and state politics, with all public offices being held by Democrats. The Republican Party in Georgia comprised some African-American leaders in Atlanta and a few isolated white cliques in the rural areas, and they dealt only with national politics. They handled federal patronage when there was a Republican president, including postal employees, revenue agents, and U.S. attorneys. The regional center for South Georgia was in Rhine, which still has a population of about four hundred. This was before the Hatch Act, which was designed to remove political activity from federal government employees, was passed in 1939 and required several more years to become effective. When Democrats lost a national election, it was necessary for a rural mail carrier or other government worker to make a trip to Rhine with a roll of bills in his pocket. If financial arrangements were successful, he kept his job. My mother's father, Jim Jack Gordy, was adept at making this accommodation, and worked for most of his adult life as postmaster and revenue agent under both major parties.

My father was a merchant and farmer and was never interested in a government job until he was elected to serve in the state legislature late in life, but he drew a sharp line between two-party national elections and purely Democratic ones for more local offices. He voted for Franklin D. Roosevelt in 1932 but supported Alf Landon, Wendell

Willkie, Thomas Dewey, and Dwight Eisenhower in subsequent elections. Daddy was a libertarian at heart and deeply resented the intrusion of the federal government into his personal affairs. He opposed the New Deal agricultural programs implemented during the Great Depression that required farmers to plow up part of their growing crops and to kill a portion of their hogs in order to qualify for "government relief" payments. I remember listening to the major party conventions on the radio, sometimes throughout the night. When Wendell Willkie was being nominated in 1940, we were still using a battery radio, and after multiple ballots the power was exhausted and Daddy cranked up his pickup truck and carried the large radio outdoors, set it on the ground, and hooked it to the car battery. He later became one of the directors of the Sumter Electric Membership Corporation, which served our area, and we soon had electric lights, kitchen stove, radio, and refrigerator. Our personal lives were transformed, and my parents began attending REA annual meetings in our county seat, Atlanta, and national meetings in Chicago and other convention sites.

FARM TO COLLEGE

I was happy on the farm, revered my father, and could have accepted a career as his successor in the community, but my parents had other plans for me. Daddy had completed the tenth grade at Riverside Academy, a military school near Augusta, Georgia, before serving as a first lieutenant in the army, and I believe this was the highest educational level that had been achieved by the men in his family. He and my mother were determined that I would finish high school and go to college. Money was scarce for everyone, but we knew that there were two notable universities in America where tuition and board were free: West Point and Annapolis.

My father did not have any special affinity for the army in which he had served, and my mother's youngest brother, Tom Gordy, was serving in the U.S. Navy as a radioman in the Pacific Ocean area. He "adopted" me as a pen pal when I was a child; we established a regular correspondence, and he sent me souvenirs from Australia, Japan, the Philippines, China, and other exotic places. It was soon decided that I would seek a naval career, with the ultimate goal being graduation from the U.S. Naval Academy. Even when I was a grammar school student, this became my avowed objective in life, and we all realized that an appointment could come only from one of Georgia's senators or congressmen, and might be based primarily on my academic record. Neither my parents nor my teachers ever let me forget, and I tried not to disappoint them. I took all the extra courses that were offered in our school, including typing and shorthand. Throughout my college years I took all my class notes in Gregg shorthand and have retained my typing skills.

Despite Daddy's best efforts, I could not get any consideration for an appointment by the time I graduated from high school in 1941, so I enrolled in nearby Georgia Southwestern College and became laboratory assistant to the science teacher, Dr. L. R. Towson. I earned a small stipend and gained an extra opportunity to learn about physics, chemistry, mathematics, and astronomy. Dr. Towson was commanding officer of the local army reserve unit, and he had drill duties twice a week during this early phase of World War II. On those days I taught freshman classes as his replacement.

I was a freshman in the junior college when the Japanese bombed Pearl Harbor, in December 1941, and was very concerned about my uncle Tom, whom I knew was stationed with about eighty other navy men on the island of Guam. After a few days, we learned that Japanese forces had invaded and conquered the small and undefended island on December 8, just one day after the war began. The duty of the navy personnel there was to relay radio signals among American ships and naval bases in the Pacific military theater, and they had been ordered not to engage the Japanese in combat to prevent unnecessary casualties among the natives of the island. We did not know what happened to Tom, but his wife, Dorothy, and three young children moved from their home in San Francisco to stay with my mother's parents west of Plains, on a farm adjoining ours. Dorothy was a very pretty woman, whom I visited whenever I came home to see my family, always hoping in vain to have some word from her husband. After about two years of assuming that Uncle Tom was a prisoner of war, Dorothy was informed officially that he was dead, and she decided to move back to California to live with her family. From her letters, we learned that her father and several brothers were all serving as firemen in San Francisco. Toward the end of 1944, she informed us that she would marry a fireman who was a friend of their family, because she needed someone to help raise her children.

Tom was found alive when the war was over, having been forced to serve on a short railroad line in Japan that brought coal from the mountains down to the main line. He had been severely abused, weighed less than a hundred pounds, and suffered from phlebitis, or varicose veins. Uncle Tom was hospitalized and near death, but according to law was promoted to the rank of lieutenant, senior grade, and paid the full salary he would have earned if he had served on active duty throughout the war. I expected Tom and Dorothy to be reunited and her second marriage annulled, which was what Dorothy proposed. However, my grandparents and all of Tom's sisters (including my mother) convinced him that Dorothy had been unfaithful and that divorce was his best alternative. By this time I was serving on my first ship and exchanging brief notes with Dorothy and sometimes with some of Tom's children, including the oldest son, who bore my name.

CHAPTER TWO: NAVY YEARS

ANNAPOLIS

After completing my sophomore year at Georgia Tech with a year of Naval Reserve Officer Training, I received an appointment and entered the Naval Academy in July 1943. During the war my Annapolis class of 1947 was expected to complete four years of classes in just three years, so we graduated in June 1946. While studying naval engineering at Annapolis, I had to learn the rudiments of electrical power, electronics, mechanical design, seamanship, and the construction and operation of ships and the equipment and armaments on them. I could have done much better in my academic work at the academy, but I depended on obtaining adequate grades from my two years of earlier college work, including the even more challenging studies at Georgia Tech. Except for choice of a foreign language, all midshipmen had exactly the same curriculum. In fact, my roommate during my first (plebe) year had already earned a bachelor of science degree from the University of Iowa, but this prior education was ignored.

There were no African-American midshipmen in my class, but during my second year at Annapolis a black student, Wesley Brown, was appointed. I became acquainted with him when he joined the cross-country team, on which I ran. I felt at ease with him, as with my old Archery friends, but was aware that many of the white midshipmen, from all regions of the country, resented his presence and were making a concerted effort among the upperclassmen to force him to leave, either by harassment or by the accumulation of excessive demerits. Similar efforts had prevented five previous African-American midshipmen from graduating. The word soon went out through the brigade that only negative conduct reports against Brown from commissioned officers would be counted by the superintendent. We assumed that this order had come from higher than the Naval Academy, perhaps from the White House. In his later biography, Lieutenant Commander Brown remembered my friendship and strong support as a fellow runner, and its special value because I was from the Deep South.

Miss Julia Coleman had introduced all her students to classical music in high school, and my roommate at Georgia Tech, Robert Ormsby, had a fine collection of records, so I was delighted my second year to room with Robert Scott, a concert pianist. He and I used all our allotted monthly spending money (seven dollars as Youngsters, and eleven dollars as First Classmen) to buy classical records. We sometimes chose several recordings of the same piano concerto by different performers to compare their techniques. (Later Vladimir Horowitz performed for us at the White House and I told him he compared very favorably to Rachmaninoff, Rubinstein, and others.) We collected and enjoyed a wide range of other classical recordings. Scott had, for those days, a high-fidelity sound system, and for special passages we turned up the volume. I remember that a group of midshipmen would invariably assemble outside our room during "Liebestod," the final aria of Wagner's *Tristan und Isolde*.

I wanted to learn as much as possible about history, literature, and facets of the U.S. Navy beyond my normal studies. I read voraciously, was an avid cross-country runner, and was fascinated with aviation.

Weekends we were permitted to cross Chesapeake Bay and go up for flights with navy aviators as they accumulated requisite flying hours in Vought OSTU observation planes and long-range PBY patrol bombers. I learned to land and take off on water, and to maneuver the two aircraft as directed by the pilots. I also spent many hours practicing the rapid identification of aircraft of many nations, as their images or silhouettes were flashed on a screen for a fraction of a second. At the time, I was determined to become a naval aviator after graduation.

Punitive hazing was permitted in those days, and during my plebe year I seemed to be the target of extra discipline by upperclassmen, especially the Yankees. As a Southerner, I refused to sing "Marching Through Georgia" or agree to any demands that reflected badly on my region of the country. Most of the time I took my punishment in good spirit, and this probably encouraged more good-natured exchanges. Among the senior midshipmen there were a few sadists, and we learned to despise and avoid them whenever possible. I became an expert at running the commando course before reveille and going to several rooms at night to do forty-seven push-ups or ninety-four deep knee bends (multiples of our class year). One of the most difficult "games" forced on us was participating in cruise box races. Each midshipman had a wooden box that we could pack and carry on a ship or use for storage of books or out-of-season uniforms. The race involved squeezing into the closed cruise box, changing uniforms, running around some designated corridors of Bancroft Hall, and then going back into the cramped space to change back to our original clothing. My being relatively small helped my performance.

For any real or alleged violation of orders, we were struck repeatedly with brooms or, much worse, the large metal serving spoons or ladles at our mess room tables. Blisters would often result. One of the claimed objectives of this mistreatment was to inure us to difficulty and to weed out those who could not stand the punishment. One of my closest friends committed suicide, and his roommate moved in with us. On our first day at Annapolis, we had been lined up and told that either we or the one on either side of us would not survive plebe year, and the attrition rate was usually even more than one out of three. If one of us showed any signs of weakness, an extra effort was made by upperclassmen and officers to encourage a resignation or induce an expulsion because of multiple demerits. I was glad to hear that most of the more brutal practices were forbidden after the war.

We made summer cruises into the Caribbean and Atlantic, with one enjoyable visit to Trinidad on the old battleship USS *New York.* Returning, we either were hit by a German torpedo or ran aground while maneuvering to avoid it. One of our propellers was damaged, and we limped back into port in Philadelphia with the stern of the ship jumping about six inches every time the propeller rotated. We midshipmen were again at sea about a year later, when we sat on deck and listened to President Truman's nasal voice announce over the loudspeaker that a formidable weapon had been dropped on Hiroshima and that he hoped this would convince the Japanese to surrender. All of us agreed with his decision, because it was generally believed that 500,000 Americans would have been lost in combat and many more Japanese killed if we had invaded the Japanese homeland and it was defended with suicidal commitment by Japanese troops on the ground. We were disappointed when we didn't return to port in time to join in the celebration when Japan surrendered just a few days later.

I was in the top 10 percent of our class

but did not really excel in any aspect of the academic or military life. The brief biographies in our yearbook, *The Lucky Bag,* were written by each midshipman's room-mate. Mine, an obvious exaggeration, included these words: "Studies never bothered Jimmy. In fact, the only times he opened his books were when his classmates desired help on problems. This lack of study did not, however, prevent him from stand-ing in the upper part of his class." I am grateful to the academy and have always ap-preciated the value of my education and introduction to military discipline.

ROSALYNN

Even more important than earning my com-mission as a naval officer, I was married a few days after graduation. I had actually known Rosalynn Smith, my future wife, since she was born. After we moved to the farm, my youngest sister, Ruth, spent a lot of time with Rosalynn, who visited our home often, so I knew her well as a teenager. I learned later, after we were married, that she and Ruth had tried to bring us together, but I was interested only in girls nearer my own age.

I had spent a month on leave in Plains as I approached my final year at Annapolis and was dating an attractive girl named Annelle Greene, who was Miss Georgia Southwestern College. On my last full night at home, she had to attend a family reunion to which I was not invited, so I was driving around with a boy who was dating Ruth, looking for a blind date for me. When we passed the Methodist church we saw Rosalynn, and she agreed to go to the movies with us. The next morning when I went into our kitchen, where Mother was cooking breakfast, she asked me what I did last night since Annelle was with her family. I responded, "I went to a movie in Americus." She asked, "By yourself?" I responded, "No, with Rosalynn Smith." She asked, "What did you think of Rosalynn?" and I replied, "She's the one I'm going to marry."

Mama and I were both surprised by my answer, because Rosalynn and I had not had any discussion about our relationship and certainly not about a future together. She was remarkably beautiful, almost painfully shy, obviously intelligent, and yet unrestrained in our discussions on the rumble seat of the Ford Coupe. She joined my family to see me off at the train station quite late the next night, after I returned from my date with Annelle, and I kissed her goodbye. I was glad to learn that Annelle mar-

Rosalynn was remarkably beautiful, almost painfully shy, obviously intelligent, and yet unrestrained in our discussions on the rumble seat of the Ford Coupe.

ried a medical student and moved to Macon. Rosalynn and I dated during Christmas vacation, and my parents and Rosalynn came to Annapolis in February for a brief holiday to celebrate the birthdays of Abraham Lincoln and George Washington. I asked her to marry me, but she rejected my proposal, then later wrote back from Plains to let me know that she had promised her father, on his deathbed, to finish college and would not marry until then. In the meantime she was dating other young men who were in college with her. I was distressed, and could only persist through my letters and an occasional telephone call. She finally accepted my proposal, and we were married the first week in July, after she graduated from the junior college in Americus. A few days later we started housekeeping together in Norfolk, Virginia, where my ship was stationed. We rented a small upstairs apartment a few miles from the navy base. This is a poem I wrote about her:

Rosalynn
She'd smile, and birds would feel that they
   no longer
had to sing, or it may be I failed
to hear their song.
Within a crowd, I'd hope her glance might
   be
for me, but knew that she was shy, and
   wished

to be alone.

I'd pay to sit behind her, blind to what

was on the screen, and watch the image
  flicker

on her hair.

I'd glow when her diminished voice would
  clear

my muddled thoughts, like lightning
  flashing in

a gloomy sky.

The nothing in my soul with her aloof

was changed to foolish fullness when she
  came

to be with me.

With shyness gone and hair caressed with
  gray,

her smile still makes the birds forget to
  sing

and me to hear their song.

BATTLESHIPS

We graduating midshipmen had to draw lots
for our first duty station, and my number
was near the bottom. My assignment was to
serve on the oldest navy ship still operating
at sea, the battleship USS *Wyoming,* which
had been commissioned in 1912, served as
a warship in World War I, then as a training
ship and for shore bombardment in World
War II with her twelve 12-inch guns. The

Wyoming then became something of an experiment station for testing the most advanced designs of radar, communications, navigation, and gunnery equipment. I was obligated to remain on this post for two years before requesting a transfer to other duties. As a young officer I had both commonplace and highly innovative assignments, including electronics officer. This was a time of severe budget restraints, when only one preproduction model of a new gyroscope compass, radar, loran (a long-range navigation system based on radio waves), fire-control system, or weapon could be afforded, and our job was to test them as thoroughly and inexpensively as possible. I was also responsible for both still and motion picture photography of towed aerial targets and shell bursts for assessing the accuracy of antiaircraft projectiles. This was during the early development of color film, a process that I learned on the ship.

Physically, my ship was something of a disgrace. The hull had been strained, perhaps by firing its main batteries during the war, and it leaked constantly. Despite the best efforts of the officers and crew to contain it, there was a small but steady stream of oil that exuded from the hull, so we were forbidden to come into the port and tie up with other navy vessels alongside the pier. Our only recourse was to anchor well out in the harbor so the surging tides would minimize the effects of our pollution. This meant that our access to the shore was in small boats that made sporadic trips to and fro when we were not operating out in the Atlantic Ocean. Senior officers and representatives of commercial firms had top priority, so the rest of us had to await our turns for boat rides. When seas were rough, of course, the small boats couldn't operate.

Our normal schedule was to spend five days cruising back and forth off the coasts of Virginia and North Carolina to perform our experimental duties, and then anchor on Saturday and Sunday. We ensigns had onboard duty as watch officers every third weekend and could go home to our families during the other two unless there were special tasks related to our permanent assignments. This was the time when new electronic equipment was brought aboard, installed, and tested for the following week's work, and as electronics officer I frequently had to perform these tasks. I worked on the new equipment, and once I was shocked quite painfully while lying under a radar power unit being repaired. Morale on the ship was very low, and I was soon fed up with navy life. I carried out my mandatory assignments and was primarily interested in spending as much time onshore as possible, either being with my family or making furniture in the large and well-equipped hobby shop on the navy base. I remember hanging a sign over my bunk that said SO WHAT?

At the end of a year, we were delighted to learn that the *Wyoming* would be retired from service and replaced by the USS *Mississippi,* which had been commissioned in 1917, served as an escort to shipping and bombarded coastlines during World War II, and was converted to its final status in 1947 to assume the *Wyoming*'s duties. Its hull had been renovated in the shipyard and was in such good condition that it was permitted to come all the way into the harbor and tie up alongside the piers! The same experimental projects were performed, and the officers and enlisted men were just transferred to our new navy home without changing our basic job assignments.

By this time I began to realize how fortunate I was to have this job as electronics officer, because I had unimpeded access to almost every technological development being introduced into the armed forces, sometimes even including the army and marines. Really for the first time, I decided to devote my full abilities to my naval career and became deeply immersed in learning everything possible about seamanship, navigation, the equipment that came onboard to be tested and evaluated, and the ship itself. I became special assistant to the executive officer and volunteered to be director of the U.S. Armed Forces Institute, which provided free courses for officers and men to complete or supplement their educations at the high school and college levels. When we could assemble a small group, I taught classes in subjects of common interest. One sailor ordered a course on painting, but he resigned from the navy before his book and art materials arrived. When they came, several of the sailors and I experimented with watercolors and oil paints, and I began to sketch scenes around our apartment. I also collected some books about famous artists and their works. I now have a large collection in my library, including the 1939 edition of Jan Gordon's *Painting for Beginners.*

I had an interest in politics during those years but adopted the officially neutral status maintained by other officers. While serving my final months on the *Mississippi,* I had learned to admire President Harry

Truman and his political courage as he made difficult decisions involving racial equality and bringing the world war to a close. This was during the early stages of the 1948 presidential campaign, and I heard that Truman's predecessor as Roosevelt's vice president, Henry Wallace, would be speaking as a presidential candidate in Norfolk. I knew Wallace was a strong critic of racial segregation, had been editor of the *New Republic* magazine, and that he was calling for an end to the Cold War with the Soviet Union. When I told the executive officer of my plans to go to the speech, he was furious that I would participate in a political event and especially for a radical like Henry Wallace. He let me know that this would be a permanent black mark in my official records. I didn't pursue the idea but continued to monitor the progress of the presidential race.

I don't remember what induced me to apply for a Rhodes Scholarship that same year. I obtained the requisite endorsement from the Naval Academy and other letters of recommendation, wrote an essay, and submitted it as a citizen of Georgia, where I thought I would have my best chance. My statement expressed hope that, as a naval officer, I might use my knowledge of international affairs, to be acquired at Oxford, as a means to promote world peace. I was notified that I was a finalist and went to Atlanta for an interview. I stayed overnight with my cousin Don Carter, where I saw my first television set. I remember that the screen was about the size of a postcard. My main challenger was a thin and stooped young man from Alabama, who said he told the Rhodes interviewers that he had focused his studies exclusively on Elizabethan literature and had no interest in anything that had happened after the death of Elizabeth I, in 1603. I had practically memorized newspapers and magazines during the previous months and answered many questions about history, geography, and current events. Not surprisingly, even to me, the Alabama scholar was chosen. He and I communicated by mail once or twice, and I was grieved to learn from his parents that he died while still a student in England.

As a young naval officer, I had to do everything possible to stretch my salary of three hundred dollars a month to cover the cost of uniforms, my food onboard ship, rent for an apartment, and other living expenses of our family, which now included our son, Jack. There was a big difference between the cost of furnished and unfurnished places, and I made full use of the elaborate hobby shops on the large navy bases, usually manned by warrant officers who were expert cabinetmakers. From them, I learned the finer points of working with different kinds of wood, making well-structured joints, using proper glues, and finishing the surfaces. In the workshops I enjoyed designing and building chairs, beds, tables, and cabinets. To save the cost of shipping, I left almost all the furniture behind when I was assigned from one duty station to another, but we brought some of the bunk beds, tables, and chairs with us when we later moved into a small unfurnished apartment in the Plains public housing project. Our nicest piece of furniture at that time was a white oak cabinet that I had built while we lived on the submarine base in Honolulu. It had mitered corners and recessed hinges and was designed to hold our high-fidelity radio and record system.

SUBMARINES

After two years I had the option of being assigned to another surface ship or applying for one of the three more special careers: intelligence, the naval air force, or submarines. By this time I had developed a strong inclination to operate at sea, so after careful consideration I decided to compete for one of the few assignments to submarines. I was selected, passed the claustrophobia and other psychological tests, and Rosalynn, our son Jack, and I moved to New London, Connecticut, for six months of intensive training with fifty other officers, a few of whom were from foreign countries. The instruction was highly practical, as we learned about the construction and diving principles of the ships themselves; assembling, storing, and firing torpedoes; operating the different guns used when on the surface; caring for the many large electric batteries that propelled the ship when submerged; and special seamanship techniques in handling the fragile vessel, with its strong and watertight inner hull surrounded by thin tanks, easily damaged.

(Note: We referred interchangeably to submarines as "ships" or "boats," and usually pronounced "submariner" with the accent on the third syllable.)

There had been a number of fatal underwater accidents during previous years, and we were required to practice escaping from a damaged submarine that could not surface. Pressurized escape hatches would let a few men at a time leave the ship and enter the surrounding sea, at depths up to three hundred feet. Rising through the water had to be done slowly and carefully to prevent the air in our lungs, which was under great pressure, being forced into our bloodstreams and causing unconsciousness or death. There was a one-hundred-foot tank at the submarine base, and we would go into the bottom, become accustomed to the high pressure, and then ascend through the water while clamping a small rope between our bare feet to control upward speed and breathing in and out through a Momsen lung. This clumsy device removed carbon dioxide from our exhaled breath and provided enough oxygen for survival. A few other trainees and I volunteered to make what was called a "free ascent," without the artificial breathing device. It was crucial to watch the exhaled bubbles and not go up any faster than they did. It was a very unpleasant experience, and it is still my most vivid memory of those early submarine days. I was determined not to permit any other trainees to exceed my performance.

At the same time, I was fascinated as never before by the submarine force, including its proud history and the mandatory intimacy of all the members of the crew. Although some of the enlisted men could concentrate almost exclusively on their own fields of responsibility as enginemen, electricians, torpedo experts, boatswains, quartermasters, gunners, or operators of navigation or fire control equipment, every officer was expected to master all these disciplines. We knew that one mistake in judgment, a lack of knowledge, or an error in opening or closing a valve could endanger everyone onboard.

I was at submarine school in November 1948 and discovered that I was the only student there who planned to vote for Harry Truman. The other officers thought that he was too liberal on economic matters, gave inadequate attention to defense issues, and had no chance to win. His commitment to racial equality was never mentioned, but it may have been a factor. Rosalynn and I became tired of trying to defend his record in the mess hall or when we were with any of the other students in our private quarters, all of whom voted for Thomas Dewey. No one wanted to talk to us after Truman's victory.

I was assigned to the USS *Pomfret* (SS-391) on graduation from submarine school and had to hurry to its base in Honolulu before it departed three days later on an extended cruise to the Western Pacific. Rosalynn decided that she and Jack would stay in Plains with our relatives for about four months until my return to our home port. The *Pomfret* was one of the 320 standard types of submarines that served during World War II, of which 132 were almost identical to it. They were designed for seventy-five-day patrols, and from Hawaii could cover the entire Pacific Ocean with their normal range of twelve thousand miles, at an average cruising speed of ten knots. Each ship had a crew of about seventy-five men and officers.

A submarine has a very strong inner cigar-shaped hull, which will withstand pressure at maximum operating depth (then about 450 feet under normal conditions), and ballast tanks surrounding this hull, which hold diesel oil or are kept empty on the surface and filled with seawater when it is time to dive. When the vessel is surfaced, about 80 percent of the pressure hull is below water level, and we had a slatted wooden deck on which the crew could walk when we were in port or cruising in calm weather. At the bow, this deck was about 10 feet above the water level, but at the stern this "freeboard" was only 4 feet. Our pressure hull was 16 feet in diameter and 312 feet long, and we lived within this space with our engines,

81

torpedoes, and batteries. On top of this hull was a small pressurized cylinder known as the "conning tower," from which we could raise the slender periscope above the surface while the ship was submerged and survey the surrounding area without being detected.

Our primary offensive armament was twenty-four torpedoes, stored and launched from directly ahead or astern of the ship, which could turn to a preset course. In addition, we had a five-inch-diameter gun located on the main deck just aft of the conning tower, 20-mm and 40-mm antiaircraft weapons above the main deck forward and aft of the conning tower, and a heavy 50-caliber machine gun that could be used against aircraft or small surface ships.

These submarines were propelled on the surface with a top speed of about fifteen knots by diesel engines, and by 252 batteries while submerged. The batteries had to be charged while on the surface. Although each of them weighed about a ton, they had very limited total energy to propel the ship and run all the equipment while we were submerged. We could cruise for about sixty miles if we crept along at only two knots, but at a maximum speed of thirteen knots — to get close to a moving target — the batteries lasted only half an hour, giving us a range of about seven miles. These limitations established our normal routine of operating on the surface when it was dark while charging our batteries and making progress toward our destination but remaining concealed and at low speed during daylight hours. At that time we had no way to draw air down into a submerged submarine to be breathed and to permit the diesel engines to run. The "snorkel" system was first made operational in a U.S. ship in 1947 but was not widely used when I began my submarine duty.

When our ship surfaced, the duty officer and two lookouts would open a sealed hatch and hurry upward from the conning tower through a steel tube to the bridge. The floor on which the officer stood was slatted like the main deck and about ten feet above the surface of the sea. The lookouts had a place to stand alongside the periscope tower, with their feet a short distance above the duty officer's head. With excellent training, we could resubmerge in about thirty seconds when necessary, by flooding the ballast tanks and turning our bow and stern planes downward as we moved forward rapidly.

I was familiar with these basic facts when I arrived on the ship, having operated on similar submarines while in training, and I was soon authorized by Captain J. B. Williams, Jr., to join the other watch officers who carried out his orders and those of the executive officer. While not on duty, each officer was responsible for supervising one of the major functions of the ship's operation. In addition, I was expected to learn from experienced enlisted men about every valve, pipe, lever, switch, hatch, torpedo, compass, wheel, or instrument that was used in the normal operation of the ship and in times of combat or other emergency.

I was designated to be the electrical officer and had spent my first two days while still in port in a cram course, primarily instructed by chief petty officers, in an effort to learn everything possible about the electrical equipment before we went to sea. When we sailed on the last day of December 1948, I began learning about my duties as a watch officer, which I would share with the four other officers who served under the captain and the executive officer. This had been an integral part of our instruction at sub school, but each ship's captain had his own idiosyncrasies. After three days I was standing watch topside on the bridge, with another officer on duty below in the conning tower. We were simulating a wartime patrol, remaining submerged during daytime and cruising on the surface at night. At our most efficient cruising speed, we proceeded about two hundred miles daily, heading toward China. This was about the same as a sailing ship in ancient days, with a fair wind.

After about a week, a storm began brewing, and I became increasingly seasick. Cigarette smoke and diesel fumes permeated the compartments belowdecks, and my nausea was uncontrollable. I was either in my bunk or throwing up in the toilet. The cold, fresh wind helped when I was on the bridge, and I stayed there whenever I could, even volunteering to take the duty from other officers a few times, so I could easily vomit over the side. Our ship was affected by the swells down to periscope depth (about sixty feet), but we could go deeper, where it was relatively calm. We remained submerged as much as possible to protect the ship from the huge seas, but it was absolutely necessary to surface during the night to charge our batteries and make progress along our assigned route. A submarine is extremely strong and rigid along its length, but its cylindrical shape makes it very susceptible to excessive rolling when wind and waves beat on it from the sides. I had experienced bad weather on midshipmen's cruises and in the Atlantic on battleships, but this storm soon exceeded anything I had known. Since my head was only about fifteen feet above the surface when I was on the bridge, I became accustomed to the salt spray and wave tops being constantly in my face. I was shivering after several hours topside in the strong January wind, even in the tropical latitude. As the waves mounted, the captain directed that we head directly into the seas to minimize the violent rolling, and this order was to save my life.

I was standing watch on the bridge about two hours after midnight, with my feet on the slatted wooden deck, when I saw an enormous wave dead ahead. I ducked down beneath the chest-high steel protector that surrounded the front of the bridge and locked my arms around the safety rail. The wave, however, smothered our ship, several feet above my head. I was ripped loose, lifted up, and carried away from the ship. I could only swim around in the turbulent water, striving to reach the surface. This was my first experience with impending death, but when the wave receded I found myself on the main deck directly aft of the bridge and was able to cling to our five-inch gun.

In the interval before the next huge wave, I scrambled back onto the bridge, where I found the lookouts hugging their protective rail, drenched above their waists. We all donned life preservers, and I tethered myself in place with a rope. If we had been traveling just a few degrees at an angle to the waves, I would have been lost at sea. It would have been impossible for the ship to return to the same site, and finding me in the dark would have been a hopeless effort. The next morning I made a report to the captain, but with a minimum of dramatic effect, just telling him that I had been swept from the bridge, landed on the afterdeck, and recovered without injury.

Our ship continued to suffer a heavy pounding, and some of the topside fittings, including our radio antennas, were washed away or damaged. After some hasty repairs, we were able to receive but not transmit messages. It was mandatory for submarines to report our status and positions at least every eight hours, but we were unable to do so. Inquiries from Hawaii began to arrive with increasing urgency and frequency when our status was not known, and eventually a message was sent to the Pacific Fleet stating that the *Pomfret* was presumed lost and all ships and planes should be on the lookout for floating debris and possible survivors in the general area westward from where we had last reported. We were then about six hundred miles south of Wake Island, and Captain Williams decided to remain on the surface and turn northward to reach the small navy base as quickly as possible. During the three days required for this journey, we realized that our families had been notified of our presumed loss. In fact, all the wives living in Hawaii were informed, but Rosalynn was still in Georgia and never received the heartbreaking news. After reporting our survival and receiving repairs for three days, during which the storm subsided, we continued our voyage.

In addition to training under simulated wartime conditions, our task was to visit the Philippines for a courtesy call and then go to the major port cities of China, where we would conduct antisubmarine warfare exercises with ships of Nationalist China, Australia, Great Britain, and the United States.

I had been especially proud of General Claire Chennault and the Flying Tigers, who fought alongside the Chinese against Japanese invaders during the early days of World War II. Later I followed the civil war in China as well as possible from the news media, hoping that Nationalist forces could prevail over Mao Tse-tung's Communist troops. Georgians were proud that Chiang Kai-shek's wife had been a student at Wesleyan College in Macon, Georgia. When World War II ended, I strongly supported President Truman's decision to send General George Marshall to China to negotiate a peace agreement between Chiang Kai-shek and Mao Tse-tung. But his mission failed, and the civil war escalated. I was disturbed later when Senator Joe McCarthy blamed Marshall and others for successes of the Communist forces and was glad when Marshall was awarded the Nobel Peace Prize.

The American government was completely committed to its alliance with Chiang Kai-shek and his forces, and our visit was designed to give them some psychological support and demonstrate that the Communist forces had not succeeded in their effort to control the mainland. It was obvious to us when we arrived that the Nationalists had already lost the war, having been driven from most of China but being permitted to remain in a few seaports along the eastern shore. We began our tour in Hong Kong, moved to Shanghai, and then to a longer stay in Tsingtao (now Qingdao). Because of the ongoing conflict and the uncertainty of its outcome, we always tied up at the pier heading out to sea and kept a substantial part of the crew onboard for a potential rapid departure. We could see the campfires of Mao Tse-tung's Communist troops on the nearby hillsides and observed the Nationalists recruiting boys and young men at gunpoint. On one occasion, the jeep carrying our captain strayed beyond the city and was hit by bullets, but no one was injured. Most of the shops were boarded in front, but potential customers were admitted through side or rear doors, and merchandise was offered at giveaway prices. When we were alongside the dock, the captain let merchants display their wares on the deck.

I had very little money and bought just a few small souvenirs of ivory and jade, but some of the officers and men purchased expensive gifts to take home. We returned to Pearl Harbor after about two months of operation in the China seas.

This visit aroused my special interest in China and its history, and I was intrigued when, just a few months later, the Nationalists were forced to evacuate to Taiwan and the People's Republic of China was formed on October 1, 1949 — my twenty-fifth birthday. After that, I monitored quite closely the events in China and Taiwan.

A few months later, still in 1949, my

The USS Pomfret *in China in 1949, with merchants on deck.*

submarine went into Mare Island, near San Francisco, for repairs, and I decided with some trepidation to visit Tom Gordy's former wife, Dorothy. On a Friday afternoon we approached the address from one of her letters, and I left Rosalynn and Jack across the street, not knowing what the reception might be. I knocked on the door, told an older woman who I was, and she exploded into shouts, "Tom's nephew is here!" It was Dorothy's mother, Mrs. McDowell, and she embraced me as Dorothy and other family members crowded around. Rosalynn and Jack joined us, and we spent one of the most delightful uninterrupted celebrations I have ever known. A long table was filled with food, dozens of neighbors were invited in from time to time, and none of us went to bed that night. I remember vaguely that everyone was drinking boilermakers (shots of whiskey with beer), many of the men played guitars and sang while the rest of us danced, and we were regaled with descriptions of their experiences with Tom during earlier days. I told them that he was regaining his health, had been steadily promoted as he managed security at naval bases in Florida, had remarried, and owned a tavern in Lake Mary, Florida, which I had visited. We took brief naps the next day, and that night Dorothy and her husband accompanied us to the stage play *A Streetcar Named Desire*.

Tom retired from the navy as a commander and lived long enough to visit us in the governor's mansion and to help with the early stages of my presidential campaign among his friends in Florida. He liked to remind me that he outranked me by several grades — but this was before I became commander in chief.

Before returning to Hawaii, our ship was assigned to operate in Puget Sound out of Seattle, and it was here that I found myself in danger again. We were tied up near the seaward end of Pier 61, and I was officer of the deck one night during a heavy fog. The lookout reported that a large ship was approaching quite close, and I went to the stern of the submarine and heard loud voices almost directly over my head. We could not see anything, and the people above me did not acknowledge my shouts as I attempted to let them know of our presence. I quickly realized that they were preparing to drop their huge anchor, believing they were in the middle of the channel. Finally, with the anchor visible just above my head and our ship, I heard the command "Prepare to let go the anchor!" Desperate, I strained my voice to the utmost and was relieved to hear, "Wait, I think there is someone down there." I was blinded by a spotlight, and the large ship backed its engines. The crisis was over.

We operated with Canadian and British ships between the fresher water of Puget Sound and the Strait of Juan de Fuca, carefully adjusting the "trim" to accommodate our relatively lighter or heavier ship in water with changing salinity. This required experimenting until we achieved neutral buoyancy during our dives. When we concluded our operations in the area and were preparing to return to Hawaii, officers on the British destroyers invited us to join them for our last night in Victoria, British Columbia, and we went there from Seattle on the surface. Our friends entertained us until dawn, utilizing their freedom to serve alcoholic drinks on their ships, and we accepted their hospitality with enthusiasm. None of us ever reached the shore.

The next morning we headed west toward Hawaii, and on the first dive one of our more senior officers, who had been drinking all night, made a terrible mistake in preparation. His job was to be sure that all the main valves were rigged to open at the same time, but he checked only those on the starboard side and was then distracted. When the captain gave the order and electrical signals were sent to the valves, the starboard ones opened and water poured into those tanks, while those on the port side remained shut. The ship began to roll over to the right as it was driven downward by our planes at the bow and stern, and we approached the point of capsizing. Only the furious blowing of high-pressure air into the tanks prevented the loss of the *Pomfret* and its crew. This was the closest our ship ever came to a total disaster. I realized how fragile was my existence, and how fallible were even the most dedicated and experienced seamen.

Afterward, our return to Hawaii was relatively uneventful, and I spent almost every moment on duty learning as much as possible about my own ship and the submarine force. All my capabilities and energy were focused on this desire to excel in my assignment. I was not motivated by any element of competition, because I was the only officer of my seniority on the ship, but I guess subliminally I realized that I would always be compared with other submariners in my Naval Academy class.

My ship was moved from Hawaii to San Diego when the Korean War began, in June

1950, and we operated along the California coast, expecting to be deployed to the war zone to conduct surveillance along the coast of Korea or to rescue downed aviators. This was a few months after our second son, James Earl Carter III, was born. He was named after me but branded by navy nurses at Tripler General Hospital in Hawaii on his wristband as Chip, a name we have used ever since. This duty in San Diego was to be our most unpleasant assignment. The navy base was overcrowded, and the only housing we could find was in a decrepit and crime-ridden area of the city. All submarines were prohibited from using the scarce docking spaces along the shore and required to tie up alongside large ships called "submarine tenders" that were anchored in the bay. We had the same delays and uncertainty with small boat travel as in Norfolk, and my time with Rosalynn and our boys was restricted. We lived in something like a garage apartment, and the landlady was intrusive and overbearing. She had a key to our quarters and would enter to go through our belongings when we were away. She criticized Rosalynn's housekeeping habits, and even expressed her displeasure about what she found discarded in our garbage. We did enjoy going to the superb

Lillian Carter and Earl Carter, 1950, San Diego, California.

San Diego Zoo, and also making some infrequent trips to nearby Tijuana, Mexico.

All members of the submarine force were informed that the navy was building its first ship of any kind since the end of the Second World War. It would be a new type of submersible, with snorkel air intake and designed to operate with extreme quiet so that it could remain undetected and attack enemy (Soviet) submarines while submerged. One officer would be assigned to Electric Boat Company (later General Dynamics Corporation) in New London to represent the government during the final months of construction. The sub would be called "Killer 1," or more properly USS *K-1*.

I submitted my application for this coveted assignment, and later that year, while my parents were visiting us in San Diego, I received orders to report to New London. I was the only officer on the detail and spent the next few months with two major tasks: helping to monitor the final building and testing of the innovative craft and devising all its future procedures for operating and conducting clandestine warfare, plus incidentals like the inventory of tools, linens, dishes, silverware, and food items. Captain Frank Andrews was chosen as our commanding officer, and he designated me as engineering officer when the other officers and men were assigned to the ship. Collectively, we quickly utilized and improved the voluminous documents I had prepared.

Our new snorkel system would permit the submarine, with the hull and conning tower a few feet under the surface, to pipe air down into the ship to be burned in the diesel engines and breathed by the crew. A valve on top of the pipe would snap shut whenever a wave washed over it, and still-running engines would use up the contained air and create an uncomfortable temporary vacuum in the ship. The unique visual feature of the *K-1* was a huge bulbous sonar array mounted forward on the main deck, which was capable of detecting the slightest sounds from distant sources in the sea. This meant that our own ship and people within it had to remain as quiet as possible. Every piece of equipment was isolated from the hull by special flexible mounts to minimize noise transmitted through the water. Our total crew was about forty men, compared to seventy-five on the *Pomfret,* and our ship was about two-fifths as large as a fleet-type submarine. Bunk sizes and food were about the same, but we had an extremely limited supply of fresh water from a small distillery. Other than for cooking and drinking, our individual allotment when at sea for long periods was only a quart per day, and we showered with salt water.

It was exciting duty because of the new

technology and because we were preparing for potential conflict during those Cold War years with Soviet submarines. We could go deep, stop propulsion, turn off all unnecessary equipment, and at these times of silence all of us removed our shoes and walked around — only when necessary — in stocking feet. We learned to hover at a desired depth by changing very slightly the seawater we displaced. When we reached a final trim, we would just elevate or lower our periscope a foot or two, which would cause our boat very slowly to rise or sink. In this condition, our huge listening device could detect ocean sounds from far away, more distant when temperature gradients were perfect and wave action was minimal. I became fascinated with the underwater character of the ocean, and read all the books on the ship about the subject. These factors were important to our survival in combat with other ships, and even during normal peacetime operations. I remember one day when we were cruising at periscope depth east of Newfoundland, in the relatively warm waters of the Gulf Stream. Suddenly, the bow of our submarine entered the much colder (and more dense) Arctic waters, and we were propelled to the surface by the strong upward force. The cold and warm waters had not mixed, even within a distance of less than two hundred feet.

We officers would sit in with the sonar specialists to become more familiar with the equipment and to monitor the more interesting sounds. In addition to distinctive propeller noises of different ships, we were interested in listening to shrimp and other creatures, especially the remarkable calls of whales. At the same time, we knew that our primary duty was to detect potential enemies before they ever realized that we were present and monitoring their movements. I wrote a poem about this contrast of peace and war.

Life on a Killer Submarine

I had a warm, sequestered feeling
deep beneath the sea,
moving silently, assessing
what we could hear from far away
because we ran so quietly ourselves,
walking always in our stocking feet.
We'd listen to the wild sea sounds,
the scratch of shrimp, the bowhead's
  moan,
the tantalizing songs of humpback whales.
We strained to hear all other things,
letting ocean lenses bring to us
the steady throbbing beat of screws,

the murmurs of most distant ships,
or submarines that might be hunting us.
One time we heard, with perfect clarity,
a vessel's pulse four hundred miles away
and remembered that, in spite of
  everything
we did to keep our sounds suppressed,
the gradient sea could focus, too, our
  muffled noise,
could let the other listeners know
where their torpedoes might be aimed.
We wanted them to understand
that we could always hear them first
and, knowing, be inclined to share
our love of solitude, our fear
that one move, threatening or wrong,
could cost the peace we yearned to keep,
and kill our hopes that they were thrilled,
  like us,
to hear the same whale's song.

K-1

I had qualified as a submariner quite early
when serving on the *Pomfret,* but now I was
senior enough to meet the requirements to
command a ship. I had already mastered
the necessary knowledge about and capabilities for submarine construction and operation, but an original thesis was also required.
I reviewed my studies of differential and

integral calculus and devised a system for determining the distance to another ship by the beat of its propellers and the rate of change of its direction from us. I was qualified to command when my plan worked in practice.

The *K-1* operated mostly in the Atlantic-Caribbean area and spent as much time at sea as possible. One interesting cruise was in the vicinity of Nassau, in the Bahamas, when we were instructed to remain continually submerged for at least thirty days. Unfortunately, after about twenty days underwater one of my electrician's mates was afflicted with increasingly severe attacks of claustrophobia. Trying not to violate our orders, Captain Andrews directed that the sailor be strapped to a bunk in the officers' quarters. But it quickly became apparent that this confinement only exacerbated the sailor's problem, as he began to thrash violently and foam at the mouth. We had to surface and have him taken to shore by helicopter.

The inside of a submarine is packed as densely as possible with equipment, leaving limited space to permit personnel to sleep, eat, and move. Even in the more luxurious officers' quarters, we slept on bunks wedged closely above one another, with a narrow opening on one side through which we folded ourselves before stretching out. When I was lying on my back, there was not enough space for a paperback book to be opened on my chest. The *K-1* was especially small, with our advanced sonar equipment making it even more crowded. Air for breathing was either recirculated through filters while we were deeply submerged or replenished while we were cruising on the surface or with our snorkel tube (about twelve inches in diameter) "inhaling" fresh air.

A fire could be deadly, especially if toxic fumes were generated from plastic or rubber insulation. All submariners had to be trained in fighting fires, and while our ships were undergoing routine maintenance in a dry dock or shipyard, we were sent to special schools to learn how best to combat this ever-present danger. On one occasion we had a fire in our engine room while submerged, and, as engineering officer, I was the leading firefighter. I donned the appropriate clothing and gas mask, discovered the source of the flames in the main motor, and directed the application of carbon dioxide and dry powder, since water or foam could not be used. I was wearing headphones and speaking into a microphone to the captain, and I reported that the fire was under control. The next thing I remember was lying on a table in the crew's mess room with a hospitalman's mate trying to get me to breathe oxygen. After a brief spell of vomiting, I was soon back to normal.

TRUMAN AND RACE

I had been serving on a ship in 1948 when President Harry Truman ordained, as commander in chief, that racial discrimination be ended in the armed forces and in the U.S. Civil Service. This was seven years before Rosa Parks took a front seat on a Montgomery bus and Martin Luther King, Jr., became famous. This change was accepted with equanimity on our ship, and I don't remember any backlash at all among the other crews with which I was familiar, but there was an outcry from many sources, especially among the members of the U.S. Congress from the South. South Carolina Governor Strom Thurmond was nominated as the "Dixiecrat" candidate in the 1948 presidential election, and his name replaced Truman's on ballots in Alabama, Louisiana, Mississippi, and South Carolina.

On the USS *K-1* three years later, I played on a fast-pitch softball team that rarely lost a game, primarily because we had a black sailor named Russell, who was our pitcher and could throw the ball with blinding speed and good control. From just forty-six feet away (twenty feet closer than a baseball mound), the ball would arrive at the batter's plate in the twinkling of an eye, and even the best batters could only guess ahead of time where the next pitch might be. Any hit was just an accident, and we would quite often win no-hitters. Thanks to a broad smile and a friendly attitude, our pitcher was the most popular man on the ship.

I was on duty when our submarine went into port in Nassau and tied up at the Prince George Wharf, and I was the officer who accepted an invitation from the governor-general of the Bahamas for our officers and crewmen to attend an official ball to honor the U.S. Navy. There was a more private comment that a number of young ladies would be present with their chaperones. All of us were pleased and excited, and Captain Andrews responded affirmatively. We received a notice the next day that, of course, the nonwhite crewmen would not be included. When I brought this message to the captain, he had the crew assemble in the mess hall and asked for their guidance in drafting a response. After

The USS K-1, *1950s. The* K-1 *operated mostly in the Atlantic-Caribbean area and spent as much time at sea as possible.*

multiple expletives were censored from the message, we unanimously declined to participate. The decision by the crew of the *K-1* was an indication of how equal racial treatment had been accepted — and relished. I was very proud of my ship.

On leave later that year, Rosalynn, our two boys, and I returned to Plains for a visit with our parents. When I was describing this incident, my father quietly left the room, and my mother said, "Jimmy, it's too soon for our folks here to think about black and white people going to a dance together." I realized how much difference there was between my life in the U.S. Navy and what it would be if I lived in Southwest Georgia. When we came to live there a few years later, we learned that she was still correct.

RICKOVER'S NAVY

After serving on the *K-1* for two years, I learned about the planned construction of two submarines that would be propelled by nuclear power. Captain Hyman Rickover was in charge of this highly secret program and was known as the world's foremost expert on peaceful uses of atomic reactors for generating electricity, providing radioactive material for medical purposes, and now for driving a ship. He would be in personal charge of selecting young submariners to lead each of two precommissioning crews to develop power plants that would be small, safe, and effective enough to be mounted in the hull of a submarine. One reactor would be built by General Electric Corporation in Schenectady, New York, and the other by Westinghouse Electric Company in Pittsburgh. Like a host of others, I applied for one of these positions, and after a few weeks I was ordered to Washington for an interview with Rickover.

Captain Rickover was highly controversial, and almost universally condemned by more orthodox senior officers for his radical disregard of navy protocol and procedures. The admirals on the selection board voted repeatedly against his promotion from captain to rear admiral, which had always meant the end of a naval career. It was the personal intervention of President Truman and some of the senior U.S. senators who approved a special law that overrode the admirals' decision and kept Rickover on duty.

I approached the interview with a lot of trepidation and had prepared as well as possible by reviewing current events, naval tactics, and other issues that I thought he might wish to discuss. I entered his office and found him sitting behind a large desk, with a single straight chair in front of it. He motioned for me to sit and immediately surprised me by asking what subjects I wished to discuss. One after another, I selected those about which I knew most at the time, including current events, naval history, submarine battle tactics, electronics, and gunnery. In each case, he asked me questions of increasing difficulty until I was unable to answer them. He never smiled, always looked directly into my eyes, and seemed to relish my obvious mental — and physical — discomfort. (I learned later that the front two legs of my chair had been shortened so I felt as if I were sliding off.)

When I responded that I read a lot of books, he cross-examined me about them. We covered some plays by Shakespeare and Ibsen, novels by William Faulkner and Ernest Hemingway, and a few novels recently on the bestseller list, going into detail about *The Caine Mutiny* by Herman Wouk. Then he asked what kind of music I preferred, and I responded rather brashly that I enjoyed country music and jazz but knew more about classical compositions. He asked for my favorite form, and I told him that I really liked piano concertos and opera. Rickover leaned forward and asked, "What is your favorite opera?" I blurted out, "Wagner's *Tristan und Isolde,*" and he asked, "Which movement do you prefer?" Fortunately, I was able to name the ending, known as "Liebestod," or "love death." I was thankful that my roommate and I had known this music and played it often at Annapolis.

Almost two hours had passed, and it seemed that the interview was about over. Rickover asked me another question, and I thought I could answer it satisfactorily.

"How did you stand in your class at the Naval Academy?"

"Sir, I stood fifty-ninth in a class of 820."

After a short pause, he asked, "Did you always do your best?"

I started to answer "Yes, sir," but I remembered who this was and all the many missed opportunities I had had to study more, participate in class activities, or strive to reach a higher level of military rank within the brigade. I finally gulped and said, "No, sir, I didn't always do my best."

He looked at me for a long time, and finally asked: "Why not?"

Then he turned his chair around to end the interview and began working on some papers on a table behind his desk. I sat there several minutes as he ignored me, and then I slowly left the room. I was disheartened on the way back to the submarine base, where I told Rosalynn I had not done well at all. But I was soon notified that I had been chosen — probably because I answered his final question truthfully. Before I received my official orders, our third son, Jeffrey, was born in the navy hospital in New London.

The other officer ordered to the USS *Seawolf* detail in Schenectady was Lieutenant Charles Carlisle, a classmate of mine who was just slightly junior to me in class standing. We had about two dozen enlisted men serving under us, and we were soon immersed in learning the rudiments of nuclear power and helping to build the prototype of the reactor that would be in the ship. This power plant was unique in that we used liquid sodium to go into the reactor and bring out heat that transformed water into steam for turbines that propelled the ship and provided power for other uses. Sodium was explosive when in direct contact with water, and the entire prototype power plant on which we worked was assembled within a steel sphere about two hundred feet in diameter and designed to contain a possible radioactive detonation if a tragic accident should occur. The major advantages of sodium were that, as a metal, it could be circulated by electric fields in pumps with no moving parts, and it would bring out much more heat than the same volume of water. Compared to that of the *Nautilus,* which would be commissioned two years earlier and used water as a heat transfer agent, our power plant was smaller, more efficient, and quieter. Designing and building one of the first high-capacity nuclear power plants and understanding the submarine in which it would be installed was a constant learning process, on the cutting edge of science. I was ordered to supplement my practical training with studies of theoretical nuclear physics at nearby Union College.

There were few people at that time who were as knowledgeable as we were about this new technology, and all of us had unique security clearances, known as "Restricted Data." When a Canadian "heavy water" nuclear power plant at Chalk River was destroyed by accident in 1952, by a reactor meltdown and subsequent hydrogen explosions, my crew were volunteered by Rickover to assist with the disassembly so it could be replaced. We traveled by train to the isolated site northwest of Ottawa and were given a briefing on the status of the disaster. The reactor core was below ground level and surrounded by intense radioactivity. Even with protective clothing, each of us would absorb the maximum permissible dose with just ninety seconds of exposure, so we had to make optimum use of this limited time. The limit on radiation absorption in the early 1950s was approximately one thousand times higher than it is sixty years later.

An exact mock-up of the damaged reactor had been constructed on a nearby tennis court, modified constantly to represent at all times the exact status of the real core underground, including every pipe, fitting, bolt, and nut. Television cameras were focused on the core, so that when any changes were made they were duplicated on the mock-up.

I divided our team into groups of three, and each trio would don the heavy white suits and masks, dash onto the tennis court, and remove as many bolts and pipes as possible in ninety seconds. These pieces would then be replaced, and we tried again and again until we were as proficient as possible. Only then did we go down into the radioactive area and do the same disassembly on the real target. We returned to Schenectady after all of us had exhausted our permissible time in the radioactive site. There were a lot of jokes about the effects of radioactivity, mostly about the prospect of being sterilized, and we had to monitor our urine until all our bodies returned to the normal range. None of us suffered any permanent aftereffects, and I was glad to learn several years later that the Chalk River reactor was back in operation.

DADDY'S DEATH

In April 1953 I had a call from my cousin Don Carter, who told me that my father was seriously ill and might not survive. He would be going to Emory Hospital in Atlanta for further tests. Daddy had always been in robust health, was a good athlete, a hardworking farmer and businessman, and at the time a member of the state legislature. I was stricken with grief and concern, especially after my mother informed me that Daddy might have cancer. I had been gone from my home in Plains since 1941, as a college student and in the U.S. Navy, and had rarely visited my parents during those years. After a couple of months, Mama let me know that Daddy was terminally ill, with pancreatic cancer, and had only a few weeks to live. I obtained permission from Rickover to leave my post for two weeks so I could be with Daddy, and drove down to Plains in July. I was looking forward to returning to my challenging and exciting work as a nuclear submariner.

My father had been moved from the hospital to his bedroom at home, and my mother and our former maid, Annie Mae Hollis, were caring for him. Except for some brief visits with my other relatives, I spent almost all my time at Daddy's bedside, having the longest and most thorough conversations I had ever had with him. He was growing weaker and had some brief spasms of discomfort but was completely cogent and eager to listen to my descriptions of navy duty and describe his work in many aspects of community life and also within the state government. What was most surprising was the steady stream of visitors who came to the house, mostly not wanting to disturb Daddy but just to bring him small gifts and relay their personal thanks for things he had done for them or their families. More than half the visitors were African-American.

I knew he was active in our church as a deacon and Bible teacher but had never realized that he served as a member of the board of education, was on the hospital authority, was active in the Lions Club, and was playing an important role in educating local farmers on better agricultural practices. He had become a statewide force in developing vocational-technical schools to supplement the more academic colleges and was a champion in helping rural communities share in Georgia's economic progress. Even more significant than these involvements in public affairs were the many reports to me of Daddy's benevolent activities, done privately and without even my mother knowing about them. It was obvious that he was putting his religious beliefs into action every day and making a profound impact on the lives of many people.

Annie Mae, who had helped my family during the 1940s, had learned about Daddy's illness and returned to Plains from California. I remember that Annie Mae was holding him in her arms when my father breathed his last tortured breath, and she never flinched when she was covered with his black vomit. Years later, in 1994, Annie Mae's home in nearby Albany was destroyed by a flood, and Rosalynn and I organized a Habitat for Humanity crew and rebuilt it.

LEAVING THE NAVY

One of the strangest and most unexpected events in my life was my slow but inexorable contemplation of resigning from the navy and returning home to Plains to assume some of my father's responsibilities and emulate his activities. I realized that I enjoyed one of the most coveted assignments that a military career could offer, and I had the prospect of unlimited advancement during the coming years. Rosalynn especially relished being a navy wife and cherished her freedom to manage our family affairs with relative independence. At the same time, I was burdened with the knowledge of the tremendous investment that had been made in my education and specialized nuclear training. Balanced against all this was the prospect of living in a tiny rural village from which I had been separated all my adult life, with uncertain economic prospects, and where I had no assurance of ever acquiring the same admirable status that Daddy had enjoyed.

I drove back to Schenectady after my father's death and burial in July 1953 and was tormented with unresolved doubts about my future. I debated the issues over and over, and finally decided that I would prefer to return home to Plains. Rosalynn was astounded and furious when I told her of my decision, but I submitted my official resignation through Admiral Rickover. He did not confront me personally, nor did he ever mention the subject to me. His reaction was disdainful; he apparently felt that it should be the highest of life's priorities for any of his subordinates to serve under him. Georgia's Senator Richard Russell, chairman of the Armed Services Committee, helped me in expediting approval of my request. I left the navy in October with mixed emotions of gratitude and guilt.

Rosalynn was not reconciled to my resignation, and relations between us remained quite cool. We shipped our few belongings home and drove through Washington to conclude my discharge procedures. She avoided talking to me as much as possible and would ask our oldest son, "Jack, tell your father we need to stop at a restroom." We had little money, and I had no prospect for an assured income, so my application had been approved to occupy one of the newly built government housing units in Plains.

We decided to take our boys to visit the Capitol, and our local congressman, E. L. (Tic) Forrester, volunteered to take us on a tour. He was an outspoken segregationist, and while with us he furiously condemned the ill-advised public housing program sponsored by racial integrationists that was going to plant unsavory and despicable people alongside decent white folks. He used racist epithets to describe the kinds of people who would occupy the units. Rosalynn and I looked at each other and didn't comment, then drove on to our new home in the Plains public housing unit.

Rosalynn and I had three sons while I was in the navy, our youngest a baby when we returned to Plains. I wanted to try again for a girl, and we had an off-and-on argument for the next fourteen years, which I finally won. Amy was born late in 1967, when our oldest son was twenty years old.

CHAPTER THREE:
BACK TO GEORGIA

LIFE IN PLAINS

I had no idea what I would do back in Georgia, except try to continue my father's work as a farmer with a small supply business that provided fertilizer and seed to other farmers and bought and stored their peanuts during harvest season. Daddy had described his warehouse activities in general terms before his death, but neither of us at that time was contemplating my leaving the navy. I presumed that my uncle Alton, whom the family called Uncle Buddy, would be in charge of settling my father's estate, and I was startled when he informed me that he would decline this responsibility and have the local judge designate me as sole executor. When I protested that I knew very little about farming or business and was acquainted with very few of the customers involved, Uncle Buddy responded that this was the best way for me to learn. He offered to help me when necessary but reminded me that he was a merchant, and not a farmer.

We were in the midst of harvest season for peanuts and cotton, our primary cash crops, and I had a crash course on the job in buying crops from farmers, collecting debts, and bringing in our own crops from the fields. It was fortunate that the seminal move to replace mules and horses with tractors had not begun, so we were picking cotton by hand and curing peanuts on stack poles just as when I had last worked on a farm, twelve years earlier. Except for a pickup truck, there were no self-propelled vehicles on the farm. Most payments for agricultural supplies that Daddy had sold during the planting and growing season were expected to be made from crops sold in the fall, and I was not adequately attentive to this facet of the business. Although there was a lot of goodwill toward our family, it became apparent that when given an option of which creditor should be paid first, many of the customers met their obligations to the one who was most demanding. There were a disturbing number of unpaid accounts at the end of the season.

Another problem was that the Internal Revenue Service decided to audit my father's income tax returns for a number of preceding years, and they demanded that I substantiate with written proof his claims that much of the income had been from the sale of timber instead of earned, and therefore subject to lower tax rates for capital gains. Contrary to more modern practices, it was customary in those days for timber to be bought by small sawmill owners, who would have fewer than ten employees and would saw lumber in the forests. Mules or oxen dragged downed logs about a hundred yards to the sawmills, which were moved frequently. There had been seven sawmill owners in Plains during the years in question, and several of them had moved away, died, or gone out of business. Their record-keeping practices were rudimentary at best. It was impossible for me to prove the sources of all the income, and the resulting penalties took up most of the cash available in my father's estate.

Despite these unexpected problems, I proceeded to settle my executor's duties to other family members. Using the best estimated valuations that my uncle and I could evolve, I divided the family holdings into five equal parts. My mother, brother, and two sisters met at Mama's home with me one afternoon, and I gave each of them an opportunity to choose their portion, in reverse order of age. Then I accepted what was left. I was glad to see 1953 come to a close, and now I was better prepared for the new year. My wide-ranging and expanding responsibilities made my previous navy life — even helping to design and build an original nuclear power plant — seem simple.

Although as a farmer I had limited access to proper woodworking facilities, I made crude but serviceable furniture for our small apartment with my hammer, handsaw, drawknife, and other simple tools of a farmer. We later gave a picnic-style table and two benches to some friends but retained some bunk beds, plus a couch and lounge chair that are still in use on our back porch. I used pine boards and wove the seat bottoms with half-inch hemp rope. We bought the cushions, and Rosalynn made the pillows. Our apartment in the government housing project was small but comfortable, our oldest son, six years old, was at ease in the same school that Rosalynn and I had attended for eleven grades, we were regularly attending the Baptist church where I had been baptized (although she was still a Methodist), and I was becoming involved in the Lions Club and some other community affairs. The Sumter

County grand jury soon appointed me to fill my father's place as a member of the board of education and the hospital authority, since these were not elective offices.

Just a fifth of Daddy's estate belonged to Rosalynn and me, but I was responsible for managing the cultivated farmland and a larger acreage of timber owned by most other heirs, including native forests and a few acres of planted pine trees. I had forgotten all I ever knew about farming, so during the winter months before planting season I learned as much as possible about managing woodlands and producing corn, cotton, peanuts, and wheat. I studied pamphlets published by the Georgia experiment stations and traveled to Tifton to attend one-day training sessions at Abraham Baldwin Agricultural College on the subjects of most interest. There were seven families living on all the combined farmland who had been sharecroppers with my father, and I talked to them about the different fields and took soil samples to determine what fertilizer formulae would be best. In addition, I made an effort to reach out to some new customers and continued trading with those who had made a good-faith effort to settle their previous debts to the estate.

With land and my future crops as security,

I went to the local bank and obtained a loan of ten thousand dollars, with which I could purchase farm supplies, and planted a crop with high hopes. A fertilizer manufacturer in nearby Dawson agreed to continue the existing arrangement to sell their products to me, and I added three dollars a ton as my profit. Most of my sales were on credit, to be paid at harvesttime. Then disaster struck our farming region, as we experienced one of the worst droughts in history. At the end of the year 1954, neither I nor many of my customers made an effort to harvest a good portion of our parched crops. I had one field of a new variety of peanuts called Virginia Bunch 67 that got a rain the first week in August and made a good yield.

Even after assigning a full value to our unpaid accounts receivable, our gross income for the year was only $280, with no salaries for Rosalynn or me. It helped that this small income qualified us to remain in subsidized housing, with monthly rent being just $31. My application for another bank loan was rejected unless I had my mother and uncle also sign the note. I didn't want to do this, so I went to Dawson and worked out an agreement with the fertilizer company to let me have a truckload (twenty tons) or railroad carload (forty tons) at a time, but on consignment. Any cash payment went directly to Dawson, and charge tickets were payable to them instead of to me. I still had no help (except Rosalynn) and had to load all the fertilizer into my small warehouse alongside the railroad tracks and then onto customers' trucks. When a forty-ton freight car came, I walked down the street and hired a man for an hour or two to help me unload it. I was really grateful when some truck drivers and customers would lend a hand. The fertilizer came either in one-hundred-pound paper bags or two-hundred-pound burlap or white cotton bags. I considered the strenuous exercise good for me and was proud of my new muscles. During harvest season I employed a number of temporary workers to help with unloading trucks of peanuts and corn. I expected to sell about 3,500 tons during the year, but I realized that I had to explore some new ideas about providing improved services to the farmers in our area and expanding my own involvement in agricultural affairs throughout Georgia.

In addition to growing cotton, corn, soybeans, and wheat, I decided to plant all our permitted acreage of peanuts as seed, and to concentrate on the Virginia Bunch 67 variety, which had done best during the previous year. I obtained as many seeds directly from the experiment station breeders as possible, so my produced peanuts could be certified the next two years as pure seed for other farmers to plant. We had normal rainfall in 1955 and were able to settle most of our unpaid accounts. We paid taxes on $3,600 of income. We first struggled just to make a living and then began to invest our profits into expanding our business. During the next few years I bought spreader trucks and began to apply fertilizer in customers' fields, and I improved the equipment used to purchase and process peanuts and corn at harvest-time. In the winter months I did as much of the work as possible in designing and building new storage facilities, dump pits, elevators and conveyor belts, and equipment to remove rocks, dirt, and sticks from harvested peanuts that came from my fields and those of customers.

Producing seed peanuts evolved into a major source of income, and I was soon contracting with other farmers to produce seed on their land for me to process in a shelling plant of my design. I sold my high-quality seed to farmers in an expanding area of Georgia, Alabama, and Florida. I also concentrated on learning everything possible about the entire seed business and was elected president of the Georgia Crop Improvement Association, responsible for the statewide production and distribution of seeds of all varieties, including corn, cotton, wheat and other grains, soybeans, grasses, and even pine trees. On my own farm and those of neighbors, I continued to concentrate on peanuts, and one year I produced sixteen varieties of this one crop. I realized later that I could have enlarged my business more rapidly and become wealthier with additional loans, but I guess the effect of growing up during the depression years made me excessively cautious about being in debt.

My mother and siblings decided to sell me some of their portions of land from my father's estate, and we were able to buy additional farms, including those that had been owned by Rosalynn's family. She and I accumulated about 3,200 acres of land, divided roughly into two tracts, one acquired by our ancestors in 1904 and the other in 1833. My mother and brother, Billy, became minor partners in the farm supply business, and our three sons, when big enough, drove trucks and helped with the handling of peanuts and other crops. I built enough warehouses to hold about fifteen thousand tons of peanuts, which were stored from harvesttime in the fall until we shelled them for commercial use or for seed. I bought a cotton gin and built storage facilities for cotton, corn, and small grains. I learned to blend specific formulae of liquid fertilizers and could fill a "prescription" for a given tract of land to match its needs after samples of the soil were analyzed. By the early 1960s, Carter's Warehouse could provide almost anything needed by local farmers, and we could purchase, process, and market the crops produced in our area. It was a family operation that evolved over twenty-three years, until I was elected president and put all our commercial affairs into a blind trust.

I became reasonably proficient in farming, forestry, business management, and leadership in statewide organizations related to these duties. I also tried to master as many skills as possible, including construction with wood, steel, and concrete, and the maintenance of our equipment. It was hard work, twelve months a year, but I enjoyed the challenges, and our multiple businesses prospered. I became deeply interested in environmental issues by meeting challenges on our own land and working with others.

We moved out of the housing project after the second year, and in 1956 rented what has always been known in our community

Producing seed peanuts evolved into a major source of income and I was soon contracting with other farmers to produce seed on their land for me to process in a shelling plant of my design.

131

as the "haunted house." It is about a mile west of Plains and on the road that goes by the farm on which I spent my boyhood. Just a couple of hundred yards from the local cemetery, this was a place to be carefully avoided after nightfall, and the people who lived in our rural community would evade the danger zone by walking down the railroad tracks instead of the dirt road. The house was built about 1835, when the first white settlers came into the area to replace the Native Americans who had been forcibly moved west to Oklahoma and beyond during the administration of President Andrew Jackson. There were reports of abnormal activities there, including numerous sightings of a white-gowned woman wandering around in the attic, holding a lantern.

A man named Tink Faircloth, who worked as a mechanic for Rosalynn's father, had lived there for a few years. I went hunting at night with him and his hounds for raccoons and opossums, and he said he was wakened several times by strange canine noises. From the bedroom window he could see a large black dog with his hounds, but each time he went through the back porch and opened the screen door, the visiting dog had disappeared. Finally late one afternoon the dog remained in the yard, looking up at Tink as he approached, wagging his tail in a friendly manner. Somewhat cautiously, Tink reached out to pet the black dog, but there was nothing there.

The owner of the haunted house later was Dr. Thad Wise, the oldest of three brothers who were physicians and owned and operated the hospital in Plains, where my mother had come to be trained as a registered nurse. The head nurse was Ms. Gussie Abrams, my godmother and a good friend of my parents. Married to another man, she had lived there for several years with Doctor Thad. Their cook, Inez Laster, reported that all of them would see a strange woman approach the house, but when they looked at her directly or spoke to her, she would turn and disappear. Inez claimed that this went on for more than a year, and that often there would be knocking on the front door but no one would be there. She would have quit, she said, but her employer reassured her about safety and she needed the income.

When Doctor Thad became quite ill, Ms. Abrams asked me to come out and stay with her, and she and I went into the kitchen one evening so she could fix me some supper. I remember that she liked to make a hole in a thick slice of bread, put it in a greased frying pan, fill the hole with a broken egg, and cook it. As I was watching this process, Doctor Thad's dogs outside began making noises I had never heard before — something like a pack of wolves howling in concert. We looked out and saw them all sitting on their haunches, looking at the sky, and producing the weird mournful cry. When we went into the bedroom, we found that Doctor Thad had just died. Somehow, the dogs were grieving for him.

Rosalynn and the boys reported many strange events and unexplained sounds while we lived there, but we never had any serious confrontations with creatures of the spirit world. One day while playing in the attic, our sons discovered a hidden room between the floor and the ceilings of the rooms below, with almost six feet of headroom. There was only a small chair in the space. We surmised that there had been a mentally impaired woman kept there by the family in earlier times, who may have wandered around with a lantern.

Rosalynn and I now had time for some recreational activities, which had rarely been possible during my navy years. We bought golf clubs and began hitting balls in the field behind our house. After a few weeks, we joined some friends and drove to Dawson, where we played on the nine-hole course that was operated by the American Legion. We heard about a square dance club that met every Friday night and were soon enjoying these sessions with almost a hundred other members from the surrounding rural area. The club's name was Meri Legs, from *American Legion*. Dancing was strenuous and challenging, as one or two new steps were added each week to our repertoire. Wearing distinctive attire, we joined other clubs at state conventions and made many new friends. This membership was to change my life.

We were also active in Plains Baptist Church, and soon both of us were teaching Bible lessons every Sunday morning. I was elected as one of the twelve deacons who were responsible for the affairs of the congregation, always submitting final decisions to be made by the assembled members. Rosalynn had been a Methodist, but she joined our church and was immersed in Baptism.

During the time I served on the Sumter County Board of Education, the schools in Georgia were still racially segregated, but within these rigid social boundaries I wanted to equalize educational opportunities as much as possible. I suggested that we five board members visit all the schools so we could better understand conditions in the classrooms, and the other members agreed. Our first visits were to the white students and faculties, and we were quite satisfied with the two schools that included students at all levels and three others in rural areas that had only elementary students. They were nice brick buildings with adequate desks, recreation, music and art facilities, and up-to-date textbooks.

The school superintendent informed us that there were twenty-six schools for black children, the large number necessary because buses were exclusively for white students and classes had to be within walking distance of black children's homes. When we visited them we quickly learned that students had to share textbooks, which were tattered hand-me-downs from white schools; classes were conducted in rooms in churches and in some of the larger houses; there was no music or art instruction and few desks. I remember most vividly that many older students were sitting on tiny stools or chairs. Absenteeism was prevalent because attendance standards were quite low and not enforced since many children had to work in the fields during school months or because their parents were illiterate and saw no benefits from classroom teaching.

After a few of these visits, the other board members declined to make any further excursions. With the advent of the civil rights movement, the state legislature began to make an effort to show that the "separate but equal" national policy was becoming somewhat more equal in order to preserve the separate. School buses were finally authorized for black students, but there was a legal requirement in Georgia that their front fenders be painted black so that everyone would know that the passengers were not precious white children. In 1955, with the first stirrings of racial unrest, the Georgia Board of Education fired all teachers who were members of the NAACP and directed that no teacher could serve who did not support racial segregation.

Although the school integration decision of the Supreme Court in *Brown v. Board of Education* came the year after we returned home, "separate but equal" was not challenged or changed in our community. Having witnessed President Truman's end of segregation in the military, Rosalynn and I supported in a relatively unobtrusive way the evolutionary process of ending the more oppressive elements of racial distinctions in our community. I volunteered to head an evangelism effort sponsored by Billy Graham, using a motion picture that encouraged all people to work together as equals in our Christian faith. I formed a biracial steering committee and was not very surprised when no white church would permit us to have racially mixed planning sessions. We met in an abandoned schoolhouse in Americus, the county seat, and followed the rules and procedures that Billy Graham prescribed, including the use of radio and newspaper advertisements. On the final evening of the crusade, hundreds of black and white people watched the film in the local theater together, and several dozen viewers accepted Jesus Christ as savior. Some of the more conservative white men participated without restraint. There were a few other prominent citizens in the county who shared our more moderate beliefs, including the president of Georgia Southwestern College, the county attorney, and the owner of the only local radio station.

As the race issue and civil rights protests became more prominent, Rosalynn and I found our previously ignored progressive attitude to be more controversial. One morning when I drove into the only service station in town, the owner refused to put gasoline in my pickup truck. I had to install an underground tank and pumping station to service our private vehicles and farm trucks. Later, about a dozen of my best customers came to my warehouse office, reminded me that they had been close friends of my father, and offered to pay my annual membership dues in the White Citizens' Council. This organization had been formed in Mississippi, rejected the violence associated with the Ku Klux Klan, and was publicly sponsored by Georgia's U.S. senators, our governor, and all other statewide political officers. I refused to become a member, and they told me I was the only white man in the community who had not joined. A sign was put on our office door one night, COONS AND CARTERS GO TOGETHER.

Our oldest son finished high school in 1965, and our family took a two-week automobile trip through Mexico. When we returned, not a single customer came into our office, and I finally learned that members of the John Birch Society had been to the county agricultural department, obtained a list of our customers, and informed each that I had been away in a Communist training camp to learn how best to integrate the public schools. I quickly visited each one and explained what we had been doing, and most of our more loyal customers returned. The college president and radio station owner remained under such pressure that they moved away. I briefly considered leaving Plains too, and accepting one of the many offers I had received from shipbuilders that would have utilized my knowledge of nuclear power and my top secret security clearance, but the economic pressures dissipated as we capitalized on the wide geographical area now covered by our seed peanut sales and other business contacts. These racial struggles now seem like ancient history.

After five years in the haunted house, we bought a lot on the edge of Plains and built a home of our own in 1961. An architect produced a design on which Rosalynn and I agreed, two skilled local carpenters supervised the construction, and some hired hands from our farming operation and I helped with the manual labor. The plans called for no moldings around the doors, windows, or at the tops of walls, so each board had to be cut to an exact fit, but the total cost was only ten dollars a square foot. With good crops, we paid off the mortgage in three years.

As the years passed, I achieved the status of an accepted community leader, as a Baptist deacon and Sunday school teacher, Boy Scout leader, chairman of the county board of education, a member of the regional hospital authority, and district governor of fifty-six Lions Clubs in our region. I had also been chosen to fill statewide positions of leadership in my farming and seed business. Unlike in Alabama, Mississippi, Arkansas, and other Southern states, our public schools in Georgia began to integrate without violence or disruption. White parents who still opposed racially integrated classrooms sent their children to one of the many private academies that sprang up throughout the South. The bitter debates and animosities subsided, and eventually almost all our customers resumed their trade with our warehouse. Throughout the 1960s, however, public school integration remained a demagogic issue among political candidates in Georgia, and Plains High School, like most others, did not enroll its first black students until 1967.

LOCAL AND STATE POLITICS

Although my father had served in the state legislature and our family members were loyal Democrats and publicly supported local and state candidates, I had never had any interest in seeking public office and took no part in politics except to join my mother — and most Georgians — in supporting Adlai Stevenson and John Kennedy. I decided to run for office in 1962, after the Supreme Court ruled in *Baker v. Carr* that all votes had to be weighted as equally as possible. This resulted in the termination of Georgia's "county unit" system, where some rural votes equaled one hundred votes in urban areas. As part of the state's response, seats in the Georgia Senate that had rotated every two years were replaced by permanent ones, with much more power and prestige. I decided, somewhat quixotically, to help save the state's public school system — threatened with closure if it was racially integrated — by becoming a senate candidate. I was changing from my khaki work clothes into a coat and tie when Rosalynn asked if I was going to a funeral. It seems inconceivable to me now, but I had not consulted her about my plans, and replied that I was going to the courthouse to qualify as a senatorial candidate and to place an announcement in the local newspaper. Rosalynn was pleased and excited by my decision, which she did not question.

The general presumption was that candidates elected under the old system would be chosen, so only ten days were allowed for campaigning before the special election. Our new senate district comprised seven counties, with a total population of about 75,000. I had some posters and calling cards printed and began to go from one county seat to another, visiting the newspaper offices and radio stations in the area and speaking to any civic club that would accept my request. It was during a slack time of year for farming, and Rosalynn and my brother, Billy, ran the office while I was away.

We were having a one-week revival at our church, and the visiting pastor was staying with my mother. When I stopped by to tell her of my plans, the preacher asked, "Why in the world would you want to become involved in the dirty game of politics?" After thinking for a few moments, I responded, "How would you like to be pastor of a church with 75,000 members?"

My opponent was Homer Moore, a warehouseman and peanut buyer from my mother's hometown whom I knew and respected as an honest business competitor. Each of us had a natural advantage in our home community, and I already knew a lot of farmers and Lions Club members. Another key factor that helped me overcome my late decision was that members of our square dancing group came from most of the same area that the senatorial district covered, and they gave me strong support.

On Election Day I was rushing from one polling place to another when I called in to Rosalynn and she informed me that a cousin of hers had reported a serious problem in Georgetown, the county seat of Quitman County, one of the smallest in Georgia. We asked John Pope, a friend of ours, to go to the courthouse to represent me. When he arrived he was dismayed to see the local political boss, Joe Hurst, ostentatiously helping my opponent. He was requiring all voters to mark their ballots on a table in front of him and telling them to vote for Homer Moore. The ballots were then dropped through a large hole in a pasteboard box, and John watched Hurst reach into the box several times, remove some ballots, and discard them.

I called the newspaper in Columbus, the largest city in Southwest Georgia, and told their political reporter what was happening. His name was Luke Teasley, and he had interviewed me after I became a candidate. I drove to Georgetown. Hurst did not seem

disturbed that he was being observed, even when I demanded that he cease his illegal tampering with the election. He responded only that this was his county, he was chairman of the Quitman County Democratic Party, and this was the way elections were always conducted. As the candidate, I was free to talk to his friend the sheriff if I had a legal complaint to register. After Hurst discounted my complaints, Teasley arrived in Georgetown, and his attitude was primarily amusement that "Old Joe" was still up to his normal tricks. John Pope stayed there and recorded what was happening during the day, and I left to visit the other counties.

I was ahead by 75 votes when the returns were received from the other six counties, but in Quitman County the vote was 360 to 136 for my opponent, although only 333 people had voted. Homer Moore was declared to be elected by the news media. The state Democratic Convention was meeting in Macon that same week, and I went there to register my complaint, which was ignored. Even some of my closest friends thought I was just a sore loser and advised me to drop the issue and decide if I wanted to run in two years. I heard my mother say to my sister, "Jimmy is so naïve, so naïve." If I had understood the strange election laws, I may have withdrawn, but I was angry. I had envisioned the recent Supreme Court rulings to be opening a new era in Georgia, based on the value of individual votes instead of votes by county, and perhaps involving a new group of legislators who could ease the way toward racial conciliation.

I went to the law office of Warren Fortson, the county attorney, and he and I examined the statutes relating to contested elections. They were almost exclusively devoted to a mathematical recount of ballots and not to fraud. In such a rare case, the appeal should be made within five days to the county Democratic Committee, of which Joe Hurst was chairman and had handpicked all the members. Our only recourse was to present the necessary appeal and then file for a recount, which would be conducted by a regional trial judge. We had a meeting in the home of my first cousin Hugh Carter, and he suggested we call his older brother, Don, who had been city editor of *The Atlanta Journal*. The newspaper soon assigned a skeptical reporter, John Pennington, to the story, and he came by to see me and then went to Georgetown, where he had a highly publicized confrontation with Joe Hurst. A series of vivid front-page articles swept the state.

Pennington learned that 117 voters had allegedly lined up in exact alphabetical order to cast their ballots. Many were dead, in prison, or living in distant places. Cartoons in the *Journal* showed graveyard voting precincts with caskets open while their inhabitants exercised their rights as citizens. We found many Quitman County residents willing to confront Hurst, and we worked day and night to accumulate a stack of sworn affidavits confirming our case. The county courthouse was packed when we appeared before the Democratic Executive Committee, but the first order of business was a motion made by my opponent's attorney that the charges be rejected, and Hurst and his committee voted unanimously to agree with the motion. No evidence was accepted. This left us with the possibility of a simple recount of ballots that were cast, and a conservative judge, Carl Crow, was designated to preside.

Since Fortson was known to be my personal friend and was quite liberal on the racial issue, he decided not to represent me at this hearing. Instead, he introduced me to Charles Kirbo, originally from South Georgia but now practicing in the large

Atlanta firm of King & Spalding, and he agreed to take my case. All we knew in advance was that a total of 496 votes had been reported (360–136) but only 333 people had cast a ballot when the polls closed. Even Joe Hurst had stated that there were no absentee ballots. Those who had conducted the election all stated that no voters had been influenced during the day, everything had been done properly, and all the ballots, stubs, and voters' lists were in the box. The big question was Where was the box and what was in it?

When the cardboard container was finally found (under the bed of Joe Hurst's daughter) and placed on the table, it was seen that the flaps were unsealed and that no documents were there — only a pile of ballots. More than 100 were rolled up together on top and encircled by a rubber band. In a lengthy statement, speaking slowly and with long pauses, Kirbo described what had been revealed and compared the situation to an account of a chicken thief who dragged a broom behind him to conceal his tracks from the sheriff. With no ballot stubs or voters' lists, Hurst had left no way to determine how many ballots should be in the box. The opposing attorneys decided not to respond, and Judge

Crow adjourned the session without comment, except that he would announce his decision the next Friday, November 2, in Albany. The Columbus newspaper reported on page 13 that "Jerry Carter from Plains, who lost to Homer Moore," would lose a recount petition.

On Friday, Judge Crow described the disparity in votes cast in Georgetown, stated that there had been no voting booths and no secret ballot, and that there was no way to determine the result of the election. All the Georgetown ballots were nullified, and the three small county precincts had voted 43 for Moore and 33 for me. This made the district total 2,811 to 2,746, in my favor. If implemented, his decision meant that I was the nominee of the Democratic Party, with no Republican opposition! We all pledged to drink only Old Crow whiskey in the future.

The state Party and secretary of state ruled that my name should be on the general election ballot the following Tuesday, but Homer Moore appealed to our local superior court judge, Tom Marshall, and he ruled late Monday night that names should be stricken from all the ballots and that the election be decided solely by new votes to be cast throughout the district the following day — beginning in about six hours. I hadn't been to bed for several days and had lost eleven pounds, but I continued to campaign during Election Day as much as possible. Two county ordinaries did not remove all names as directed, and in most counties the result was similar to the first one. In Quitman County, however, the voters felt for the first time in many years that they were free from oppression, and there were 448 to 23 votes in my favor. The overall tally in the district was 3,013 to 2,182.

Homer decided to appeal directly to the members of the Georgia Senate, whose presiding officer was Lieutenant Governor Peter Zack Geer, a close friend of Homer and Joe Hurst who had always carried Quitman County by ten-to-one margins. There was another contested election in Savannah, Georgia, and the lieutenant governor refused to discuss either one before the legislature convened. We knew that he had absolute control over the senate and would be assigning the newly elected members to committees and other posts. In effect, Peter Zack would decide between Homer and me. The issue was still very much in doubt.

I notified my fellow school board members

that I would resign as chairman if elected, and would concentrate on educational matters as a senator. After sleeping for a full day, I began studying the senate rules and procedures and other issues of importance in the district. I went to Atlanta in late November to meet the lieutenant governor, and Peter Zack received me politely. He said he couldn't discuss any possible contest, noted that I was about the last one to come to see him, and asked for my committee preference. Homer Moore had already made his requests. I said my only preference was the education committee, and he was surprised that I didn't ask for rules, appropriations, judiciary, or industry and trade. He said there should be no problem. The top positions were filled, but if I liked to write, he might make me secretary. I accepted and started to leave, then asked if there was a subcommittee on the university system. There was not, and I asked if one could be formed. He called the upcoming committee chairman, who had no objection to my being head of the new subcommittee on higher education — if I should be a senator.

It is the custom in Georgia to have a wild hog supper the night before the legislature convenes, and Rosalynn and I went to the affair in the old Biltmore Hotel in Atlanta. As we approached Peter Zack's suite, we met Homer Moore and his attorneys leaving, with broad smiles on their faces. We hoped that the lieutenant governor had just told a joke. The next day we were nervous and discouraged when the senate was called to order, but I was sworn in without question. I was also on the agriculture committee and, after a few weeks, on appropriations. I worked hard, read all the bills, and enjoyed the few weeks each year when we were in session. I wrote a book later called *Turning Point* to describe this entire event, which was my introduction to politics. I had learned a lot in just a few weeks.

My two personal legislative goals were to improve election procedures and to secure a four-year college in Southwest Georgia. Now, having a lot of experience on the voting issue, I worked with a small group of lawyers from the judiciary committee to draft a comprehensive reform package that incorporated effects of recent Supreme Court decisions and clarified procedures to be followed in cases of fraud. I remember that one floor amendment was proposed by a senator from Enigma (I envied his hometown's name) that would "prohibit any citizen from casting a ballot in a primary or general election who has been dead more than three years." A good-spirited debate included claims that wives or children could decide fairly accurately how their deceased loved one would still vote after such a brief time. The reforms were overwhelmingly approved, without the proposed amendment.

The other issue was much more important in my district, because the nearest senior college was Auburn University in Alabama, where our students had to pay out-of-state fees. The two junior colleges eligible for promotion were Georgia Southwestern in Americus (my county seat) and a larger institution in Columbus. The elected governor, Carl Sanders, had promised the people of Americus that he would support their request but had backed down under pressure from Columbus. Their supporter, Bo Callaway, was our district representative on the Board of Regents. He was wealthy, politically influential, and chairman of the committee that decided on the academic status of all colleges. I was at a great disadvantage, except that I was chairman of the subcommittee that would have to approve any funding for the university system. The governor wanted a new dental school in his hometown, and I had the proposed legislation in my pocket. Following some quiet but intense negotiations between me and the governor, he used his influence among the regents, the dental school was funded, and Georgia Southwestern became a senior college. Primarily because of this achievement, I was reelected in 1964 without opposition for another two-year term. But it left some bad feelings between me and Callaway.

RELATIONS WITH ROSALYNN

From our marriage in 1946 until I decided to become a candidate for the state senate, in 1962, I maintained a loving and respectful relationship with Rosalynn but followed the example of my father and other men I knew by making the primary decisions in our family. From the beginning, she was quite shy and never wanted me to leave her side at navy cocktail parties or other events when strangers might be present. I was at sea a lot during those early years, and trusted her to manage our family budget and finances and to make most of the decisions about household affairs and raising our children. At the same time, I felt that it was my exclusive responsibility to make final judgments about other, more far-reaching affairs. I cannot understand in retrospect why I didn't at least consult her concerning decisions that affected all our family, including leaving the navy, dividing my father's estate, and running for public office.

As I began to expand our agricultural supply business by visiting potential new customers and becoming involved in professional organizations, I needed someone to run the office while I was away, and Rosalynn offered to help me. She studied a book on accounting, and she and our boys began working at the warehouse in the afternoons. Over time she accommodated our return to Plains and proved to be an invaluable partner in managing Carter's Warehouse, with hundreds of decisions to be made every week concerning our multiple customers and their reliability in repaying their accumulated debts as they bought seed, fertilizer, pesticides, and feed for animals. She also kept the books for our purchases and sales, and was able to ascertain which of our many enterprises were profitable or losing money and what might be done to improve their performance. I became heavily reliant on her judgment and learned to consult her routinely.

When she joined me in political campaigning — always appearing without me — she was effective in securing support from doubtful voters, and I soon realized that people were more inclined to express their beliefs or concerns to her than to me. I was surprised to discover that she liked the art of politics: analyzing issues, allocating funds, devising strategy, formulating proposals, traveling, arranging nightly accommodations on the strenuous campaign trail, initiating radio and television interviews, and even delivering speeches. In fact, she liked the entire political process more than I did.

For the first time in our marriage, we became real partners in every aspect of our lives — but still managed to give each other plenty of space to do our own things.

CONGRESSMAN OR GOVERNOR?

As the 1964 general election approached, there was the beginning of a political revolution in our state. Because of President Lyndon Johnson's successful promotion of civil rights, he was very unpopular in the Deep South.

A number of Georgia's officeholders defected from the Democratic Party and became Republicans. It would be many years before the Republican Party became dominant, but this was the beginning. One of the defectors, Bo Callaway, was the state chairman of Barry Goldwater's presidential campaign against Johnson in 1964 and also became a Republican candidate to represent our congressional district. Both won handily. My mother was Johnson's campaign manager in our county and took a lot of abuse. Her headquarters was in the old Windsor Hotel in Americus, and at the end of a working day her parked automobile was often covered with graffiti or her radio antenna bent or broken. My sons were roughed up at school and sometimes came home crying, but Rosalynn and I consoled them, and they continued to have Democratic stickers on their book sacks and lunch boxes.

Secretary of Agriculture Orville Freeman came to our county to campaign on Johnson's behalf, and Mother arranged for a political rally at the local baseball field. We attended, along with about a hundred white citizens and two thousand African-Americans. Vice President Hubert Humphrey and his wife, Muriel, also made a tour through Georgia, and Mama was asked to accompany them. One of their stops was in Moultrie, where Humphrey was to speak to a joint session of civic clubs. Muriel was scheduled to meet with women for luncheon in a local hotel. Rosalynn was with them, and my sister Gloria Spann was driving. As they approached the hotel, Muriel stated that she would not attend the meeting if it was not racially integrated. With a secret wink, Mama said, "Gloria, go in the hotel and make sure everything is okay." Gloria returned after a few minutes, gave a thumbs-up sign, and they attended the luncheon. When it was over, the black maids put their aprons back on and cleaned up the dining hall. Mama was proud of both Muriel and Gloria.

Racial attitudes were unclear in Plains, with most of our white citizens remaining silent. This changed when black activists began to enter churches with white congregations to demand participation in worship services. There was a confrontation at the Methodist church in Americus that aroused international attention when black Christians were refused admission and knelt in front of the church, surrounded by cameras from the major television networks. Although we had not had any altercation at our church, the eleven other deacons decided, over my objection, to establish a policy that black worshipers could not enter Plains Baptist Church. Like all important decisions of Baptist congregations, the issue had to be determined by a vote of the entire church membership. Rosalynn and I were attending a wedding of my niece north of Atlanta on Saturday, and we had to get up early and drive back to Plains before the Sunday morning service. Only about forty members normally attended a church conference, but about two hundred were present for this debate and decision. There was a vote after the chairman and I made our conflicting presentations, and 6 people, including 5 in our family, voted against the recommendation of the deacons. Fifty voted aye, and all the others abstained! That afternoon, many church members called to say that they agreed with me but didn't want to aggravate other members of their families or alienate their customers. For my family, this demonstration of conflicting opinions was the real turning point and proved to be indicative of the general attitude in Georgia. One by one, the two hundred local school districts accepted the mandate of the U.S. Supreme Court during the years ahead, and none of our governors defied the federal government by standing in the schoolhouse door, as governors had in Arkansas, Mississippi, and Alabama.

As my second state senator's term was ending, I decided to oppose Bo Callaway in his reelection campaign for Congress, despite his great advantage as a wealthy and relatively popular incumbent who had been showered with special favors by the Republican Party. Our personal differences were exacerbated by his being a Democratic defector and a graduate of West Point. I was campaigning almost full-time when, just a few weeks before the primary, Bo decided to withdraw from the congressional campaign and run for governor, leaving me with no opposition. Our Democratic gubernatorial candidate, former governor Ernest Vandiver, withdrew from the governor's race, for health reasons, he claimed. I went to Atlanta and tried to recruit other prominent Democrats to run but was unsuccessful. I feared that the primary choice would be between Callaway and the archsegregationist Lester Maddox, who had become infamous by standing in the door of his Atlanta restaurant with a pick handle, threatening to use it on any black person who attempted to enter his establishment. He was a fiery orator and vowed that there would be no racial mixing in Georgia if he became governor.

With pledges of support from a few young Democrats, I decided to relinquish my assured seat in the U.S. Congress and run for governor. Hamilton Jordan and his girlfriend Nancy Konigsmark, both students at the University of Georgia, volunteered to help me and were key staff members throughout my political career. I made rapid progress in my brief statewide campaign, but without any prepared organization and with very little money, I failed in my attempt, and Lester Maddox was nominated as the Democratic candidate with Callaway as the unopposed Republican. These two met each other in the general election, along with former governor Ellis Arnall, who ran as an independent. When no one achieved a clear majority, the Georgia constitution authorized the state legislature to choose the governor, and the overwhelmingly Democratic legislators selected Maddox. They believed, correctly, that they could take over many of the powers that Georgia's governor had always enjoyed. Until then the governor had chosen the speaker of the house, made final decisions on top committee assignments, and decided when or if proposed legislation would be brought to a vote.

PIONEER MISSIONS

I was deeply disappointed and disillusioned with politics and with life in general. My sister Ruth Carter Stapleton was a famous evangelist and author who was living in North Carolina, and she came to help me overcome my bitterness and despair. Using Bible verses to strengthen her appeal, she pointed out that everyone was destined to failures, disappointments, embarrassments, and sorrows, and advised me to forget about myself for a while, strengthen my religious faith, learn from my political defeat, and become stronger, more confident, resilient, and prepared to reach some well-considered alternative goals in life.

I took Ruth's advice and volunteered to participate in what Baptists call "pioneer missions." I was directed to go to Lock Haven, Pennsylvania, where my partner would be a farmer from Texas named Milo Pennington. With a small budget and a long-distance telephone service that could be used only at night and on weekends, a group of volunteers at Pennsylvania State University had called everyone in the Lock Haven telephone book. They identified those who had no religious commitment but might be willing to discuss the subject. About one hundred families were found, and our task was to visit each one and talk to them about our faith. Milo had been on other missions of this kind, but this was a new experience for me.

I was nervous and somewhat embarrassed, but when I met Milo he tried to reassure me. "We don't have to worry about the reception we will get or the results of our efforts. We'll pray a lot, do our best, and depend on the Holy Spirit to determine the outcome." This attitude was foreign to me, accustomed to accomplishing almost every goal I had sought. Milo and I found a three-dollar-a-day double room and met a state game and fish ranger who was a Christian and would be our host and adviser. With names and addresses on a handful of three-by-five cards, we went from one home to another, always pausing to pray before knocking on the door. With some exceptions, we were invited in to meet with the family members after we explained our mission. Milo was a simple, relatively uneducated man, blessed with supreme self-assurance. I agreed that he should be the primary witness, and he would explain, in basic words, the plan of salvation: All of us fall short of the glory or perfection of God and deserve punishment; but God loves us, and through his grace and our faith in Christ, not because we have earned it, we are offered complete forgiveness. Jesus has taken on himself our punishment, and through repenting and accepting this forgiveness, we are reconciled with God and, with the Holy Spirit dwelling within us, can have a full life now and forever.

Some families refused to let us enter, some said they were already Christians, others seemed amused, and still others seemed to have been eagerly awaiting our message and invitation. I was at first uncomfortable with the way Milo made his presentations. He used simple examples from the lives of people he had known, and his own religious experiences. I was amazed, therefore, at the emotional response of many of the people, who were often in tears. We would join them in prayer as they pledged to change their lives and accept the faith we described to them. I knew the Holy Spirit was present. One night that week, I called Rosalynn and described some of the visits. I told her that I had no trepidation about our future encounters and, strangely, no sense of responsibility for the results of our often awkward presentations. I added, "I feel that it's in the hands of God." And the results we achieved — the transforming experiences we shared with the people to whom we witnessed — were my first encounter with the remarkable effect of Christian faith.

Not all our efforts succeeded. Once we climbed some outside stairs to see a woman living by herself in a small apartment. When we began our presentation, she jumped up from her chair and shouted, "Not me! I don't transgress against God, and I certainly do not deserve any punishment." Despite our further efforts to explain, she ordered us out of her home. We knocked on the front door of a fine house owned by the local General Motors dealer, and he refused to let us enter or speak to him or others in the home. Another memorable visit came later that week, in the poorest part of the city. When we asked a Salvation Army worker how to find our targeted address, she told us it was above some stores, then asked if we *really* wanted to go there. As we began to ascend the steps from an alley door, we heard a stream of invective coming from above — language I'd heard only in the navy, but this time in a female voice. Milo and I looked at each other and finally decided to continue. A young woman received us with amusement and soon let us know that she was the madam of a small whorehouse, with three other "girls" as her partners.

She obviously enjoyed arguing with us and asking leading questions, which we answered as effectively as possible. Eventually, we began to talk about her background and found her to be especially bitter toward her straitlaced parents, on whom she blamed her present plight. Her father, she said, had made improper sexual advances, and as a teenager she'd finally had the nerve to tell her mother. An angry and tearful family confrontation resulted, and both parents accused the girl of lying and being obsessed with sexual fantasies. She ran away from home and became a prostitute "to support myself," she said. She had had no contact with her family for eight years. We had been there almost two hours when she said we would have to leave but invited us to come back the next day — our last one in Lock Haven.

We prayed for guidance that night, but our return brought no miracles. We read John 8:2–11, where Jesus forgives the woman "taken in adultery" and says to her accusers and would-be executioners, "Let him that is without sin among you cast the first stone." After everyone has left, he tells the woman, "I do not condemn you. Go, and sin no more." Despite our best efforts, this woman could not consider herself worthy of God's forgiveness — because at that time she was not willing to "sin no more." She did agree to call her parents and actually dialed their number while we were there. When there was no answer, she promised to try again later. I have prayed often that she was reconciled with God and her parents. Despite these apparent failures, more than forty people in Lock Haven agreed to start a new church, and we helped them rent an abandoned building near the end of the runway of Piper Aircraft Company. I came home from Lock Haven with a heightened sense of the possible intimacy between a human being and God.

I later went on a similar missionary trip to Springfield, Massachusetts, and my assignment was to witness to Spanish-speaking families, most of whom were from Puerto Rico. They were very poor and lived in ramshackle, almost abandoned apartment buildings near a large textile mill that had closed. Those who were lucky enough to find work would travel in buses to labor in nearby fields of vegetables and shade-grown tobacco. My partner this time was a Cuban-American named Eloy Cruz, pastor of a small Baptist church in Brooklyn, New York. I was proud when I was chosen for this task because I knew the language, but I soon realized that the Spanish vocabulary I had known and used in the navy was quite different from the one we were now using to teach the gospel. Reverend Cruz did almost all the witnessing, and my contribution was limited to reading the Bible verses that we chose in advance of each visit. I was amazed at how effective Cruz was in reaching people's hearts. They would become emotional and sometimes weep when he explained to them some aspect of Jesus' ministry and how his life could relate to them.

Once a woman opened her door surrounded by five or six children. When we told them the reason for our visit, her husband, who was sitting across the cluttered room, immediately tried to hide a half-empty beer bottle behind his chair. We told him that Jesus had no objection to drinking wine. As Eloy Cruz explained the story, I read from the book of John about Lazarus, Mary, and Martha, three of the closest friends of Jesus. Lazarus had died, and Jesus was preparing to restore him to life. This was a dramatic story, even with my inept reading of the Spanish scripture. After Jesus wept, and then called to Lazarus, our listeners waited breathlessly. When the dead man came forth from the tomb, everyone broke into cheers. Later, they knelt with Reverend Cruz and me and accepted Christ as savior. I had wonderful experiences every day as I worked with this remarkable man. He always seemed to know exactly what to say and formed an instant intimacy with the poor people whose homes we entered. With the simplest words, he could capture their imaginations and souls.

I was embarrassed by the deference with which Eloy Cruz treated me. For one thing, I owned an automobile — something he'd never dreamed of having. Furthermore, I had been a state senator, and even a candidate for governor (he seemed to ignore my defeat). He considered himself "just" a Cuban, and a refugee, but I knew the opposite; he was a great man. As we prepared to say good-bye at the end of the week, I asked him what made him so gentle but so effective as a Christian witness, and he was quite disconcerted. He finally said, *"Pues, nuestro Señor no puede hacer mucho con un hombre que es duro"* (Well, our Savior cannot do much with a man who is hard). He noted that Christ himself, although the Son of God, was always gentle with those who were poor or weak. He went on to say that he tried to follow a simple rule: "You only have to have two loves in your life: for God, and for the person in front of you at any particular time."

Eloy Cruz's words have had a profound effect on my life, and I often remind myself of them. There are times when courage is required, and genuine humility is not easy to retain for those of us who are blessed with almost every possible advantage. To put myself on an equal basis with a homeless person, a drug addict, a destitute African family, or some neighbor who might be lonely or in need tends to make me feel uncomfortable. But when I succeed, I find that I am ennobling them — and myself. This is not just an idealistic theory, because I know from a few such occasions in my life that it has been true.

I learned some profound and lasting lessons from the combination of my political defeat and my recovery from it, which can best be encapsulated by advice given to us as schoolchildren by our teacher Miss Julia Coleman. She would say, "You must accommodate changing times but cling to unchanging principles." (I quoted her when I was inaugurated as president and when I received the Nobel Peace Prize.) I have tried, at least most of the time, to set high objectives, to accept failures and disappointments with relative equanimity, to acknowledge and try to correct my mistakes and weaknesses, and then to set different and sometimes higher goals for the future. I seek as much help and advice as possible, and if these ambitions are worthwhile and seem to be justified, I just do my best and don't fear the potential adverse consequences. My experiences in Lock Haven and Springfield have helped me apply my Christian faith much more regularly to my secular life, and to resolve the apparent conflicts more easily and consistently.

Chapter Four:
Atlanta to Washington

1970 Election

After a brief respite, I continued with my business and community affairs but began another campaign for governor, which I did not intend to lose. At the end of most days I would drive to places throughout Georgia, making speeches or participating in public events before returning home late at night. I took a course in remembering names and stayed in touch with as many influential people as I could remember, and we sent personal notes to many of them. When three years had passed, I was thoroughly familiar with our state and the issues that seemed important to our people, and had accumulated a voluminous list of potential supporters. There were a large number of farmers and others I had known in my seed business, and a total of 208 Lions Clubs in Georgia where I was well known. I didn't have any billboards or public announcements during this time, just campaigned quietly and without publicity. I was concerned by a public opinion poll that showed former governor Carl Sanders with an 84 percent favorable rating.

During the early summer of 1970, we could spare more time away from the warehouse with planting season over, so Rosalynn and my sons began campaigning also. There were many textile manufacturers and paper pulp mills in Georgia, and we were at their main entrances handing out pamphlets when employees went to work early in the morning. My cousin Hugh was in charge of financing, and we had a goal of ten cents per person in each county (which we reached in only a few places). A man named David Rabhan owned a twin-engine Cessna airplane and volunteered to fly me around the state. He had a wide range of friends among black leaders, including Martin Luther King, Sr., and arranged for me to meet with them and speak in their churches. Many high school and college students volunteered to help, including Jody Powell, a former cadet in the Air Force Academy and now a graduate student at Emory University. Hamilton Jordan served as campaign chairman.

There were many memorable events during the campaign, but one that I can't forget occurred in Bainbridge. I had first visited with Sam Griffin, the editor of the local newspaper, which was founded by his father, former governor Marvin Griffin, and then I went through the business district, going in all the stores and offices to shake hands and hand out my pamphlets. I did the same thing when I encountered someone on the sidewalk. As I approached one burly young man, he turned away and looked toward the wall. I presumed that he recognized me and was either supporting my opponent or just kidding me. When I touched his shoulder, he turned and struck me on my jaw with all his force. I stumbled backward and fell in the middle of the street. While automobile traffic stopped, I slowly recovered my senses and some people helped me to my feet and to a bench on the sidewalk. The police detained the young man and asked if I wanted to press charges. By this time, Sam Griffin had arrived, and after a few minutes he explained that my assailant was a former U.S. marine who had been discharged because of mental problems. He told the police that he thought I had been sent to take him to "an insane asylum," and I told Sam to apologize to him and his family and that I was the one who might have been at fault. I drove home and rested for a day before going back on the campaign trail. I had difficulty speaking, but an X-ray revealed that my jaw was only cracked and not broken. I remember that *The Atlanta Constitution,* which was supporting former governor Sanders and derogating all his opponents, had the headline U.S. MARINE PUNCHES CARTER, describing my being knocked into the street but giving no explanation of the circumstances.

As I gained in popular support, the Atlanta newspapers did everything possible with both news coverage and editorial comments to picture me as a racist. They failed to report my many meetings with black citizens, and attributed to me the aspersions cast on Sanders as a liberal by any conservative persons or news media. My campaign commercials emphasized my background as a former submariner and now a full-time peanut farmer, with photographs of me and our sons working in my fields and warehouse. Sanders extolled his successful life, emphasizing his exalted social and economic status, with a pervasive slogan: CARL SANDERS OUGHT TO BE GOVERNOR AGAIN. I remember long TV commercials showing him flying his own airplane and including a series of endorsements by political and business leaders from Atlanta. We relied on personal contacts by my family with people in their own communities and at work sites. My emphasizing my working-class background made it almost inevitable that class distinctions would be drawn. I welcomed the support of more conservative Georgians, including Marvin Griffin, who had been defeated for governor in 1962, but I was never tempted to indicate any deviation from the moderate racial beliefs I had always exhibited, in the navy and during my time in Plains.

We always lacked money, but our family members, almost always in different places, joined my efforts in meeting people and distributing pamphlets in factory shift lines, at all-night singings, at professional baseball and football games, and along the streets of as many of Georgia's six hundred towns and cities as possible. By Election Day we figured that Rosalynn and I had shaken hands personally with 600,000 Georgians. I received 48 percent of the Democratic Party votes on the first ballot, and defeated Sanders handily in a two-man runoff. In the general election I prevailed over the Republican candidate, Hal Suit, a prominent television personality from Atlanta.

During the final days of the general election campaign, I was flying from Brunswick to Newnan, Georgia, sitting in the copilot's seat alongside Rabhan. He was taking a nap and I was controlling the plane when both engines stopped. He pretended to still be asleep while I punched him hard with my left elbow. He awoke, waited until the Cessna had lost a few hundred feet of altitude, then reached over casually and switched a valve to connect standby fuel tanks and bring the engines back to life. I was furious while he laughed at my discomfort. Finally, I also joined in the merriment, and we had a conversation about the impending end of the campaign. He had helped me very generously, and I asked David what I might do to repay him. He asked if I had a paper and pencil, and I found an aviator's map of Georgia with some blank space on it. He dictated, "The time for racial discrimination is over in Georgia," and said, "This is what I want you to say when you are inaugurated."

I worked hard on my inaugural address. In eight minutes, I said that I had probably traveled throughout Georgia more than any other previous candidate, "and I say to you quite frankly that the time for racial discrimination is over. No poor, rural, weak, or black person should ever again have to bear the additional burden of being deprived of the opportunity of an education, a job, or simple justice." There were several young and progressive governors elected in Southern states in 1970, but this statement made news. A drawing of me was on the cover of *Time* magazine with the headline DIXIE WHISTLES A DIFFERENT TUNE.

GOVERNOR

There were momentous events during my first years in public office as state senator and governor. In 1963 Martin Luther King, Jr., made his historic "I have a dream" speech to a massive crowd in Washington. King, Bobby Kennedy, and President John Kennedy were assassinated, Richard Nixon was forced to resign as president, and the U.S. Supreme Court ruled in *Gideon v. Wainwright* that state courts are required under the Fourteenth Amendment to provide counsel in criminal cases to represent defendants unable to pay their own attorneys. My expectations were raised that this decision would address a serious flaw in our criminal justice system by eliminating the gross difference of treatment of black defendants that had stemmed from their having been excluded from voting or even jury duty during the generations of racial discrimination. In my brief speech at the Lincoln Memorial in Washington on the fiftieth anniversary of the King speech, I pointed out that there were more than 835,000 black inmates in our nation's jails, five times as many as when I left the White House, in 1980. I said that a young black boy in America has a one-in-three chance of being a prisoner during his lifetime.

When we moved into the governor's mansion we found that all the servants and yard workers were "trusties" from the state penitentiary. They were intelligent and dedicated to this assignment as a positive alternative to spending their days behind bars. Within a few weeks one of the cooks, named Pearl, came to Rosalynn and asked to borrow $250, claiming that she had been sentenced to life imprisonment unless she could pay a fine of $750 and had already served four years. This was almost unbelievable, but she had a letter that indicated she could be released from prison with this final payment to the court in her hometown. I investigated the case and found that her husband had been an abusive drunkard, who was at home only on her paydays as a dental assistant, that he beat her and took almost all the money. One day she fought back, and in the scuffle she killed him with a butcher knife. Immediately after her trial, her court-appointed lawyer was getting married and the judge wanted to go on vacation. They decided that she should go to prison only until she paid a fine of $750, but while she was an inmate her mother had been able to raise only $500. I had the attorney general intercede, and Pearl was set free within a few days.

We learned about an even more egregious case on a visit to Cumberland Island, off the coast of Georgia. We had lunch with an affluent African-American couple, friends of ours. The husband had worked for Air France for almost twenty years, and they owned one of the rare private dwellings on the large and isolated island. He told me of a servant who lived on the mainland who had lost possession of fifty acres of land that had been in her family for several generations. She had needed some money to put up bail for her son who was charged with a minor crime, and the justice of the peace offered to give her a loan of $225. She was illiterate and put her mark on what she was told was a promissory note with her property as collateral. When she went to repay the loan, she learned that she had signed a warranty deed and in fact had sold her land, for $4.50 an acre! I took a boat over to the Camden County courthouse and found that the report was accurate but that there was a pending legal case and it would be improper for the governor to intercede. The Georgia Supreme Court later ruled against the woman, and she lost her property.

One of the most competent and attractive servants at the mansion was a young woman named Mary Prince, who helped care for our three-year-old daughter, Amy. She was serving a life sentence, but she convinced us of her innocence. She had lived in the city of Columbus in Southwest Georgia and had visited her cousin in nearby Lumpkin. There was an altercation one night, and a man was shot and killed. As the only nonresident there, Mary was accused of the crime, although several observers knew that she was not guilty. They were not asked to testify. According to the mandate of the *Gideon v. Wainwright* ruling, she was assigned an attorney, whom she never saw until they met at the courthouse for her trial. He advised her to plead guilty and promised that she would receive a light sentence. She took his advice, and her penalty was life in prison. The trial judge happened to be Tom Marshall, a friend of mine who had graduated from the Naval Academy before resigning from the navy and going to law school — and the same one who had wiped our names off the ballot the night before the senate election. When I was elected president, the Georgia State Board of Pardons and Paroles approved my request to be assigned as Mary's parole officer and to take her to Washington with us. By then Tom Marshall was chief justice of the Georgia Supreme Court. Eventually, a retrial was ordered, and the authorities were persuaded that Mary was innocent. She was granted a full pardon and since that time has been an integral part of our family.

I had known that one of my fellow Georgia senators, although not a lawyer, was earning a tidy income by collecting twenty-five dollars monthly from a large number of poor families who could not afford an attorney but had succumbed to his promise of getting one of their relatives out of prison by using his influence with the pardon and parole board. Whenever an inmate was released through normal procedures, usually without any involvement of his, he would claim credit in a letter to his "customers." There were several lawyers in Atlanta who preyed on the state prisoners whom they knew were eligible for parole by charging onetime fees similar to the monthly ones collected by my senate colleague. Rosalynn went to the women's prison and collected the names of these attorneys, and I reported them to the bar association. They were censured but not fined or disqualified. The excessive punishment of prisoners and the use of the death penalty in the United States, alone in the developed world, have continued to fall most heavily on the poor, mentally ill, and people of color. It was on this subject that I made the best speech of my life.

The state constitution limited me to a single four-year term, but those four years were some of my most pleasant and productive. The Georgia governor is known to be the most powerful in America. The legislature can be in session only thirty-five or forty-five days on alternating years, and I could veto bills with almost no possibility of a legislative override. Georgia is required to have a balanced budget (unless we are threatened with invasion from another state), and I could strike out any line items in the final budget bill. The lieutenant governor's authority was limited to managing some issues in the senate, and the second in command in the executive department was my executive secretary, Hamilton

Jordan, whom I appointed without legislative involvement. When I traveled, he acted with full authority on my behalf. My personal choice of cabinet officers was final. Although they covered a wide range on the political spectrum, more than 95 percent of house and senate members were Democrats. I took full advantage of this authority to restructure the antiquated government.

I went to Washington early in my term to attend a National Governors Association conference, and all of us were invited to an evening banquet at the White House. Ronald Reagan, Nelson Rockefeller, George Wallace, and most others were more famous than I, so I was surprised that President Nixon shouted out my name as soon as I entered the East Room. Billy Graham was standing at his side and reached out to shake my hand. He said, "I have always wanted to thank you personally ever since you headed my campaign so successfully in Americus, Georgia. May I have the honor of introducing you to the president?" Nixon was the first president I met.

After months of study by experts and panels of distinguished citizens and then a long series of legislative battles, we were able before I left office to reduce more than three hundred state agencies and departments to twenty-two, and to consolidate almost twenty issuers of bonds to just one. Ever since that time, Georgia has enjoyed triple-A bond ratings. My biggest headache was that former governor Lester Maddox had been elected lieutenant governor, since he was limited to one four-year term as governor. We were not compatible, and his influence in the senate made many legislative victories more difficult than they should have been. Still, I was able to meet many of the needs in education, health care, taxation, and the environment that I had determined to be important during my recent campaign and two terms as senator. Being especially interested in international affairs, I expanded Georgia's relations with foreign countries, brought more foreign diplomats to Atlanta, persuaded Asian and European companies to invest in new businesses in our state, and established Georgia trade offices in Canada, Japan, Germany, Belgium, and Brazil. We visited these and other countries, including Israel and the West Bank, where General Yitzhak Rabin and Prime Minister Golda Meir welcomed us as personal guests. I even hosted a rare annual session outside Washington of the Organization of American States. I was asked to serve as a member of the Trilateral

Commission and learned as much as possible about international issues.

I knew the potential presidential candidates, including my fellow governors Ronald Reagan, Nelson Rockefeller, George Wallace, Jerry Brown, Terry Sanford, and Milton Shapp, and as the 1972 presidential campaign year evolved, I invited other presidential hopefuls to visit Atlanta, the trade and communications center of the Southeast. These included Senators Hubert Humphrey, Edward Kennedy, Edmund Muskie, Henry "Scoop" Jackson, George McGovern, and Eugene McCarthy. All these Democrats spent nights with us at the beautiful new governor's mansion. They were eager to talk about their own plans, and I asked them questions about important domestic and foreign issues. Most of them had traveled overseas less often than I, and it was obvious that other governors and I who were implementing laws relating to welfare, education, taxation, and transportation were more familiar with these issues than senators who may have drafted or voted on the legislation several years earlier.

Senator Jackson asked me to nominate him at the 1972 Democratic Convention in Miami, and I was honored to do so. George McGovern was an admirable man and the favored Democratic candidate, but all of us Southern governors knew that he would have little support in our states. When he was nominated, that consideration did not prevent me and other governors from desiring to be chosen as his vice presidential running mate and pledging to support him in the general election. He offered the position to Ted Kennedy and several other liberal Democrats, who declined. After a chaotic voting procedure, McGovern chose Senator Thomas Eagleton of Missouri, who was finally approved. He was forced to resign when it was revealed that he suffered from depression and was on psychiatric medication, and Kennedy's brother-in-law Sargent Shriver was chosen. McGovern and Shriver received 37 percent of the total popular vote against Richard Nixon and Spiro Agnew, with less than 25 percent in Georgia.

PLANNING THE BIG RACE

My political adviser and publicist, Jerry Rafshoon, and Dr. Peter Bourne, a psychiatrist and prolific author who was my "drug czar" in Georgia, took the initiative in shaping my future political career. In late 1972, Peter outlined in some detail how we might mount a campaign for president in 1976, with the presumption that I would fill the political middle ground between the expected Democratic opponents, conservative George Wallace and liberal Ted Kennedy. I shared this letter with my press secretary, Jody Powell, and Hamilton Jordan. Rosalynn and I decided to have some private discussions that also included Charles Kirbo, attorneys Landon Butler and Philip Alston, and my cousin Don Carter. We had several meetings to discuss how a campaign might be mounted despite little name recognition, and without any prospect of raising much money for the primary contest. We would have to use the same strategy that had been successful in the 1970 race for governor: maximum personal contact with voters, recruitment of new political activists, and the committed involvement of other family members. After these early discussions I was still somewhat embarrassed by and leery of the whole idea. As I remember, we never used the word "president" but just referred to "national office."

One morning I received a call from Dean Rusk, our most distinguished Georgian. He had served as secretary of state under both John Kennedy and Lyndon Johnson, and was now in semiretirement in Athens, Georgia, where he was teaching international law at the University of Georgia. He wanted to come and talk to me, and I invited him to the governor's office. He responded that the subject of his discussion was not appropriate for an official location, so we arranged for him to come to the governor's mansion late that afternoon. We sat in rocking chairs on our back veranda and shared an appropriate Southern libation. Without any introduction, he began the conversation by saying, "Governor, I think you should run for president in 1976." I knew him to be an intimate friend of the Kennedy family and thoroughly knowledgeable about national politics, and was taken aback. I didn't let him know that we had been talking about that possibility but listened intently as he outlined a carefully planned, step-by-step procedure that he thought I should follow.

I didn't make any positive response but just said I would consider his ideas, and then made careful notes and shared them with Rosalynn and the few other conspirators. The encouragement from Dean Rusk removed our remaining doubts, and we began to study the new Democratic Party rules for primaries, the political situations in all fifty states, the names and attitudes of key news reporters, potential sources of funding, and possible competitors. At my request, Hamilton Jordan put together a seventy-page strategic notebook, encompassing all our tentative and highly secret plans. At the same time, I continued my all-out effort to reorganize the state government.

In March 1973, as time for the 1974 campaigns for governors, senators, and congressmen approached, National Democratic Party Chairman Robert Strauss came to Atlanta to give a speech and asked if he could talk to me. Charles Kirbo had become my closest friend and adviser and was serving as chairman of the state Democratic Party, and he joined us at the governor's mansion. Strauss asked if I might consider being responsible for the nationwide effort to elect candidates of our party. Concealing my interest, I listened as he explained how I would be thoroughly instructed by experts in all facets of running a campaign, informed about the most important contests, and could send one of my assistants to Washington to join in top-level strategy sessions of the Democratic Party. I could accommodate my own schedule in choosing the candidates I would personally assist. The national party would, of course, pay all my expenses.

I agreed without much delay, sent Hamilton Jordan to Democratic Party headquarters in Washington, and appointed Frank Moore as my executive secretary in Georgia. I began my duties as campaign coordinator during days I could be spared from the governor's office. By election time in November, I had participated in thirty-seven campaigns throughout the country, with excellent results. Undoubtedly helped by the Watergate scandal and President Nixon's resignation, we Democrats gained four senators and forty-nine representatives, giving us a two-thirds majority in the House. I learned a lot and made hundreds of valuable contacts. Just before I announced publicly my plans to run for president, there was a Democratic "mini-convention" designed to adopt a new charter for the party that made the primary system much more transparent and democratic. We prepared one thousand color campaign pamphlets that cost a dollar each and distributed them to key Democrats. George Gallup had recently published a public opinion poll that contained thirty-two names of potential Democratic nominees. Mine was not included. We had a lot of work to do.

One potential candidate, Ted Kennedy,

arrived at the mansion to spend the night before Law Day in May 1974. He was scheduled to address the entire University of Georgia student body the next morning. As governor I was asked to speak at noon to a small group of law school alumni. I labored over my speech, but when I listened to Kennedy, I realized that my talk covered almost the same points. I borrowed a desk and hastily scratched a few notes on an envelope, expressing my deep concern about inequities in the criminal justice system, and I described some of these cases.

Hunter S. Thompson, who was traveling with Kennedy, took a seat in the back of the dining hall where I was speaking. He was famous as the author of *Fear and Loathing on the Campaign Trail '72* and for unorthodox statements such as "I hate to advocate drugs, alcohol, violence, or insanity to anyone, but they've always worked for me." His neighbors at the table later told me that he repeatedly freshened his glass of iced tea with shots from a bottle of Wild Turkey whiskey, but that he seemed transfixed when I began my remarks. Afterward, he obtained an audio recording of my speech and began to extol it in his *Rolling Stone* articles and media interviews. He later told me that he made visitors to his home in Colorado listen to the tape. When Hunter died, in 2005, he left my speech on YouTube, and it is part of his Internet biography.

One enjoyable project that I began as governor was to make a special effort to bring moviemakers to Georgia, and it was highly successful. Some of the most well known of our twenty-six films were *Deliverance, The Longest Yard,* and *Smokey and the Bandit.* I traveled to Hollywood and New York to sell our state to producers, and on one of my trips I had my first introduction to a nationwide audience with an appearance on *What's My Line?* No one recognized me, but after a number of humorous questions Arlene Francis and other panelists finally identified me as a governor. On another occasion I visited Radio City Music Hall and watched the Rockettes practice a routine that involved a submarine. They invited me to join their chorus line, and a photographer snapped a picture of me standing on one foot with my other leg as high as I could raise it. I returned to Atlanta late that night, and the next morning Rosalynn asked me what I did in New York. I replied that I worked hard all day trying to promote another movie to be made in Georgia. She said, "It was not all work," and showed me a photograph in the morning newspaper, of me in line with the Rockettes and almost falling over backward!

NATIONAL OFFICE

My term as governor expired in January 1975, and almost immediately I began to make a few forays around the nation with Jody Powell to take advantage of state Democratic conventions and other speaking opportunities. We had very little money and shared a small hotel room only on the rare occasions when we couldn't find some supporter with a spare bed for the night. It was very discouraging at first, because nobody knew who I was and few people were even thinking about the presidential election, which was still eighteen months in the future. A young man from New Mexico named Tim Kraft was hired as campaign manager in Iowa, and after spending a few weeks in the state we decided to have a press conference and reception in a Des Moines hotel. We rented a large ballroom and bought soft drinks and some sandwiches and cookies, but only one reporter and three inquisitive potential supporters came. I spoke to them briefly, and then Jody and I walked to the city hall and county courthouse and handed out my pamphlets in every office.

We visited more than 120 Iowa communities, arranged meetings in people's homes and in college classrooms, and were thrilled when as many as twenty people attended. We were always looking for someone with a microphone or even a reporter's scratch pad, hoping to get some news coverage. Jody snored a lot, and I usually managed to be asleep before he came to our shared room for the night. Once he woke me and reported excitedly that I would be on television early the next morning. He avoided answering my questions, just responding that he would explain later and that we had to be up at five o'clock. On the way to the TV station, he asked if I had a favorite recipe, admitting that I would dress up like a chef and be interviewed on a cooking show. I donned an apron and a floppy white hat, and gave the audience one of my favorite ways to prepare fillets of any kind of fish. I demonstrated how to cut them into strips the size of French fries, marinate them overnight in some kind of steak sauce, dip them in flour, and deep-fry them to be served hot or cold. After I began to win primary elections, the video of this session was resurrected and played over and over, along with reruns of *What's My Line?*

Operating on a financial shoestring and not facing any serious opponents during those early months, we were never really discouraged by the lack of attention. Our strategic plan was clear, with the only serious change having been the decision by Kennedy not to enter the race after polls showed that too many people still remembered his role in the accidental drowning of a girl at Chappaquiddick. In addition to Iowa, we concentrated on New Hampshire, with New Mexicans Chris and Georgia Brown in charge, and Florida, with Plains native Phil Wise as state campaign manager. Accepting speaking invitations when possible, Jody and I visited all fifty states during the primary period. Since most of the other candidates were better known and had lined up the support of active Democrats, we recruited a wider and wider circle of young people and relative newcomers to politics. The few who worked for us full-time received small stipends and had to arrange for their own lodging, sleeping in their automobiles or in people's homes, or paying for a cheap motel room from their own funds.

One of the earliest and most persistent questions when I began campaigning was

"If elected, will you tell us the truth?" Having served as a legislator and governor, I knew how difficult it was to keep this promise, especially when facing influential constituents who held opposing opinions on subjects important to them. Nevertheless, I decided to make the commitment, and would tell my small audiences that I would make the same declarations to them and to all my other listeners. Often I would close by saying, "If I ever lie or even make a misleading statement, don't vote for me." Depending on the audience, I would talk about my experience as governor, my varied educational background, my service in the navy, my knowledge of farming, and my commitment to manage the federal bureaucracy with a technique known as "zero-based budgeting." I always gave the audience a full opportunity to ask me questions, which helped me decide what to include in future appearances.

I received applause when I reported that I had been a submarine officer and was still a farmer — and not a lawyer. I sought out livestock sale barns in Iowa and other agricultural states, and often the auctioneer would let me say a few words to the assembled buyers and sellers of cattle and hogs. To them and to interviewers from newspapers and other media, I could answer questions about agricultural issues, including details of fertilizer prices, seed, and the current marketing of corn, soybeans, and pork. I soon realized that my opponents, mostly from the U.S. Senate, would address questions about welfare, health, education, or transportation by referring to Senate Bill 643 or another number and its proposed impact. I could describe how the same federal laws were helping or obstructing progress among the people at home in Georgia.

I reported regularly on progress and discussed the issues that were being raised with some young lawyers who had helped me in the governor's campaign, led by Stuart Eizenstat and Jack Watson. We studied Social Security laws, the farm bill, health legislation, and especially the controversial subject of abortion. I had to be careful to maintain the same position in conservative Iowa and more liberal states in the Northeast. Hamilton and others laid out our itinerary for the week after listening to my suggestions. Sometime in April, Rosalynn agreed to make a foray into Florida, and she campaigned as she had during my race for governor. She drove from one community to another, stopping at courthouses, newspaper offices, livestock sale pens, and especially radio stations. She would spot an antenna, go into a news room or the broadcasting booth, and tell a reporter or disc jockey that her husband was running for president and she wanted to talk about him. If, as often happened, he didn't know anything about politics, she provided a written list of questions he could ask her, and she responded with her carefully rehearsed answers. In all, she was to spend seventy-five full days in Florida, visit 105 communities in Iowa, and expand her crusade into forty other states.

CAMPAIGN TECHNIQUES

When I began campaigning, it soon became obvious that there was a serious distrust of top political leaders in Washington. Our oldest son, Jack, had left his study of nuclear physics at Georgia Tech and volunteered for service in Vietnam. When he returned home on leave as an enlisted man, he was ridiculed by his friends and college classmates for being foolish and naïve, and chose not to wear his uniform. It was widely known that a stream of false statements was being promulgated from the White House and Department of Defense about the issues that had caused America's involvement in that conflict, our massive bombing campaign, and our relative successes against the Vietcong. A general sense of alienation was, of course, exacerbated by the Watergate revelations and President Ford's full pardon of Nixon.

After a few months, we had seven separate family campaigns going on, with Rosalynn; me; all three of our sons with their wives; my mother, Lillian; and her youngest sister, Emily Dolvin — all in different parts of America. Rosalynn and I usually met in Plains and shared our experiences at our home on Saturdays, attended church on Sunday, and then went to Atlanta for strategy sessions that grew steadily in size. Hundreds of Georgians formed what was known as the "Peanut Brigade" and traveled to key states at their own expense to knock on people's doors and explain why I should be elected president. As the other Democratic candidates began campaigning, almost all were still bogged down in the Congress or managing their states' affairs, campaigning just part-time and focusing on a few key primaries where each thought he could do well. I was the only one who sought delegates in every state, hoping at best to come in first but at least to gain a few convention votes.

Some of my Democratic opponents from Northern states began to raise the issue of race relations, emphasizing my having come from the Deep South, where the tinges of racial segregation still lingered. On my first campaign trip to Massachusetts, I visited one of the Revolutionary War sites and permitted some news reporters to ask a few questions. The first was "Why should anyone from Massachusetts vote for a governor from Georgia?" I responded, "Well, when John Kennedy ran for president, he received a higher percentage of votes from Georgians than from the people of your state, and I expect the same treatment." In a meeting in Washington of campaign leaders, there was a question about how well we were including black people in full-time positions on our staffs. Most of the others pointed out that they had either one or two, or were searching to find some who were qualified. When they asked Andrew Young about my campaign, he responded, "I don't know exactly how many Governor Carter has now, but last month there were twenty-two." I was questioned about the race issue frequently, and made a serious gaffe when asked about housing patterns in big cities, where families with ties to Italy, Greece, Ireland, or other

European countries concentrated their homes. I said that, in general, I thought it was all right for people who shared the same languages, religions, and customs to choose to live near each other. There was an uproar in the news media about my espousing racially pure neighborhoods, but it died down when Daddy King, Andy Young, Benjamin Mays, and others defended me.

To everyone's surprise except ours, we came in first in Iowa and New Hampshire and then concentrated on Florida, where the segregationist George Wallace was expected to repeat his 1972 victory and Scoop Jackson was certain to prevail among more conservative voters and Jewish citizens. Primarily to stop Wallace, Andy Young, the Martin Luther King family, and some of the more liberal labor unions endorsed me, and I carried the state. Then I went on to beat Senators Lloyd Bentsen, Fred Harris, and Adlai Stevenson III in their home states of Texas, Oklahoma, and Illinois, and to gain enough other support to give me a clear majority at the Democratic Convention.

VICE PRESIDENT
I decided that I needed a vice president who was familiar with Washington and the

Congress, which eliminated other governors and local officials. I met with potential running mates before the convention; most of them visited at my home and toured Plains with me. These included Senators Ed Muskie, Frank Church, John Glenn, Walter Mondale, and Scoop Jackson. I watched how they related to my neighbors on the streets, and to the customers who gathered in my warehouse office. "Fritz" Mondale was the least well known but was quite compatible with me and had the most thorough and ambitious ideas about how the vice president could play a greatly expanded role. I chose him, and approved all his suggestions, many of which had evolved after his extensive meetings with Governor Nelson Rockefeller and Senator Hubert Humphrey, his predecessors in the office.

Before we began the frantic two-month general election campaign on Labor Day, Fritz and I hosted a series of all-day sessions on the most important topics of the time. Groups of the foremost experts we could identify would assemble in Atlanta and then come to Plains in chartered buses, and we would meet in my mother's isolated Pond House for discussions about taxation, welfare, education, transportation, the mili-

With Vice President Mondale in Rose Garden, April 13, 1978. Fritz Mondale was compatible with me and had the most thorough and ambitious ideas about how the vice president could play a greatly expanded role.

tary, and relations with the Soviet Union, Israel, China, and other countries. In addition to learning as much as we could, we had a chance to get to know these leaders and later to choose from among them the cabinet officers to serve with us. Many of them realized our dual purposes, and all of them were on their best behavior.

I had known Zbigniew Brzezinski as director of the Trilateral Commission when I was a member, and he helped brief me before the presidential debate on foreign affairs. Later — after my election and during the early months in office — he assisted me in preparing an ambitious agenda regarding other nations. It included the inevitable challenges but also a few that had not been at the forefront of the campaign issues or emphasized in the news media. I decided on a major effort for peace in the Middle East, the end of apartheid in South Africa, and majority rule in other nations; reduction of nuclear arsenals, normalization of diplomatic relations with the People's Republic of China, open communications with Cuba, and resolution of the Panama Canal issue. This last was highly publicized, because in the Republican primary there had been a strong demand by Ronald Reagan that we "should not give away our canal." I also decided that human rights would be the centerpiece of our foreign policy.

GENERAL ELECTION

After President Gerald Ford narrowly overcame a right-wing challenge from Ronald Reagan and was nominated as the Republican candidate, he and I waged a vigorous but mutually respectful contest, and we both survived three national television debates. Ford had been hurt previously by political attacks from Reagan and by his pardon of Nixon, but I never raised this issue. During our debate on foreign issues, he had also insisted, inexplicably, that the Soviet Union did not dominate any of the East European countries that were occupied by Soviet troops. My own campaign suffered, perhaps even more, from an ill-advised interview I granted to *Playboy* magazine, in which I was explaining Jesus' Sermon on the Mount and stated that, like other men, I had "lusted" for women. I could not think of an effective way to further explain my blunder and decided just to live with it. Within a few days, I dropped almost 15 percentage points in public opinion polls.

Ford and I chose not to raise any campaign funds from corporate or private contributors but to finance our general election campaigns from the dollar each taxpayer could designate for this purpose. (That contribution has been raised to three dollars but has not been used by presidential nominees since 2004.) We had neither the money nor the desire to purchase negative commercials, which have more recently become the key tactic in winning elections. I respected Ford very much, for his integrity and his encyclopedic knowledge of the federal government and its agencies.

Our family and other close members of our political team assembled in Atlanta for election night and watched as returns began coming in from the East Coast and then moved westward, mostly by time zone. In general, I carried most of the Eastern states and Ford swept states in the West. We were almost tied until late returns from Mississippi came in last, to give me a slight margin of victory in popular votes and 55 percent of the electoral votes. The entire campaign was described in more than thirty books. Two of the most complete and accurate are *Marathon* by Jules Witcover and *Running for President, 1976: The Carter Campaign* by Martin Schram.

CHAPTER FIVE:
LIFE IN THE WHITE HOUSE

FIRST FAMILY LIFE

My inauguration speech was one of the briefest on record for the first inauguration of a president. It began with thanks to Gerald Ford for "healing our nation" and expressed two of the major themes of my administration: keeping the peace and strengthening human rights. Even though I had been preparing to be president, I was genuinely surprised when the Episcopal bishop from Minnesota pronounced "blessings on President Carter." The phrase "President Carter" was startling to me, but I was ready and eager to assume the responsibility, and we looked forward to life in the White House. My first official act was to pardon the draft evaders from the Vietnam War.

I wrote in my diary: "The quarters at the White House are quite similar to those we enjoyed as the governor's family in Georgia, but I have been constantly impressed — I almost said overwhelmed — at the historical nature of the White House, occupied for the first time by our second president, John Adams. When I see a desk or a writing cabinet or a book or a sideboard or a bed that was used by Thomas Jefferson or Abraham Lincoln, Franklin Roosevelt or Truman or Kennedy, I have a feeling of almost unreality about my being president, but also a feeling of both adequacy and determination that I might live up to the historical precedents established by my predecessors."

That first night we had a very relaxed and informal meal with our family. Earlier when Rosalynn had visited the White House some of our staff asked the chef and cooks if they thought they could prepare the kind of meals we had enjoyed in Plains, and the cook said, "Oh, we've been fixing that kind of food for the servants for a long time." The meals in general were superb, but we were shocked to learn that for the first few days our food bill in the White House was six hundred dollars, and that the president pays for all meals for the family and personal guests.

On inauguration night we attended eleven parties, but we moved fast, danced a few times for our own enjoyment and that of tens of thousands of partygoers, met all our commitments, and got back home in time to go to bed about 1:30 A.M. Rosalynn had decided to wear the same evening gown that she had worn for my inaugural ball as governor. She was criticized by the news media for not choosing a new model from a famous designer, but I approved her choice and was very proud of her beauty and grace.

During the following days we shook hands with thousands of people in receiving lines to thank those who had helped us during the campaign and to cement ties with members of Congress, diplomatic officials, and also with members of the armed forces. I was particularly impressed by how many generals and senior enlisted men came by and made some reference to peace, their prayers for us, or just said, "God be with you."

The first reception was for more than 750 people in whose homes members of our family had spent the night on the campaign trail. These meetings were emotional because some of the families had taken us in when few people knew or cared who I was. We gave each couple a small brass plaque stating that a member of my family had stayed with them.

We decided that, as much as possible, we would make the White House into a pleasant family home, and our private life there was eventful and enjoyable. The building had been completely renovated and repainted when Harry Truman was president, while he and his family moved across the street into Blair House. He was not much of an athlete, and his exercise was vigorous walking, but his friends installed a one-lane bowling alley in the basement as a birthday gift. In 1969 President Nixon, who was an avid bowler, replaced it with a more modern version. An outdoor swimming pool and cabana were installed in 1975, while Gerald Ford was president, to replace a pool alongside the Oval Office used by Lyndon Johnson and then covered over to provide space for the White House press corps. The tennis court had a longer history, having been first built in the early 1900s and used by Theodore Roosevelt, Woodrow Wilson, Warren Harding, and Calvin Coolidge. It was moved to its present location in 1975. All the members of my family and many of our invited guests enjoyed these facilities.

A small but luxurious family theater was built in 1942, and all presidents have used it for practicing speeches, holding private group meetings, and viewing motion

Carter family at the State dinner on the occasion of the peace treaty signed between Israel and Egypt, March 26, 1979.

pictures. The first films that we watched were *One Flew over the Cuckoo's Nest* and *All the President's Men,* about the Watergate scandal, which contributed to my election. We could order any movie, and often received new films before they were shown in public theaters. The projectionist's records show that our family watched 480 movies (about 2 per week), many requested by Amy to share with her school classmates. On Friday nights the students would often stay up until dawn, watching one film after another, and then sleep until noon before going to the swimming pool or bowling alley.

Amy was nine years old and the center of media attention, and it was less well known that we had three older sons, two of whom lived with us. Our oldest son, Jack, his wife, and one-year-old son, Jason, stayed in Georgia. Our youngest, Jeff, was with us, and he attended George Washington University. Our middle son, Chip, helped both me and the Democratic Party with political affairs. Our mothers visited often and always stayed in the Queen's Bedroom, across the hall from the Lincoln Bedroom.

When there was no official White House function, we arranged to have our family together at suppertime, and had our meals in a small dining room adjacent to the upstairs kitchen. As at our home in Plains, our family had frank and often contentious discussions around the table. They all had experiences I couldn't share, and it was obvious that American citizens expressed their own points of view to my family members much more freely than to me. Rosalynn and the boys traveled a lot and attended many events, and Amy brought home accounts of life in her elementary school, located in the Foggy Bottom neighborhood, about a mile from the White

House. She had no hesitation in sharing her opinions and provided our family with sound assessments of life in the public school system. In addition to her classmates she had close friends among the children of White House staff members who had served with me when I was governor.

I left for the Oval Office early every morning, read the morning newspapers and any personal messages that were waiting for me, and had an intelligence briefing about eight o'clock from Dr. Brzezinski, who was now national security adviser. Sometimes we were joined by the CIA director or other specialists. I usually had lunch there or in a small adjacent office and quite often invited the vice president, cabinet officers, staff members, or leaders from Congress to join me. Rosalynn lunched with me every Wednesday so we could discuss personal affairs and I could answer her persistent questions about official issues.

I was determined to be strict on expenditures for the nation, and to set an example in my personal life. I decided to sell the presidential yacht *Sequoia,* and to minimize the playing of "Ruffles and Flourishes" when I arrived at public meetings. I was surprised when some of these changes proved to be quite unpopular, and to learn how much the public cherished the pomp and ceremony of the presidency. I also planned to cut back on expenditures for the hideaway at Camp David, which had been established by President Franklin Roosevelt. This is an enclosed area of 120 acres, located in the Catoctin Mountain Park, about sixty miles north of Washington. Toward the end of February, Chip's wife, Caron, began having labor pains, and we took her to Bethesda hospital, where a son was born, named James IV. After holding him for a while, we drove on to Camp David for our first visit. As did most other presidents, we fell in love with the place, and I told my budget director not to touch its funding and not to let me know what it cost to operate. Also, I didn't want any more construction done there without my personal approval. Subsequently, our family and sometimes special guests went to Camp David on almost every free weekend.

At other convenient times we were able to go home to Plains or the coastal islands and other restful places in Georgia, to fish for striped bass and bluefish along the Eastern Seaboard, and to enjoy some of our national parks. We took our boys down the Salmon River in Idaho and then fished the Snake River while staying in the Grand Tetons. It was on this trip that Rosalynn learned to fly-fish.

One of my boyhood hobbies that our family cherished was collecting Indian artifacts. When we returned home to Plains from the governor's mansion or the White House during winter months, Rosalynn and our three boys would almost immediately change clothes and go to a favorite field where Native American villages had existed. There were a half dozen of these locations that I had previously known to be productive. After a crop has been harvested or the land plowed in preparation for new planting, a few rains will wash away the topsoil and leave pieces of flint stone exposed. We would slowly walk back and forth across the field, about fifteen feet apart, and search the ground carefully. On our best day we found twenty-six unbroken points. My total collection includes about fifteen hundred arrowheads and other stone pieces and clay pottery, which has been analyzed by professors at the University of Georgia to ascertain the Indian tribe, kind of stone, probable site of manufacture, and estimated age. A number of the arrowheads are almost identical and seem to have been produced at a central location and traded to distant places. Their ages range from two hundred to six thousand years. The Yuchi tribe of Lower Creek Indians was forced to leave our area in 1828, and our ancestors moved here five years later. This was exactly one hundred years after the first English settlement was established on the Georgia coast, two hundred miles to the east.

I had been a fisherman all my life, but I didn't learn to fly-fish for trout until I was governor and living near the cold waters of the Chattahoochee River, which flows through Atlanta. Quite often on weekends at Camp David, I fished in Hunting Creek at the base of the mountain while Rosalynn practiced her casting technique in the pool behind our cabin. Our most gratifying recreational excursions were to Pennsylvania, where we sought out a convenient place to go fly-fishing on weekends. As guests of a private hunting and fishing club, we traveled by helicopter and landed on the farmland of a dairyman, Wayne Harpster, who owned or leased a good portion of Spruce Creek, about twenty-five miles south of Penn State University. We formed an immediate friendship with him and his entire family, and began to go there quite regularly.

We would helicopter to Camp David, be met by a horde of news reporters as we disembarked, and then proceed to our cabin while they went to nearby motels to await our return to Washington. We changed clothes, collected our fishing gear, returned to the helicopter, and flew another thirty-five minutes to the Harpster farm, where we landed in a remote pasture near our cottage. We did this during our last two years, and these fishing expeditions were never detected by the news media. This has continued to be an annual visit by us, and Wayne has become a regular companion when Rosalynn and I go fishing on other exotic streams in the world. Our most recent fishing excursions have been to Mongolia to fish for taimen, the largest species of trout; to the Kola Peninsula east of Murmansk, Russia, for Atlantic salmon; and to Argentina (for the fourth time) to fish for trout and other species.

My family helped make my off-duty times in Washington very pleasant, with visits to museums, theaters, and many historic sites, and also just loafing around the White House playing tennis, swimming, bowling, and watching movies. I spent a lot of relaxing hours tying trout flies while listening to good music. All of us are also avid readers, and it was during the weekends that I had a chance to catch up on back reading and prepare for the week ahead, frequently studying voluminous briefing books from my staff. During the first few months, our family and a number of staff members took a speed-reading course every Friday night, which made it much easier for me to read what my secretary informed me was an average of three hundred pages of official documents each day.

Rosalynn and I decided that Amy would attend one of the nearby public elementary schools, which aroused some comment in the news media because it had been assumed that she would go to one of the more elite private institutions. I had been deeply involved in education as a member of the county school board, state senator, and governor, and was committed to the public school system. Rosalynn and I wanted Amy to be deeply involved in the Washington community and with children of diverse backgrounds. At Thaddeus Stevens Elementary School she had classmates who were from a wide range of families, including blacks, Hispanics, and children of the servants in foreign embassies.

I was still a parent. In July 1977, I received word that our son Chip was renting a home from a man whose close friend was going to be receiving a large quantity of marijuana in the Gulf of Mexico on a fishing boat. I called Chip, and, without telling him what the problem was, I asked him to come home. I learned that he had been invited to go fishing on the boat that was soon to receive the marijuana. The marijuana was transferred, the bust was made, and three tons of marijuana was confiscated. Chip's contact turned out to be a federal government informer.

I was running every afternoon from five to seven miles, and I usually extended this distance to at least ten miles a day on weekends. During my maximum running times I was averaging about forty miles a week. I kept a careful log of distances run and times required, but this was one of three things we lost when we went back to Plains. (Two superb bamboo fly rods were stolen.) I really enjoyed this daily break from my official duties. By the way, I never ran with Secret Service agents but always with my military aide, who provided constant communication access between me and agencies of the government and the outside world. White House physician Dr. William Lukash, members of my family, and a few guests would sometimes join me. Willie Nelson would run five miles with me when he spent the night at the White House.

I lost some weight, and Rosalynn complained that I was too thin. I remember that when I had my first annual physical examination, Dr. Lukash reported that my heart rate was forty-one beats per minute. When some of the news reporters questioned him, a second count was forty.

In September 1979 I decided to enter the ten-thousand-meter race on Catoctin Mountain, near Camp David. I ran the course twice in advance to become familiar with the difficult terrain and timed myself at a few landmarks along the way. On race day I decided to cut my previous best time by four minutes, which proved to be a serious mistake. The weather was unusually warm and humid, and I overexerted and had to drop out of the race, overcome with heat exhaustion. I recovered quickly and handed out the prizes at the awards ceremony. Although I felt a little weak, I didn't have any aftereffects. I should have played it safe to make sure I finished, because the news media had a field day with my failure, with photos of my sagging body in many newspapers.

Nobody in our family had ever even seen skis, but we decided to take up cross-country skiing during our weekends at Camp David. There were several convenient places inside the fenced compound, and the surrounding country roads and park area provided excellent trails. Catoctin Mountain Park Superintendent Tom McFadden gave lessons to all the members of our family. I had two notable falls during this time. On a late Sunday afternoon in February 1979 we were going down a steep slope on a newly constructed section of highway. The groomed trail was narrow, and there was about an inch of ice on both sides. My right ski went under the ice sheet, and I fell over on my face. My forehead, cheeks, lips, and chin were slashed. We radioed Dr. Lukash and learned that he was treating Superintendent McFadden, who had had a spill and cut his face even more severely. I rode back to Camp David on a snowmobile, bleeding badly. Dr. Lukash treated all the superficial cuts on my face, and we skied the next day. The big problem was that I was scheduled to make a speech at Georgia Tech on Tuesday. We called Lillian Brown, who was a superb artist with cosmetics, and she applied several layers of greasepaint and powder and accompanied me to Atlanta. I got through the ordeal without embarrassment, but I had to be careful to avoid any broad smiles, which caused the thick makeup to crack.

My other accident occurred two days after Christmas in 1980. With only two inches of snow on the ground, I went out to ski on the steep nature trail behind our cabin at Camp David, and my ski hit a rock. I fell, jammed my left elbow under my body, and broke my collarbone. I went to Bethesda hospital to get it X-rayed and strapped up, then returned to Camp David. This left me partially handicapped during the final few days of my term in office. It didn't hurt much at first but was uncomfortable when I experienced vigorous handshakes. This happened when we had a reception for the fourteen hundred staff members who worked in and around the White House and also when I went to the Sugar Bowl game in New Orleans and Georgia's star player, Herschel Walker, clasped my hand and almost lifted me off my feet. It was six years later, when I was sixty-two years old, that Rosalynn and I became avid downhill skiers.

Amy and I spent a lot of time together, swimming, bowling, and hitting balls on the tennis court. She said she wanted a tree house, and we looked at possible places on the South Lawn. I didn't want to damage any of the historic trees, so we decided to place the sleeping area up in the tree but supported from the ground. She outlined what she wanted, and I drew the plans, ordered the necessary lumber, and Amy and her friends were soon spending nights up in the green foliage — watched carefully by the Secret Service agents. Later, when Bob Hope came to visit us, he made a wisecrack about being a Republican and I announced that he would be moving from the Lincoln Bedroom to sleep in Amy's tree house.

Our youngest son, Jeffrey, was an amateur astronomer and borrowed a fine tracking telescope that he set up on the roof of the White House. He studied the various constellations and galaxies and could describe what we were observing. Jeff became friends with Dr. Carl Sagan, who invited us in December 1977 to visit the naval observatory adjacent to the vice president's home. The Mondale family joined us as Dr. Sagan gave a slide presentation on outer space, including his speculation about life on distant planets. We enjoyed the stargazing, and I wrote a poem about the lovely sight of a flock of geese flying over Washington, their breasts reflecting the city lights.

A Reflection of Beauty in Washington

I recall one winter night
going to the White House roof
to study the Orion nebulae,
but we could barely see the stars,
their images so paled by city lights.
Suddenly we heard a sound
primeval in its tone and rhythm
coming from the northern sky.
We turned to watch in silence
long wavering V's,
breasts transformed to brilliance
by the lights we would have dimmed.
The geese passed overhead,
and then without a word
we went down to a peaceful sleep,
marveling at what we'd seen and heard.

We were enjoying the White House but missed the large veranda that surrounded the governor's mansion in Atlanta. The Truman Balcony overlooked the South Lawn, Jefferson Memorial, and the distant Washington airport, and was furnished with little glass tables and straight-back chairs something like those in a soda fountain. We decided to import some comfortable rocking chairs and ordered six from Georgia. After that, our family had a pleasant vantage point from which we could observe a por-

226

tion of Washington, and we went there especially during late afternoons and at night. This is where I would take important foreign visitors when I wanted our discussions to be relaxed and completely private.

I remember one session with British Prime Minister James Callaghan, who asked for a conversation that would be totally off the record. We had a cocktail while enjoying the new rocking chairs, and he described Great Britain's economic troubles and told me that the International Monetary Fund was putting pressure on him to reduce their deficit with what seemed to be draconian actions. I interrupted to offer my help in easing the IMF demands, and he said, "No, no! I want you to support their restraints. I want them to force me and my government to do what I know is right but is not politically popular."

Over the years we invited thousands of our friends to the White House to spend the night, for South Lawn events, concerts, and official entertainment of foreign dignitaries. Rosalynn and her aides and the State Department worked together to prepare the guest lists and did a fine job. We also enjoyed having children and grandchildren of former presidents, but for some reason we made one glaring omission by failing to invite Margaret Truman, whose father was the president I most admired. We later apologized to her, but I will always regret this mistake.

MY FAMILY HELPS

The president of India died when I had been in office just a few weeks, and I called Mama to see if she could represent our country at the funeral. She had been a Peace Corps Volunteer in a village near Bombay when she was seventy years old and had become well known in the country. When she answered the phone I asked her what she was doing. She said she was sitting around the house looking for something to do, and I said, "How would you like to go to India?" She said, "I would love to go someday. Why?" And I said, "How about this afternoon?" She said, "Okay, I'll be ready." When I described the purpose of the trip, she asked me to have an appropriate black dress ready when she arrived in Washington, and I agreed. She was accompanied to the service by our son Chip and some members of Congress who had a special interest in India, and I authorized the plane to fly the funeral party to Bombay (now Mumbai) after the services, to let Mama visit her former Peace Corps post. It was a town of about twelve thousand people named Vikhroli, and when they arrived at its entrance only a few people were there to meet my mother. She was disappointed but asked to visit the little room where she had lived. When they turned a corner, thousands of waiting villagers, who had been perfectly quiet, burst into wild applause when they saw the woman they called Lilly.

My family spared me a lot of overseas travel, as Rosalynn, our sons, and my mother attended the funerals of President Jomo Kenyatta in Kenya, Prime Minister Golda Meir in Israel, and the presidents of India, South Korea, and Algeria, plus historic birthday events in England, Australia, Canada, and several countries in Latin America. On one occasion, when I had a number of difficult diplomatic challenges in South America and couldn't make the trip myself, Rosalynn toured seven nations for meetings with presidents and other top officials. After careful briefings from the State Department and the CIA, she carried personal messages from me urging President Ernesto Geisel of Brazil to abandon his plans to reprocess nuclear fuel for weapons and the leaders of Peru and Chile to reduce their purchases of armaments, and to inform the president of Colombia that one of his cabinet officers was accepting bribes from drug cartels. Rosalynn was, if anything, more frank and forceful in her presentations than Secretary of State Cyrus Vance or I would have been.

ENTERTAINMENT

Rosalynn went out of her way to plan entertainment for foreign dignitaries that was most likely to please them. She checked in advance with the CIA, State Department, and the visitor's embassy in Washington and ours in the foreign country, and the performances at state banquets accommodated the interests of our guests. Carmen Romano, wife of Mexican President José López Portillo, was a concert pianist, so at our dinner for them Rudolf Serkin played several selections and then Carmen surprised our guests with her performance. Japanese Prime Minister Masayoshi Ohira liked informality and popular music, so Bobby Short sang while we served barbecue on the roof of the West Wing, overlooking the Rose Garden. President Anwar Sadat said he watched western films every day and requested that the Statler Brothers perform. The New York Harp Ensemble played while King Baudouin and Queen Fabiola of Belgium dined with us, and a group of young Suzuki violin students, including Amy, played. Then a few of the more advanced violinists, some as young as seven, joined the U.S. Marine String Band as an impromptu finale. As a special treat for all Americans, Rosalynn arranged a series of Sunday afternoon performances that were recorded and televised by PBS.

The artists who performed at the White House during my time in office included Beverly Sills, Isaac Stern, André Previn, Sarah Vaughan, Dizzy Gillespie, George Shearing, Shirley Verrett, Itzhak Perlman, Pinchas Zukerman, Frank Sinatra, Leontyne Price, Tom T. Hall, Sarah Caldwell, the Romeros, André Watts, the Guarneri String Quartet, the Alvin Ailey American Dance Theater, Andrés Segovia, the Boston Pops, Willie Nelson, John Denver, Mstislav Rostropovich, Bill Monroe, Mikhail Baryshnikov, Vladimir Horowitz, Dolly Parton, Eubie Blake, and many others. We also had concerts on the South Lawn of the White House and special performances inside. I especially enjoyed recitations by twenty-one of our nation's most notable poets. Andre Kostelanetz led a full orchestra of military bands in Tchaikovsky's 1812 Overture, with its grand finale of cannons and fireworks.

Whenever appropriate, we joined in the

performances, often dancing together and especially enjoying the practice sessions before the formal events. I sang "Salt Peanuts" with Dizzy Gillespie and joined Willie Nelson in either "Georgia on My Mind" or "Amazing Grace." (He turned the microphone as much as possible toward himself.) I remember during a practice session that Baryshnikov leaped high enough to hit one of the chandeliers in the East Room, and we had to find a lower stage and move it to a different place. Our most memorable event was when Horowitz came to play, fifty years after he first performed at the White House, for Herbert Hoover. He was concerned about harsh reverberations, even after we closed all the curtains, and insisted that nearby carpets be brought in to cover part of the polished wood floor. He was still not pleased, and two of our sons went up to the third floor and brought all three Oriental rugs from the hall to the East Room before he was satisfied. When Rosalynn came in, she saw Horowitz and me on our hands and knees, unrolling the rugs and adjusting them around the piano. The White House photographer missed a notable picture.

We were delighted in 1978 to participate in the initiation of the Kennedy Center

Honors program, which has continued since that time. I commented then that the five people chosen would receive recognition but, more important, "come here to honor us and all the people of the world." The artists named during our three years were Marian Anderson, Fred Astaire, George Balanchine, Richard Rodgers, and Arthur Rubinstein in 1978, Aaron Copland, Ella Fitzgerald, Henry Fonda, Martha Graham, and Tennessee Williams in 1979, and Leonard Bernstein, James Cagney, Agnes de Mille, Lynn Fontanne, and Leontyne Price in 1980. Andrés Segovia became a special friend, and when we visited a nightclub in Spain on a later trip, he made a surprise appearance, performing for us and other patrons. Later he gave us a special casting of his hands as they played the classical guitar.

These many events occupied a lot of Rosalynn's time, but the lives of our family and many others were brightened by knowing these talented people and enjoying their performances.

WORSHIP, AND FOREIGN LEADERS

My religious faith had become a minor issue during the campaign, when I responded "yes" to a reporter's question, "Are you a born-again Christian?" Some reporters implied that I was having visions or thought I received daily instructions from heaven. My traditional Baptist belief was that there should be strict separation between church and state. I ended the long-standing practice of inviting Billy Graham and other prominent pastors to have services in the White House, and our family assumed the role of normal worshipers in a church of our choice. When I became governor, Rosalynn and I decided to join the Baptist congregation nearest our new home, and this same decision brought us into membership in First Baptist Church, just a few blocks from the White House. Our Sunday school teacher, Fred Gregg, asked me to teach a Bible lesson on occasion, and I decided to do so a few times each year if it could be done without prior notice or publicity. Here is a March 20, 1977, excerpt from my diary:

"I taught Sunday school and broached the idea to the Sunday school . . . class that Baptists and other evangelical groups ought to adopt the same policy that the Mormon Church has: to send large numbers of young men and women volunteers around the world for a year or two of service to the church, working with missionaries. I have an inclination to pursue this more in the future when I have time to put my thoughts together."

Later, I proposed this to Jimmy Allen, president of the Southern Baptist Convention, and the idea was adopted in 1978 as Bold Mission Thrust. Unfortunately, it was never fully implemented after the convention became divided over a struggle for power and control between traditional and more conservative leaders.

At Camp David there was no chapel at the time, and worship services were held in a small room normally used for motion pictures. I invited the chaplains at nearby army bases to lead our Sunday services, and they sometimes brought tape recordings of their choirs to augment our voices in singing hymns. We used the same room, rapidly modified, for worship services on Friday, Saturday, and Sunday to accommodate the Muslims, Jews, and Christians who were assembled for the Middle East peace talks. A small chapel was built with donated funds while George H. W. Bush was president.

Several of the leaders I met as president were interested in my Christian faith. Except for a summit meeting in London, my first foreign visit in 1977 was to Warsaw, Poland, which was then dominated by the

Soviet Union. We were received graciously by First Secretary Edward Gierek, who served as the national leader under his masters in Moscow. After several hours of discussing official issues in the presence of our staffs, he asked if he could speak to me in his private office. He said that he espoused atheism as a Communist, but that his mother was a Christian and had recently visited the Vatican. Then, somewhat ill at ease, he asked me if I could explain the foundations of my Christian faith. He listened as I responded, and then I asked him if he would consider accepting Jesus Christ as his personal savior. I had done this hundreds of times as a deacon and in my lay mission work. He replied that he would like to remove this distance with his mother, but he was prohibited from making any public profession of faith. Polish Cardinal Karol Józef Wojtyła was elected as Pope John Paul II in 1978, and the following year he requested permission to visit Poland. Gierek was warned by Soviet President Brezhnev "not to do something he would regret." The Pope's request was granted in June 1979, and Gierek was removed from power. I never knew what his decision was about becoming a Christian before his death in 2001.

Later we went to South Korea, where I first visited a U.S. military base for discussions with our military leaders and took an early morning run with our troops. After we proceeded to Seoul, I had meetings with some of the most notable human rights heroes in the country and worshiped in one of the world's largest Baptist churches. I spent the next two days with the head of state, General Park Chung-hee, congratulating him on the economic progress being realized, and then arguing for hours about several other contentious issues, including his avoidance of responsibility for his nation's military defense and his gross abuse of human rights. These were probably the most unpleasant discussions I ever had with one of our supposed allies, but the atmosphere was somewhat brightened by the presence of his young daughter, Park Geun-hye, who was acting as first lady after her mother had been killed by a North Korean assassin.

When we concluded our official discussions, General Park asked for a private meeting with me and, as had First Secretary Gierek, he wanted to talk about my Christian faith. He said that his wife and some of his children were believers (not all Christian) and had urged him to talk to me. After

I made a brief presentation and answered his questions, he requested that I ask one of my Baptist friends to come to the Blue House to explore how he might become a Christian. I did this before leaving South Korea, and I was later informed that the requested meeting occurred. General Park was assassinated the following year. (In February 2013, Ms. Park Geun-hye became president of South Korea.)

I initiated the most significant exchange I had concerning Christianity with a foreign leader. When I normalized diplomatic relations with China, I invited Vice Premier Deng Xiaoping to visit me in January 1979. We and our officials had intense negotiations on dozens of controversial issues that had accumulated during three decades of estrangement between our two nations, and many of the new agreements had to be approved by Deng and me personally. At the end of our official state banquet, the Chinese leader said, "President Carter, you have been very helpful to the Chinese people, and I wonder if there is anything special that we may do for you." I thought for a few moments and then responded, "Well, when I was a little boy my supreme heroes were Baptist missionaries who served in China, and I used to give five cents a week to help build hospitals and schools for Chinese children. Since 1949, missionaries, Bibles, and worship have been prohibited in your country, and my request is that these three things be permitted." Deng seemed to be taken aback by my request and said he would have to wait to make a decision. The next morning, he told me that he could never permit Western missionaries to return to China because they had been critical of native culture and lived in a superior way. However, he would grant my other two wishes.

Rosalynn and I were able to visit China about six months after we left the White House and were delighted to witness the rebirth of Christianity there. We worshiped in a church in Shanghai that had five Anglican priests and learned from them that Bibles were being distributed freely. On one occasion there had been a shortage of the special thin paper normally used in Bibles, and the government had helped to provide their needs. There was established a "three-self" system for Christian churches, meaning self-governance, self-support, and self-propagation. The National People's Congress officially guaranteed freedom of worship with no limit on the location or number of congregations, but each new church is supposed to register with the government. Over the years hundreds of congregations have refused to comply with this ruling, but most of them are ignored by officials unless their pastors or members make public claims or comments that are provocative. I have worshiped in both "three-self" and unregistered "house" churches on my many visits to China, but my multiple requests to Chinese leaders to remove this registration rule have not been honored. The result of Deng Xiaoping's decision is that China is now the fastest-growing Christian nation, with an unofficial estimate of more than 50 million worshipers, and there are more than a dozen seminaries in the country where new pastors are trained. The basic doctrine of the two types of Chinese churches is the same as in our churches in Plains: a belief in the Trinity; Christ being both human and God; Jesus' virgin birth, death, and resurrection; and the second coming.

NEWS MEDIA AND CONGRESS

From the start of my presidency I was determined to give access to members of the Congress and leaders in the news media. During my first two years in office, I held forty-one press conferences for the national press corps. Frequently, I had special groups of newspaper editors and publishers, as well as news directors and owners of regional television and radio stations, come to the White House for extended luncheon discussions with me. In May 1978, I added Jerry Rafshoon to my staff and at his suggestion began holding intimate dinners with leading national media figures and, sometimes, their spouses. Rosalynn and I enjoyed these sessions with news media stars, including Walter Cronkite, Carl Rowan, Katharine Graham, and James "Scotty" Reston. Off the record, I would answer all their questions.

My efforts to woo the news media were not successful. A scholarly analysis of presidential news coverage revealed that, overall, I had negative coverage in forty-six of the forty-eight months that I served — the only exception being the first two months, including when my family and I walked down Pennsylvania Avenue. This was a problem we could never understand or resolve but we just decided to accommodate what we couldn't correct. Some of the most influential analysts never anticipated my election, and others could not accept having a governor from the Deep South in office. There was a running debate about whether I was a liberal or a conservative, with the conclusion that I was being devious about my basic philosophy. Also, a negative attitude toward the presidency carried over from the Watergate revelations about President Nixon, with perhaps a suspicion that we too had something unsavory to hide. We remember most vividly that *The Washington Post* had a full page of derisive cartoons showing me, my mother, and other members of our family with straw coming out of our ears, frequenting outdoor privies, and associating with pigs. At the end of my term, one of the most prominent columnists wrote that finally the Reagans would "restore grace to the White House." One of my top advisers, Charles Kirbo, referred to my pledge never to lie as throwing down a red flag. He said, "We just lost the liar vote."

Throughout my term we arranged private meetings with all Democratic and Republican congressional members and individually with senior members of the key committees. During the first two years I had broad congressional support among Democrats, and Senator Ted Kennedy was especially helpful. This changed dramatically late in 1978, when he decided to run for president. He became one of my most persistent opponents, seemingly determined to minimize my achievements. Kennedy recruited a number of the more liberal Democrats to support him.

The most memorable occasion of Kennedy's opposition to my proposals came in 1979, concerning our national health plan, which was the result of months of work by my cabinet officers, economic advisers, White House staff, and congressional leaders. Except for Kennedy, we had full support from chairmen of the six key committees in the House and Senate, and all six had been involved in its preparation. Our plan protected all Americans from catastrophic illness costs; extended comprehensive health coverage to all low-income citizens; gave total coverage to all mothers and babies for prenatal, delivery, postnatal, and infant care; promoted competition and cost containment; and provided a clear framework for phasing in a universal, comprehensive national health plan. Its total startup costs were included in my annual budget proposal, and it was to be fully implemented over a period of four years, with funding assured. Senator Kennedy had his own preferred plan, which was so expensive that there was no prospect of congressional support, but his committee members participated with us until the week of announcement, when he decided to oppose the legislation. Kennedy's opposition to our plan proved fatal; his was a powerful voice, and he and his supporters were able to block its passage. We lost a good chance to provide comprehensive national health care, and another thirty years would pass before such an opportunity came again, with just partial implementation.

I turned more and more to moderate Republicans, with minority leaders Senator Howard Baker and Congressman John Rhodes as key allies when my commitments were compatible with theirs. These included streamlining the government bureaucracy, tightening control over intelligence agencies, instituting zero-based budgeting, initiating free trade agreements, and cutting back on unnecessary weapons systems.

Almost every substantive legislative act on domestic affairs was drafted in the White House under the leadership of Stu Eizenstat, a young Atlanta attorney who had headed the group that studied issues during my campaign. We invited Democratic committee chairmen and senior Republicans, or their staff members, to participate. Frank Moore, my top assistant as governor, coordinated relations between me and members of the House and Senate. These efforts were successful in getting multiple proposals passed by Congress, where I had a very high percentage approved, with strong support by both parties.

Chapter Six:
Issues Mostly Resolved

There were a number of issues I faced in the White House that were not passed on to my successors, either long-standing problems that I was able to resolve or matters that were transient in nature. Everybody warned me not to take on too many projects early in the administration, but it was almost impossible for me to delay things that I thought needed to be done.

Syrian Jews
Sometimes I got involved in matters beyond my constitutional duties or authority, such as this special request from a congressman described in my diary: May 4, 1977: "Met with Congressman Steve Solarz, who is primarily interested in the Syrian Jews being able to leave and in particular five hundred young women who are unmarried. Some of the young men have been permitted to immigrate to this country, but they can't find

wives, and the women who are still in Syria can't find husbands. I'll discuss this with President [Hafez al-] Assad when I get to Geneva."

Assad permitted the young women who could arrange marriages to come to New York, and a number of them found husbands here. I was invited by one elated groom to be his best man but was unable to accept the job. Assad later bragged about the majority having the good judgment to remain in their permanent home.

MAJORITY RULE IN RHODESIA

One of our major goals was to help institute majority rule in southern Africa and to strengthen the commitment to human rights throughout that continent. I chose Andrew Young as my ambassador to the United Nations because he was universally admired as a top lieutenant of Martin Luther King, Jr., and had a deep interest in Africa. When Andy made a tour of the region in February 1977, my instructions were to find out what the leaders wanted or needed from the United States, and to see what could be done to encourage democracy and human rights. He reported that the situation was "very confused" but that we should put heavy pressure on Rhodesian President Ian

Smith and South African Prime Minister John Vorster to accept majority rule. He said the British had practically no remaining influence, but it would be best to keep them in the forefront of diplomatic efforts. I put his recommendations into effect and soon had a message from Vorster that Smith might be ready to consider a change, but that it was too early in South Africa.

I wrote in my diary on March 3, "It's a little frustrating to be dealing with Ian Smith through Vorster, and to be deferring to the British, who've shown a remarkable incapacity to put the thing together so we know which way to exert our influence." On March 23, I wrote that "I decided to ask the Vice President to take responsibility for this southern African question, which is a complex matter. My own thought is that we might get ourselves, Great Britain, South Africa, and some of the frontline presidents — maybe [Samora] Machel (Mozambique), [Kenneth] Kaunda (Zambia), and [Olusegun] Obasanjo (Nigeria) — to agree on an overall approach to Rhodesia and Namibia, and then just ram it through and in the process get a commitment from South Africa to . . . liberalizing attitudes towards blacks, moving toward ultimate full participation by black citizens of South Africa."

In May I sent my vice president to meet with Vorster, and Fritz called publicly for "one man—one vote" in South Africa. When he returned, he reported that Vorster might help us with Namibia and that the government of Zimbabwe/Rhodesia would be based on majority rule. "Vorster retained his own long-standing commitment to apartheid, insisting that the blacks were a different kind of human beings." I added a diary note: "My own guess, however, is that our quiet but persistent pressure along with other nations might force evolutionary changes in South Africa."

Joined by many other nations but opposed by some "white supremacists" in our own Congress, these efforts were eventually successful. Direct elections caused Rhodesia to become Zimbabwe before I left office. Namibian independence took longer, and it was thirteen years before South Africa had its first free elections and Nelson Mandela became president.

Andy Young was a superb ambassador, who always supported freedom and human rights, and I trusted him completely. His opinions were compatible with mine, but he spoke loudly and publicly in New York and in foreign countries, often without approval or instructions from me or the State Department. On several occasions, Secretary of State Cyrus Vance came to the Oval Office to complain about Andy's independent comments, and a white congressman from Georgia made an unsuccessful effort to have Ambassador Young impeached. After a couple of years there was a UN resolution that related to the Palestine Liberation Organization (PLO) with which Andy had to deal. In the process, he met with a PLO representative, which violated an official commitment that our government had made while President Nixon was in office: not to deal with the PLO until after they recognized Israel's right to exist. I actually believed this commitment was misguided, because open negotiation seemed to me to be more likely to bring about desirable results. Nevertheless, while Andy did not in this case violate the commitment because he was acting as president of the Security Council, he did neglect to confer with me or the secretary of state before holding the meeting.

I was out running late one afternoon when Secretary Vance, his deputy Warren Christopher, Hamilton Jordan, and Jody Powell interrupted me to say that Andy could no longer serve. They said he had misled Vance about meeting with the PLO. This presented me with one of my most difficult decisions as president: between my secretary of state and my personal friend who was an ambassador. After meeting with Andy and some of my trusted African-American advisers from Georgia, I decided to let him resign. I have never been sure that this was the right decision. He made a public statement: "It is very difficult to do the things that I think are in the interest of the country and maintain the standards of protocol and diplomacy. . . . I really don't feel a bit sorry for anything that I have done." This unfortunate incident has never lessened our close and personal friendship.

IDI AMIN

There is never any way for a president to avoid the twenty-four-hour-every-day responsibilities of the job, staying in communication with heads of departments and ambassadors from their posts around the world and subject to scrutiny by more than a thousand White House reporters during times of crisis. During our first weekend at Camp David, Idi Amin, the deranged and brutal president of Uganda, responded to my criticisms of his multiple assassinations and other human rights violations. After ordering all Americans living in the country to come to Entebbe to meet with him, he singled out the more than one hundred Christian missionaries and announced that he was going to execute them, one by one, until I apologized to him. He gave me a deadline, and I was in a quandary. I decided to call for help from the king of Saudi Arabia, who had great influence on Amin with potential financial gifts and as a fellow Muslim, and Amin then announced that the missionaries were free to leave Uganda. I was thrilled, but not surprised, when all of them refused to abandon their missionary duties and decided to remain in the country.

ALEXANDER HAIG

It had been customary in the past for the regional military commanders to confine their reports to the secretary of defense, but I wanted to learn as much as possible about what was happening in their major geographical areas. I instructed Secretary of Defense Harold Brown to have them come by to see me when they were in Washington. The first to report was General Alexander Haig, supreme commander of our forces in Europe, including NATO. He had played the key role in negotiating between President Nixon and Vice President Ford concerning a full pardon for Nixon if he would resign. As he and I discussed issues in the European Theater, I had difficulty understanding what he was trying to say and was concerned about his partisanship and derogation of my policies emphasizing peace and human rights. After thinking about it for a few days, I suggested to Secretary Brown that Haig be removed from this command, which was highly political in nature. Reluctantly, and mistakenly, I yielded to Brown's plea that this decision be postponed. Haig resigned in 1979 and entered politics on his own, later serving as Reagan's secretary of state for a few months and then seeking to become the Republican nominee for president. During the campaign he called George H. W. Bush a "wimp." Bush went on to be elected.

MAINE INDIANS

One of the most interesting legal cases I had to address was a defensible claim by Native American tribes in Maine that they owned a substantial portion of the state. The area in question amounted to 12.5 million acres and was inhabited by more than 350,000 people, mostly of European descent. The Interior Department seemed to be siding with the Indian tribes, and the Maine congressional delegation wanted to pass legislation that would wipe out all aboriginal claims with a payment based on land values in 1796, no interest added.

I asked William Gunter, a friend who had just retired as chief justice of the Georgia Supreme Court, to mediate the dispute. His proposal provided the basis for a final settlement that protected the rights of the Passamaquoddy and Penobscot claimants. This was an important matter for the state, directly involving almost two-thirds of its area and about one-third of its people. Political candidates in Maine were drawn into the debate, and Senators George Mitchell, William Cohen, Ed Muskie, and Bill Hathaway had to handle it with great sensitivity to survive in office. I signed the legislation in October 1980, after the Congress appropriated $81.5 million in federal funds to purchase clear title to 305,000 acres of woodland, and to provide about $27 million in a trust fund for the Native American tribes. In effect, each tribal member received the equivalent of $25,000 and 275 acres of land. Since then, the trust funds have been wisely invested.

REORGANIZATION

Building on my experience as governor, my first request to the Congress was to authorize me to simplify and streamline the federal government, subject to a subsequent veto by the House and Senate. No Democrat in the House would introduce the bill because the powerful chairman of the Government Operations Committee did not wish to share this authority with me and claimed it was unconstitutional. I convinced Republican members to sponsor the legislation, and it finally passed in April 1977. During my term I made eleven careful recommendations to make government more simple and effective, ten of which were accepted. I also proposed the creation of two cabinet-level departments to replace multiple smaller agencies that were confusing and unmanageable. The Energy Department was headed by former Secretary of Defense James Schlesinger, and the first secretary of education was former Court of Appeals Judge Shirley Hufstedler. I wanted this new department to be as free as possible from previous obsession with racial lawsuits, or domination by the teachers' unions. Ronald Reagan promised during the 1980 campaign to abolish these departments, as have other Republican candidates since then, but both of them have survived.

SUMMIT IN ENGLAND

Even on official missions, we had some good times. To prepare for my first summit meeting with six other leaders in London, I studied five big briefing books on political and economic matters. I was especially concerned about measuring up in the fiscal discussions because the leaders of Great Britain, Germany, France, Japan, and Italy had all served previously as finance ministers. I accepted an invitation from Prime Minister James Callaghan to arrive in London a few days earlier than the others. My plans were to visit Laugharne, the Welsh home of Dylan Thomas, my favorite poet, but Jim pleaded with me to go instead to Newcastle upon Tyne. This was the ancestral home of George Washington and the site of a crucial election the day after I was there. The reception was enthusiastic, and I spoke to a crowd of about thirty thousand. (This was one of the few places where the Labour Party prevailed.) I planted a poplar tree descended from one at Mount Vernon planted by Washington, but I could see it had been frozen in the hold of Air Force One and was dead. (Later, Rosalynn's brother replaced it with a live one.) By the time our G7 group assembled, I had become familiar with many of Britain's domestic issues and received good publicity in the news media. I continued that early arrival policy for my other three summit meetings, in Germany, Japan, and Italy.

On that Sunday we visited Westminster Abbey to worship, see where the King James Bible was produced, and to visit Poets' Corner. I asked where Dylan Thomas was honored, and the archbishop responded that he was too disreputable to be included. We had an argument about the relative characters of Lord Byron, Edgar Allan Poe, and others that was widely reported by the reporters with us, and Dylan's widow, Caitlin, later wrote to thank me. Jim Callaghan warned me that any political influence on this subject would be counterproductive, but I wrote the archbishop and his committee a letter when I returned to Washington, extolling the poet's remarkable works. During my last week in office, Dylan Thomas was accepted for commemoration, and I taped a message for the BBC that was played at the ceremony. Citizens of Laugharne later brought me a duplicate of the stone marker in Westminster for my presidential library.

One foreign leader with whom I was having a somewhat contentious relationship was Chancellor Helmut Schmidt of

Germany. I had met him when I was governor in 1973 and he was finance minister. I was trying to get Volkswagen to establish a manufacturing plant in Georgia and also wanted to set up a trading office in Bonn. We had a productive meeting because he was eager to have my assessment of the ongoing Watergate hearings. More recently, he had been critical of some of my policies as president, obviously thinking that my insistence on human rights in the Soviet Union was naïve and counterproductive. I wanted him to stop providing Brazil with equipment and technology for processing plutonium, and to stimulate Germany's economy as the other Western leaders were doing to address a worldwide economic slump. I met with his foreign minister to try to resolve these issues before the June summit meeting. We eventually succeeded, but these irritants were always replaced with others during my term in office, including the size and composition of nuclear weapons in Europe, the degree of economic stimulus in the United States, and my strong reaction when the Soviets invaded Afghanistan. In summary, I wrote in my diary in 1980, "He's a strange man and a good leader of Germany. I'm afraid he has a problem in his attitude toward me. Privately to the news media and to others he's constantly critical of the United States, of our resolve, our fairness, our commitment, our honesty, and so forth. He knocks me and Brzezinski and Vance and Muskie and others."

The G7 meeting (now expanded to G20) was interesting and productive. Among many items on our agenda, the two most difficult and time-consuming were human rights and nuclear nonproliferation, where we and the Canadians were criticized as too strong. I was impressed by how eager the other leaders were to have bilateral meetings with me and to associate their nations with ours. One very enjoyable event that caused me some pain a year or two later was a beautiful banquet with the British royal family. I sat with Queen Elizabeth, and we had a delightful chat about serious matters and also personal things. She complained about having seven different uniforms she had to wear on annual occasions and how difficult it was to fit into them when her weight tended to increase. We decided it might be good to shift to centimeters on everything except waistlines, which would continue to be measured in inches. After supper I was approached by the Queen Mother, and we discussed how our families were affected by immersion into public affairs. As we said good night, I kissed her lightly on the cheek and she thanked me for coming to visit. More than two years later, there were reports in the British papers that grossly distorted this event, stating that I had deeply embarrassed her with excessive familiarity. I was distressed by these reports, but couldn't change what had happened — nor did I regret it.

B-1 BOMBER

During the 1976 campaign, both Jerry Ford and I had known that whichever of us was elected would have to decide whether to build the proposed B-1 bomber. As president, I set June 1977 as a deadline and worked on this issue for months, having numerous discussions with experts and interested parties on both sides of the question. Secretary Harold Brown, the joint chiefs, and I eventually decided that the extremely expensive new bombers would not be worth the cost and that our defense needs could be met for another fifteen or twenty years by the existing B-52s and other smaller planes, combined with the new and extremely accurate cruise missiles, which could be launched from land, submarines, surface ships, and airplanes. What we couldn't reveal at the time was the top secret development of "stealth" technology that would make our planes invisible to radar. This would be incorporated into fighter planes and the B-2 bombers a few years later. House and Senate leaders supported my decision, but defense contractors were disappointed. When Reagan came into office, he got approval to build one hundred unnecessary B-1s, which cost about $200 million each. Although B-1s have been used in combat on rare occasions, upgraded B-52s are now expected to continue in service until 2040 and the B-2 until 2058. Making such long-term decisions about very costly military items is always a difficult task for presidents, especially when manufacturing jobs are carefully located or promised for constituents of powerful legislators.

DEREGULATION

As governor I had seen how costly and unnecessary were some of the federal regulatory agencies, whose purpose over several decades had changed from protecting consumers to defending monopolies and restricting competition in the marketplace. At the same time, the regulated businesses were discouraged from introducing better products or services. This economic blight extended over railroads, electric power, oil and gas, bus lines, trucking firms, airlines, banks, insurance companies, and even television, telecommunications, and radio networks. For instance, each airline had its own exclusive and protected routes, and if large pay increases or other costs were implemented, the Civil Aeronautics Board (CAB) would routinely pass the added costs on to passengers and prohibit competition.

I began to study these industries more closely, working with interested members of Congress, my cabinet officers, and Alfred Kahn, a remarkable economist. He came to serve on the Civil Aeronautics Board and later helped as my "inflation czar." When we implemented his ideas about aviation, the CAB ceased to exist. In effect, we were able to deregulate all the industries I've named and permit competition in each commercial area, while preserving the safety of consumers and protecting them from abusive business practices, especially by the large banks.

NEUTRON BOMB

A decision on whether to deploy the neutron bomb was one of my most difficult, and it provoked public debates and hard feelings with the Congress and also with some of our NATO allies, especially Germany. Harold Brown, Jim Schlesinger, and I were quite supportive of technological improvements in weaponry, including precision bombs, cruise missiles, nuclear ship propulsion, and stealth aircraft. Another potential advance was an atomic explosion that could minimize destruction of buildings and equipment but kill as many people as possible with high radiation of deadly neutrons. The original concept was first tested in 1963, and our military had initiated a schedule of production. When the complete concept was explained to me, I decided that the weapon should not be deployed either by our own military or by those in NATO. I consulted with European leaders, and German Chancellor Schmidt became quite angry and criticized my decision publicly. I notified him that I would reconsider if he would endorse the weapon's deployment in Germany, but he was not willing to share the responsibility, and my decision prevailed. President Reagan resumed production of this "enhanced radiation weapon," and a few of them were deployed among U.S. forces, but the last one was dismantled by President George W. Bush.

COLD WAR

The Cold War was raging, and the Soviet Union and the United States were engaged everywhere in intense competition. There was not a country, no matter how small or remote, where we each didn't strive to obtain more influence than the other. This was often beneficial to the local people as we offered them better trade relations, some forms of foreign aid, or improved military capabilities. My goal was to demonstrate the advantages of freedom and a commitment to human rights in contrast to the Soviet system of Communism and oppression. There were vivid examples of these unpleasant and dangerous policies in Poland, East Germany, Czechoslovakia, Romania, Hungary, Yugoslavia, and Albania — and in Afghanistan when the Soviets invaded, in December 1979. The most obvious example was the domination of people who lived within the Soviet Union.

Perhaps the turning point in my presidential campaign had been when President Ford denied in a debate that the Soviets were dominating any countries in Eastern Europe. To demonstrate my concern about their plight, my first overseas visit, after the London Economic Summit, was to Poland. I began calling for the release of the imprisoned human rights activist Natan Sharansky, and I had highly publicized personal correspondence with Andrei Sakharov and his wife, Yelena Bonner. I presented persistent demands through Soviet Ambassador Anatoly Dobrynin to his superiors to permit oppressed Jews to emigrate to Europe and America. Later, when I met directly with President Brezhnev, he knew that human rights would be on my agenda and would have a written response ready that he simply passed to the interpreter to read. Although Soviet leaders never acknowledged that they denied any rights or that this was a legitimate subject of discussion with me, our policy had some tangible effects. The number of Soviet Jews permitted to leave the country almost quadrupled to 51,320 in 1979, and there is no doubt that Soviet citizens were strengthened in their demand for additional freedoms.

I went to Vienna in June 1979 to meet with President Brezhnev and his team to negotiate a reduction and future limits on nuclear arsenals. Protocol called for the Soviets to come to the United States for this session, but Brezhnev was ill and could not fly at high altitudes. He was accompanied by Foreign Minister Andrei

Gromyko; Konstantin Chernenko, second in command and future Soviet leader; and Defense Minister Dmitry Ustinov. We concluded the SALT II agreement, with a projected life of five years, when a more drastic reduction in nuclear armaments was contemplated. Although not ratified by the U.S. Senate, SALT II remained in effect beyond its expected time. The most interesting event was when Brezhnev said, at the beginning, "If we do not succeed, God will not forgive us!" As leader of an atheistic regime, he was embarrassed by the resulting silence, and Gromyko finally said, with an attempt at humor, "Yes, God above is looking down at us all."

I was delighted to see the Cold War end when Soviet leader Mikhail Gorbachev introduced reforms known as *perestroika* and *glasnost* (reorganization and openness) and withdrew Soviet troops from Afghanistan in the 1980s. The Berlin Wall was torn down, the Communist Party lost control, and the USSR was dissolved in 1991. This left Russia as a major regional player, but the United States remained as the world's only superpower.

SAVING NEW YORK CITY AND CHRYSLER

In July 1977, Mayor Abraham Beame came to see me about the financial plight of New York City. I had met Abe during my campaign and had reaped rich dividends when the New York *Daily News* published a glaring headline: FORD TO CITY: DROP DEAD! after a previous plea for assistance had been denied. Abe had worked heroically to reduce projected budget deficits of $1.5 billion, and he wanted me to consider declaring the city a disaster area, realizing that a more long-term solution was needed. I brought in Treasury Secretary Michael Blumenthal, and we finally planned a federal loan to the city. Beame was one of the most dedicated public servants I ever knew, working in a completely modest way for the well-being of the people he represented. A power blackout later that month probably cost him reelection, but we went ahead with plans to help the city. Senator William Proxmire, chairman of the Committee on Banking, Housing, and Urban Affairs, was adamantly opposed to the "bailout," but we finally got it approved with adequate financial guarantees for the U.S. Treasury.

The only other issue like this that I had to face was the prospective insolvency of

Chrysler Corporation, a major defense contractor and the employer of more than 165,000 workers. Chrysler was in desperate financial condition when Lee Iacocca became CEO, and I eventually agreed to grant a guaranteed loan of $1.5 billion to prevent its bankruptcy, an immense increase in unemployment and other costs, and Chrysler's possible takeover by one of the aggressive Japanese automobile manufacturers. I required, however, strict business practices and labor union concessions to be supervised by the treasury secretary, plus full repayment of the loan at the going interest rate. When Chrysler later recovered, the federal government reaped substantial dividends.

MIDDLE EAST PEACE

During my 1976 campaign many Americans asked questions about the Middle East, but most were merely seeking assurance of my good intentions toward Israel. I became increasingly interested in bringing permanent peace to Israel and its neighbors, and soon after being elected I discussed this privately with Zbigniew Brzezinski, whom I had chosen as national security adviser. There was little information available about how Syria, Jordan, Egypt, or even Israel would react to such a proposal, so I decided to meet with all their leaders as early as possible.

Israeli Prime Minister Yitzhak Rabin came first, on March 7, and was surprisingly negative about initiating peace talks. I learned after his visit that he and his wife were being accused of having an illegal bank account in America, and he was also facing strong opposition for reelection from Menachem Begin.

Anwar Sadat came from Egypt on April 4, and I found him to be receptive. He didn't believe he could ever recognize Israel as legitimate or permit Israeli ships to use the Suez Canal, but he promised at least to listen to my future proposals and try to be flexible.

King Hussein of Jordan was at the White House on April 25, and he was reluctant to aggravate other Arab leaders by engaging with Israel but willing for others to explore possibilities.

Syria's President Hafez al-Assad declined my invitation to visit the United States, but I arranged to meet with him in Geneva, Switzerland, in June. He was supportive of my ideas but insisted that a broad spectrum of Arab leaders should participate and that

Peace Treaty, Sadat, Begin, Carter, *painted October 2003.*

the Soviet Union should co-host any peace talks.

After taking office as prime minister of Israel, Menachem Begin made some very harsh statements that almost precluded any necessary compromises, but he made a fine impression on all of us when he came to visit in July. We had long private talks, and I had the impression that he would not abandon his basic commitments to his supporters in Israel but would be as accommodating as possible to my proposals concerning peace with Egypt and Palestinian control over their own affairs.

At this time it was assumed that there would be a multinational peace conference in Geneva, in accordance with UN Security Council Resolution 338. This plan soon proved to be too bureaucratic for implementation, and the planned involvement of both the United States and the Soviet Union aroused strong opposition from Israel and Egypt.

One weekend when our family was enjoying Camp David, Rosalynn suggested that this would be an ideal place for negotiating teams to benefit from the privacy and quiet atmosphere. I agreed with her and sent handwritten invitations to Begin and Sadat in August 1978 to join me for comprehensive peace talks. They both accepted.

I described our thirteen days together in *Keeping Faith,* and several other books have been written about our negotiations at Camp David, but I would like now to describe some of the more personal relationships that developed there.

I had practically memorized the maps of disputed areas and the voluminous briefing books prepared on the biographies of Begin and Sadat by our intelligence agencies. These included their early lives, political careers, promises and obligations to powerful political groups, and psychological analyses predicting how they would react to pressure while negotiating and after they returned home.

When Begin arrived at Camp David in September 1978, he made it clear to me that he was prepared only to outline some general principles and then turn over the responsibilities to our cabinet officers for future detailed negotiations. I disagreed and found that Sadat was willing to support my more ambitious plans for peace talks. I got both leaders to agree that if we failed I would make public my final proposal and let each of them explain why he accepted or rejected it. Another agreement was that we would not share our daily discussions with the outside world, and we did not deny a rumor among the two negotiating teams that all the outside phone lines were tapped.

At first I thought I could bring both men into a small room in my cabin and get them to discuss with me all the advantages that a peace agreement could bring to their people. But I found this to be impossible, because both of them would ignore my proposals and revert as soon as possible to vitriolic exchanges about things that had happened during the four wars between their countries during the previous thirty years. On occasion, they would go back to Biblical days. Finally, after three days had been wasted in loud arguments, I decided that they should be kept apart, and we maintained this arrangement for the remaining days together. I had created a single document that outlined my concept of a comprehensive peace agreement. I would take it, usually first to the Israelis and then to the Egyptians, modifying the text only when absolutely necessary. Progress came slowly but surely, paragraph by paragraph.

Tensions became so great that I thought we should take a break, and we all agreed to visit the nearby Civil War battlefield at Gettysburg. All officers trained for military duty had studied this conflict in detail, as had I and almost all the top leaders from Israel and Egypt. There were excited comments as we were guided from one location to another — except from Begin, who had never received military training. I began to worry about his relative isolation in the group, but then we reached the place where Abraham Lincoln made his historic address. Everyone got respectfully quiet to contemplate the scene, and after a few moments Begin began to recite Lincoln's words: "Fourscore and seven years ago . . ." This was an emotional experience, the most memorable of the day.

Late at night on the ninth day I became concerned about Sadat's safety. He was ahead of all his delegation in accommodating my proposals, and we knew that some of the Egyptians were fervent in their hatred and distrust of Israel. His foreign minister had resigned in protest and returned to Egypt, and some of his other top officials were on the verge of rebellion because of concessions he had made. I had sent word that I wished to see Sadat late that afternoon and was told that, uncharacteristically, he had already gone to bed and did not wish to be disturbed. I was doubtful about the truthfulness of this response, and for one of the few times in my life I could not go to sleep. I finally arranged through Zbig Brzezinski to have security arranged outside Sadat's cabin, and I was relieved to see him the next morning.

On the eleventh day, I was meeting with Secretary of Defense Harold Brown about some important budget issues when Secretary of State Cy Vance burst into the room and said that Sadat had his luggage on the porch of his cabin and had asked for a helicopter to take him back to Washington for a return to Egypt. This was one of the worst moments of my life. I knew that he was doubtful of our potential success after Israeli Foreign Minister Moshe Dayan told him that Israel would make no more concessions. I went into my bedroom, knelt and prayed for a while, and for some reason I replaced my T-shirt and blue jeans with a coat and tie for the first time since I'd arrived. Only then did I go to Sadat's cabin, where he and I had a terrible confrontation. I used all the arguments and threats I could muster, and eventually he agreed to give me one more chance.

By the thirteenth day there were only a couple of unresolved issues, which were of paramount importance to Prime Minister Begin. One concerned the status of Jerusalem and the other removal of all Israelis from Egyptian territory. He would not yield on either, and he was very angry with me. We all decided that our only option was to return to Washington, acknowledge failure, and plan for some possible future efforts. My secretary came to me with a request from Begin that I sign photographs of the three leaders as souvenirs for his eight grandchildren. Without telling him, she had called Israel and obtained their names, so I inscribed them, with love, to each child. I went to Begin's cabin, and he admitted me with a polite but frigid attitude. I gave him the photographs, he turned away to examine them, and then began to read the names aloud, one by one. He had a choked voice, and tears were running down his cheeks. I was also emotional, and he asked me to have a seat. After a few minutes, we agreed to try once more, and after some intense discussions we were successful.

On the way back to Washington we called Presidents Richard Nixon and Gerald Ford to give them the good news, and followed this with a press conference at the White House.

PANAMA

My first knowledge of Panama came when I was a student at Georgia Tech, an engineering school that concentrated on relations with Latin American countries. There were several students from Panama, my first acquaintance with anyone from a foreign country, and I was able to practice my rudimentary Spanish. They were proud of the Panama Canal, which provided good job opportunities for them and a permanent connection with the United States. As a naval officer serving on ships that operated in the Pacific and Atlantic Oceans, I became more aware of how valuable the canal was to international traffic, in times of peace and war. It was during my time as a state senator that I became aware of serious disharmony between Panamanians and Americans. My friends from Panama told me about the arrogance of some Americans who lived in the Canal Zone, prejudice against Panamanians with dark skin, and preference in hiring and pay practices that made local workers feel inferior. As president, I began working on a settlement of the Panama Canal arguments as early as possible. I will describe this process in some detail because it would become the most difficult political challenge of my life, even including being elected president.

The canal had been a divisive issue between America and the people of Panama and Colombia for seventy-five years. Construction of a canal had begun under the French in 1881 but was later abandoned because of increased costs and the deaths of many workers from typhus fever and other diseases. The United States had signed a treaty with Colombia in 1903 to take over the canal project, but when it was not ratified, President Theodore Roosevelt indicated to rebels in the Panama area that the United States would support their independence from Colombia. This strategy succeeded because of the exercise of

American military force. The United States unilaterally drafted a favorable treaty with Panama, which was hurriedly signed on the night of November 18, 1903, in Washington, just a few hours before a delegation from Panama could arrive and examine the text. Panamanians were ostensibly represented by a Frenchman who had last visited Panama eighteen years earlier. The huge engineering feat was completed in 1914, and the canal was operated under American supervision, with many Panamanian workers.

There were constant altercations relating to sovereignty over the Canal Zone, culminating in a confrontation during the early months of Lyndon Johnson's presidency. President Eisenhower had pledged to the Panamanians that no U.S. flags would fly over the zone, but some American students raised a flag on January 9, 1964, and massive rioting by Panamanians erupted. American troops responded with force, and twenty Panamanians and four Americans were killed. Johnson called Panamanian President Roberto Chiari to express his regret, and Chiari demanded that the treaty be revised. Johnson promised to consider Panamanian grievances, and he launched negotiations for a new treaty.

However, opposition from the U.S. Congress was so great that he never submitted the agreement for ratification.

Negotiations continued under Presidents Nixon and Ford, but neither proved willing to send a treaty to Congress. Meanwhile, Panama and a number of other Latin American countries pressured the United States to act. Positions on both sides hardened. In 1973 Panama took the issue to the UN Security Council, where the United States exercised its veto over a demand that a new, "just and equitable" treaty be negotiated. The "unaligned" nations, not just in the Western Hemisphere but around the world, all supported Panama's demands.

During the fall of 1975, thirty-eight senators introduced a resolution against any revision in the existing treaty, aware that thirty-four could block any effort. Polls indicated that only 8 percent of the American public was willing to relinquish control of the canal, and conservatives saw this as a prime issue. Both Ronald Reagan and the John Birch Society launched nationwide crusades in 1974 with speeches and video and audio tapes. This was a challenge that I inherited.

After studying the issues, I concluded that

Panama had legitimate claims and initiated substantive negotiations. General Omar Torrijos was then the ruler of Panama; I learned to respect his political courage and honesty and to consider him a personal friend. I had two experienced and respected negotiators, Ellsworth Bunker, former ambassador to Argentina and several other countries, and Sol Linowitz, who had been chairman of Xerox. They reached a successful formula early in August 1977. One treaty would apply from 1979 through 1999, when the Canal Zone would cease to exist and the area would belong to Panama. The other would be a permanent guarantee that the United States would protect the canal and have priority of using it in a time of emergency. Now I had to persuade sixty-seven senators to vote for a highly unpopular agreement that many of them had promised to oppose.

My first effort was to recruit Presidents Ford and Nixon, and Senate leaders Robert Byrd (Democrat) and Howard Baker (Republican) as allies, and then convince other senators that their most influential home state political leaders would be supportive, or at least neutral. We began inviting as many as two hundred prominent citizens from individual states to the White

House, where military commanders, cabinet officers, and I would explain the canal's history and outline the advantages to our country if the treaties were implemented. My cabinet members and other senior officials made more than fifteen hundred appearances throughout the nation, and I induced forty-five doubtful senators to visit Panama and see how vulnerable the canal was to sabotage and how able were the Panamanians who provided most of the technicians in charge of its operation. Our military commanders in the Canal Zone and General Torrijos, with the demeanor and frankness of a sergeant, proved to be excellent salesmen.

I invited national leaders from the hemisphere to attend a signing ceremony of the negotiated documents in September 1977, and eighteen presidents and a number of other top officials attended the emotional event. As Torrijos and I prepared to enter the large auditorium from a side room, he burst into tears and wept for a few minutes on his wife's shoulder until he regained composure. Unfortunately, we had to wait until the following year for the Senate to begin substantive hearings in the committees on foreign affairs and defense, and then have extensive floor debates. The public endorsement by Senators Byrd and Baker was a positive factor, but massive pressures were put on senators who expressed an inclination to oppose the treaties. By this time, opinion polls showed that 34 percent of Americans approved the treaties.

Assisted by Frank Moore, I kept a notebook on my desk with all pertinent information I could obtain about each senator, including twenty or more names of people or organizations that were most influential with each one. I kept a running tally of those committed to vote either for or against the treaties. I knew their primary involvements in state or national affairs, and whether they had any personal interests in the canal. There were nine "undecided" Republicans whom President Ford agreed to call, though only one of them finally voted yes. There was a flood of crippling amendments, and Senators Robert Dole and Jesse Helms charged publicly and falsely that Torrijos and his family were drug dealers and that high officials in the United States had been bribed. The Senate had closed sessions where these charges were refuted. A vote on the first treaty was scheduled for March 16 and the other a month later. With a week to go I had fifty-nine promised votes. Eleven senators were still unsure, and I had to have eight of them. Here are some key concerns that had to be addressed:

Mark Hatfield (Montana) was worried that former senator Mike Mansfield, now ambassador to Japan, might support his opponent in the next election.

Dennis DeConcini (Arizona) wanted a separate amendment to say more forcefully that the United States could use military force in Panama to defend the canal if necessary after 2000.

Sam Nunn (Georgia) said his fellow senator Herman Talmadge would have to support the treaties and the DeConcini amendment would have to be approved.

Henry Bellmon (Oklahoma) wanted my promise not to veto a costly desalinization plant in his state.

Howard Cannon (Nevada) had mail running twenty to one against the treaties, and he feared condemnation from Mormon newspapers.

James Abourezk (South Dakota) resented having been excluded from congressional meetings on the energy issue and insisted that I not let cabinet members attend them.

James Sasser (Tennessee), a personal

friend, was angry about my vetoing the Clinch River Breeder Reactor and other issues in his state.

S. I. Hayakawa (California) wanted to be consulted personally on foreign affairs and wanted me to recognize the Ian Smith regime in Rhodesia. He had written a semantics textbook of which he was very proud.

We finally prevailed, with sixty-eight votes, because I met the demands of Nunn and DeConcini with language that didn't change the treaties; got Mansfield to assuage Hatfield; agreed with Bellmon on his desalinization plant; induced Mormon editors (who opposed the treaties) not to condemn Cannon; got the king of Saudi Arabia to intercede with Abourezk; invited Sasser to the White House to meet a vast array of stars at the twentieth anniversary of the Country Music Association; and read Hayakawa's book on semantics, discussed it with him, and invited him to meet with me several times to "confer" on international affairs.

This was the most courageous vote in the history of the U.S. Senate. Of those twenty who voted for the treaties and were up for election that year, only seven retained their seats, and eleven supporters — plus one president — were defeated two years later, in 1980. Reagan used this as one of the decisive issues against me in his campaign, and the decision remained unpopular, even later.

American officials still wish to stay clear of the controversy. When the time came in 2000 to grant sovereignty to Panama, neither President Bill Clinton, Vice President Al Gore, nor the secretary of state wanted to attend the ceremony, so Clinton asked me to represent the United States. Even later, when President George W. Bush was in office, I received another unexpected request: that I represent the United States in beginning a massive expansion of the canal's capacity. Panama's President Martín Torrijos (son of Omar) and I pushed the plunger to explode the first dynamite. In both cases, I was grateful for the honor.

HUBERT HUMPHREY

Senator Hubert Humphrey had been a hero of mine since I watched him lead the 1948 Democratic Convention fight over civil rights. The "Dixiecrats" withdrew and formed their own party, choosing Strom Thurmond as their nominee, with the goal of taking Southern votes away from Truman.

Truman won, and Humphrey was elected the first Democratic senator from Minnesota since the Civil War. I met Hubert when I was a state senator. He came back from an African trip to visit the home of a supporter of mine in Atlanta. He began describing his experiences at about 9:00 and was still talking at 2:30 A.M., when I had to leave and drive home to Plains. When Lyndon Johnson ran for election in 1964, he chose Humphrey as the vice presidential candidate. As I mentioned earlier, Hubert and his wife, Muriel, came to Georgia to campaign, and my mother volunteered to be their host.

Johnson decided four years later not to run for reelection, and Humphrey was nominated as the Democratic candidate, with Richard Nixon as his opponent. He had inherited an unpopular war in Vietnam, and he decided not to criticize or disavow responsibility for any of the decisions that had been made concerning the war. This cost him votes among Democrats on the left, and many conservative votes went to George Wallace, who ran as an independent. Humphrey lost a close election. He was reelected as senator in 1970 and served in that office until the end of his life.

As one of the Democratic hopefuls who

came to visit me in 1972, Hubert really made himself at home in the governor's mansion and proved to be our favorite visitor. We have a delightful photograph of Amy sitting on his lap as a four-year-old, feeding him part of her brownie, and both of them have it smeared all over their faces. Once again, he was defeated in the presidential race that year, when Democrats nominated George McGovern.

When I selected Walter Mondale to be my vice president, he turned to Senator Humphrey for advice on what the office might comprise, and Hubert helped him prepare a bold and unprecedented set of proposals. They involved situating his office near mine, having an unrestricted and automatic presence in all discussions, complete briefings with me on the handling of nuclear weapons, meetings with any members of Congress without prior approval, and freedom to go on overseas trips including meetings with heads of state and with an unlimited press entourage. I was surprised to learn that these were privileges and responsibilities that had never been granted to Vice President Humphrey. I added a few perquisites for Fritz, like setting his own times for vacation periods and freedom to go to Camp David whenever he and his wife, Joan, wished. Senator Humphrey was a staunch friend and supporter and was especially helpful in giving me advice concerning how best to approach other senators when I faced sensitive issues such as dealing with Israeli supporters or getting votes for the Panama Canal treaties.

When Hubert was suffering from terminal cancer, I learned that he had never been invited to visit Camp David and asked him to go with me for a weekend. I stopped in Minneapolis on the way back from a visit to the West Coast in December, picked him up, and we spent a cold and rainy weekend together. We watched a couple of movies and spent hours in front of a warm fire in our cabin, which I described in my diary as "one of the most enjoyable and interesting weekends I've ever spent."

MOUNT SAINT HELENS

In May 1980 the biggest natural explosion ever recorded in North America occurred when Mount Saint Helens volcano in Washington State erupted. My science adviser, Frank Press, and other scientists had been monitoring activity on the site for several months, and people had been warned of the danger, but fifty-seven people were killed when the entire north side of the volcano blew away and spread ash in fourteen states. I decided immediately to visit, accompanied by Dr. Press; the secretaries of interior, agriculture, and the army; and the directors of the Federal Emergency Management Agency (FEMA) and the National Institutes of Health. We found that one cubic mile of the mountain had been pulverized, 28 feet of silt had clogged the Columbia ship channel, and every tree had been leveled in an area of 150 square miles. As we approached the still-smoldering mountain in a large helicopter, we could see that there was nothing left beneath us except a sea of boiling lava, still containing chunks of ice the size of houses, which had been blown off the peak. Thousands of people would have perished without the early warning, and Dr. Press expressed regret that scientists had underestimated the power of the explosion, which was equivalent to a ten-megaton nuclear bomb. Nearby Spirit Lake was filled with 400 feet of ash and lava, and the level of its surface was raised 150 feet. As we flew around the mountain, several miles away, we saw some large pieces of lava fall beyond our helicopter, and we agreed with the pilot that our observation tour should end.

After consulting with my advisers, I

decided not to do any unnecessary renovations but to let nature heal itself. I didn't see how anything could grow in the devastated area, but twenty-five years later, in 2005, I was leading a group of volunteers in building Habitat for Humanity homes in Benton Harbor, Michigan, when a truck drove up loaded with boards suitable for framing the roof trusses. The lumber had been cut from new-growth trees from the base of Mount Saint Helens, and the timber company wanted us to use it on these homes for poor families.

CHINA

One of the most compelling facets of my life has been my relationship with China. As a boy, I shared the admiration of all Baptists for missionaries who served there, whom we considered our ultimate heroes. People would drive long distances to listen to a missionary who was home for a rare vacation, and I remember pledging a nickel a week to help build hospitals and schools for Chinese children. We still honor Lottie Moon, our missionary who died in China from starvation because she gave her food to needy families. My interest in the region was rekindled with my early visit as a submariner, and I continued to follow

Chinese history.

In February 1972, President Nixon made a historic trip to China, which resulted in the Shanghai Communiqué. This agreement acknowledged that there was only one China, but our diplomatic ties with Taiwan remained intact through the balance of Nixon's time in office and during Gerald Ford's years. This issue was rarely discussed during my campaign for president, but I was increasingly convinced that the United States should acknowledge an obvious fact: that the People's Republic of China was the government that should officially represent the Chinese people. I knew that the U.S. Constitution gives sole authority for diplomatic recognition to the president, and I was determined to exercise it if an adequate agreement could be reached with Chinese leaders regarding treatment of the people of Taiwan. I began to explore this possibility as soon as I was in office, but there were other, more pressing international issues on my agenda. Also, it was not clear to me which leader had the authority to speak for the Chinese government.

On February 8, soon after my inauguration, I met with Huang Chen, the chief of the Chinese liaison office, who told me that their top officials could never come to Washington officially as long as we had an ambassador here from Taiwan but were eager to visit as soon as the Taiwanese left. There was a lack of trust between the United States and the People's Republic of China, as indicated by a misunderstanding between Secretary of Defense Harold Brown and Huang Chen, who was critical of proposed changes in our strategic planning from an ability to fight two and a half wars to one and a half. He thought we were reducing our vigilance against the global threat from the Soviet Union but had no more objections after Harold pointed out that the war for which we would no longer plan was against the People's Republic of China.

Instead of choosing a professional diplomat to represent me in Beijing, I decided to send Leonard Woodcock, president of the United Auto Workers. What I needed was not a smooth-talking diplomat but the toughest negotiator I could find.

Woodcock arrived in China in July, and I sent Secretary Vance in August for consultations with the leadership. The results were discouraging, and there was virtually no progress toward normalization for months. In May 1978, I sent National Security

Adviser Brzezinski to see what he could do. He hit it off with the leadership, and Woodcock was able to continue the process. There were a number of people in our State Department who were deeply committed to Taiwan, so we never sent any substantive messages from there to Woodcock. To maintain secrecy, all dispatches were approved by me and transmitted from within the White House.

There had been a leadership struggle going on in China, but it became increasingly clear that Deng Xiaoping (then spelled Teng Hsiao-ping) would prevail over Hua Guofeng. Although his title was vice premier, in late 1978 Deng was the real Chinese leader with whom we were negotiating. I had basic demands on which I was not willing to compromise, and we were pleasantly surprised on December 13, when Woodcock informed me that the Chinese would accept our key proposals, all relating to the status of Taiwan. Amazingly, the secret was kept until Deng and I announced our agreement simultaneously from Washington and Beijing two days later. I wrote in my diary:

"We were very favorably impressed with Teng and the rapidity with which he moved and agreed to accept our one-year treaty with Taiwan, our statement that the Taiwan issue should be settled peacefully would not be contradicted by China, and that we would sell defensive weapons to Taiwan after the treaty expires."

Except for diehard Taiwan supporters, the joint statement was remarkably well received in the United States and throughout the world. Because commercial and political ties with Taiwan were strong, I had expected strong congressional opposition, but it did not materialize. That same week Deng announced a profound policy change within China to "openness and reform," tied directly to the new relationship with the United States. My invitation to Deng Xiaoping to visit Washington was quickly accepted, and his charisma, frankness, and quick wit went a long way toward overcoming the widespread aversion to the "Red Chinese Communists" on the mainland. Measured by long-term global impact, this was probably the most important diplomatic decision I ever made.

During his visit, Deng and I signed numerous agreements to recover from the thirty years of alienation and incompatibility between our nations. We discussed the steady series of wars in Asia that we had known, including those between Japan and

China, World War II, the Korean War, and the more recent conflicts in Vietnam and Cambodia. Deng confidentially alerted me that he planned a punitive strike against Vietnam. I objected to this, but he assured me that it was to be a short-term conflict. China has maintained peace internally and with its neighbors since then. Its economy has boomed into the second largest in the world, and its diplomatic and trade relations have been extended to almost every other nation.

I have visited China regularly since leaving office, and The Carter Center has been given major requests for assistance. We planned and helped design a large prosthesis factory in Beijing and carried out a five-year project to bring special education teaching skills to the schools of China. We trained hundreds of instructors who would teach the teachers how to address the needs of the approximately 51 million Chinese suffering from disabilities. Beginning in 1996, our greatest program effort was to monitor and encourage the small villages of China as they chose their leaders with democratic elections. For twelve years we worked to bring this opportunity to what were initially almost a million villages (which are not part of the government system). After a few years of trial, we made recommendations for improving the original law. Candidates can seek office whether or not they are members of the Communist Party, there is a secret ballot, and officials can be reelected after completing their three-year terms. Rosalynn, I, and other representatives of our Center have personally observed many of these elections. One interesting feature is that candidates are usually permitted to give three-minute campaign speeches immediately before votes are cast. These sometimes are recorded and played again three years later if the elected official seeks a new term. The turnover rate has been quite high.

We established websites (in Chinese and English) that posted analyses and assessments of these elections. As the websites became more popular, students and scholars of Chinese government, as well as ordinary citizens, submitted articles and commentaries on the necessity of more political reform. The websites were transformed into something of a platform for democracy debate in China, and the government began to impose restrictions.

Many disturbing altercations have arisen between freely elected village officials and Communist Party leaders regarding use of land, routing of roads, and location of factories. Our role in promoting village elections was slowly but steadily rolled back. As Chinese leaders grew distrustful of activities designed to expand the debate on democracy, we have turned our attention to enhancing bilateral relations, encouraging exchange of students and tourists, and working with the government on common interests in developing countries, especially in Africa.

As I write this, in September 2014, I have just returned from a ten-day visit to Beijing, Xi'an, Qingdao, and Shanghai, for conferences with business and political leaders and students from four universities. The year 2014 was the thirty-fifth anniversary of normalized relations between our countries, 110 years after Deng was born, and 65 years after my first visit to China and the foundation of the People's Republic of China.

HUNGARIAN CROWN

One of the most surprisingly controversial presidential decisions I made was to return the Crown of Saint Stephen to the people of Hungary. It was said to have been given by the Pope in the year 1000 to Stephen, the first king of Hungary, as a symbol of political and religious authority and was worn by more than fifty kings when they were vested with power. A distinctive feature was that the cross on top was bent. As Soviet troops invaded Hungary, toward the end of the Second World War, some Hungarians delivered to American troops the crown and other royal regalia, which were subsequently stored in Fort Knox alongside our nation's gold. The Soviets still dominated Hungary when I announced my decision to return the crown. There was a furor among Hungarian-Americans and others, and I was denounced as accepting the subservience of the occupied nation. I considered the crown to be a symbol of the freedom and sovereignty of the Hungarian people. I returned it in January 1978, stipulating that the crown and insignia must be controlled by Hungarians, carefully protected, and made available for public display as soon as practicable. A duplicate of the crown was brought to The Carter Center as a gift for me in March 1998 and is on display in our presidential museum.

Rosalynn and I led volunteers to build Habitat houses in Vác, Hungary, in 1996, and we were treated as honored guests of the government and escorted to the Hungarian National Museum to see the crown and the stream of citizens who were going past it, many of them reciting a prayer as they did so. We were told that more than 3 million people pay homage to the crown each year. A few years later it was moved to its permanent home, in the Hungarian Parliament Building.

ALASKA LANDS

During my administration there was another serious controversy over an environmental issue where resolution was long overdue. This may have been the most significant domestic achievement of my political life. Alaska had been admitted to the Union as the forty-ninth state in January 1959, when a debate began over how some of its vast federal lands should be divided among the indigenous Indians and Eskimos, deeded to the state government, or retained as national forests, parks, and wilderness areas. President Dwight Eisenhower and his successors avoided the controversial issue, and the discovery of oil and the growth of commercial fisheries had added an important factor: the contention over enormous wealth. I decided to begin discussions that might resolve the issues, but I quickly learned that the congressional delegation from Alaska was deeply committed to the oil industry and other commercial interests, and senatorial courtesy prevented other members from disputing with Senators Ted Stevens (Republican) and Mike Gravel (Democrat) over a matter involving their home state. Former Idaho governor Cecil Andrus, my secretary of interior, and I began to study the history of the controversy and maps of the disputed areas, and I flew over some of them a few times.

Environmental groups and most indigenous natives were my allies, but professional hunters, loggers, fishers, and the Chambers of Commerce were aligned with the oil companies. All the odds were against us until Cecil discovered an ancient law, the Antiquities Act of 1906, which permitted a president to set aside an area for "the protection of objects of historic and scientific interest," such as Indian burial grounds, artifacts, or perhaps an ancient church building or the site of a famous battle. We decided to use this authority to set aside for preservation large areas of Alaska as national monuments, and eventually we had included more than 56 million acres (larger than the state of Minnesota). This gave me the bargaining chip I needed, and I was able to prevail in the subsequent debates.

My efforts were extremely unpopular in

Alaska, and I had to have extra security on my visits. I remember that there was a state fair where people threw baseballs at two targets to plunge a clown into a tank of water. My face was on one target and Iran's Ayatollah Khomeini's on the other, and few people threw at the Ayatollah's.

Congress passed the Alaska National Interest Lands Conservation Act (ANILCA), which set aside an area larger than California, in December 1980, doubling the size of our national parks, tripling wilderness areas, and protecting twenty-five free-flowing streams. At the same time we clarified ownership of remaining lands and opened all offshore areas and 95 percent of land areas to oil exploration, excluding a pristine area known as the Alaska National Wildlife Refuge. After several decades, the decision has become increasingly popular in the state.

THE HOSTAGE CRISIS, AND FINAL YEAR

My last year in office was the most stressful and unpleasant of my life. From November 4, 1979, American hostages were held captive by Iranian militants, supported by the Ayatollah Khomeini and his government. This crisis was of overriding importance for me, and I severely restricted my travel and met frequently with families of the captive diplomats to share whatever information we had. I sent a warning to the Ayatollah during the first month that I would close all access by Iran to the outside world if a hostage was harmed and would attack militarily if one was killed. He took my warning seriously and was careful with the well-being of the Americans. One of them was quickly released when his arm seemed to become paralyzed, and he was returned to his home in Maine.

Our goal was to free the hostages through diplomacy, but we believed we needed to be prepared for other alternatives. We began planning how to rescue the hostages after they had been in captivity for about two months. Our special forces practiced and refined the process in the American desert. Final plans were to fly seven large and long-range helicopters from an aircraft carrier to an isolated place in the Iranian desert, called Desert One, where they would be refueled from a C-130 airplane. The rescue team would then fly into Tehran at night, overwhelm the captors with as little violence as possible using night-vision equipment, and the hostages and rescuers would helicopter to a nearby airport, where a large passenger plane would land and bring them to safety. Our regular observations from space revealed the captors' habits, so we knew which ones were on duty at any time by the parked cars. A cook from Greece had been working in the embassy, and he gave us information about the location of the hostages and their daily routine. It was imperative that we have six helicopters to bring out all the hostages and the rescue team, because any left behind might be executed. Everyone on my national security team agreed to these plans after we studied and improved them during meetings in the secret "situation room" of the White House.

We were ready to proceed when the rescue team was trained, the desert landing place had been surveyed by sending a small airplane to land there, and the weather was right. In early April 1980, the Iranians failed to follow through with an agreement to transfer the hostages, and on April 11 I called my advisers together and we agreed to move ahead with the rescue mission. My last suggestion was that we add another helicopter, giving us two more than necessary. Secretary Cy Vance and all others had participated as we planned the rescue procedure, step by step. However, Cy was on vacation when the final date was set, and on his return he expressed his disapproval. I called another meeting on the issue. He explained his objections, we had a thorough discussion, and all other participants again voted to proceed.

Everything went as planned, except that one helicopter inexplicably returned to the aircraft carrier and another went down in a sandstorm, which left us with the required six at Desert One. After refueling, one of the helicopters swerved on takeoff and ran into the C-130, damaging them both and killing eight crewmen. I was forced to order the team to abandon the rescue attempt. It was a tragedy and a bitter disappointment, which I reported on television after sleeping a few hours.

Vance resigned from our administration after the effort failed. Although Cy was closest to me in overall policy toward peace and human rights, he was very protective of the State Department and had threatened to resign on three previous occasions when he thought that the White House staff exerted too much authority or that I did not implement his recommendations. He explained that he objected to the rescue attempt because it involved excessive risk of armed conflict and loss of life, but I felt that his resignation was the result of pent-up complaints. We maintained our friendship, and I spent several nights with the Vance family in New York City after I left the White House.

The failed rescue attempt had terrible political consequences for me. Senator Ted Kennedy mounted a major challenge to me during the Democratic primary campaign, and Ronald Reagan also raised the issue strongly in the general election. Since I had refrained from exerting military force to punish the Iranians, the failure to secure the freedom of the hostages made me vulnerable to their allegations that I was an ineffective leader.

While Iranians were weakened by the international sanctions imposed on them because of their illegal act, they were attacked by forces of Iraq's Saddam Hussein. I condemned the invasion because it interfered with my efforts to free the hostages, but it caused additional problems as the substantial oil exports from both countries were cut off, causing skyrocketing oil prices and global inflation, and high interest rates resulted.

QUICK-WITTED CIA

During the hostage crisis we sent a number of secret delegations into Iran, which was fairly easy to do because the Iranian leaders wanted to maintain as normal an environment as possible and relished all the favorable publicity that resulted from visits by foreign news media. Even the Ayatollah Khomeini gave personal interviews to American journalists. On one occasion we had a few CIA agents in Tehran who were traveling with false German passports, since many Iranian leaders had been educated in Germany. As our people were leaving, one of them had his credentials checked and was waved past by the customs officials. He was called back, however, and the official said, "Something is wrong with your passport. I've been here more than twenty years and this is the first time I've seen a German document that used a middle initial instead of a full name. Your name is given as Josef H. Schmidt and I don't understand it." The quick-thinking agent said, "Well, when I was born my given middle name was Hitler, and I have received special permission not to use it." The official smiled, nodded, and approved his departure.

HUMAN RIGHTS AND
LATIN AMERICA
My commitment to human rights was derogated by many Republicans and some

foreign leaders as naïve and a sign of weakness. One of my primary concerns was with the military dictators in Latin America and their fervent American supporters in the commercial sector, along with congressional lobbyists and key people within the State Department and other branches of our government. For generations the official U.S. policy had been to support these regimes against any threat from their own citizens, who were branded automatically as Communists. When necessary, U.S. troops had been deployed in Latin America for decades to defend our military allies, many of whom were graduates of the U.S. Military Academy, spoke English, and sent their children to be educated in our country. They were often involved in lucrative trade agreements involving pineapples, bananas, bauxite, copper and iron ore, and other valuable commodities.

When I became president, military juntas ruled in Argentina, Bolivia, Brazil, Chile, Ecuador, El Salvador, Guatemala, Haiti, Honduras, Nicaragua, Panama, Paraguay, Peru, and Uruguay. I decided to support peaceful moves toward freedom and democracy throughout the hemisphere. In addition, our government used its influence through public statements and our votes in financial institutions to put special pressure on the regimes that were most abusive to their own people, including Chile, Argentina, Paraguay, Nicaragua, and El Salvador. On visits to the region Rosalynn and I met with religious and other leaders who were seeking political change through peaceful means, and we refused requests from dictators to defend their regimes from armed revolutionaries, most of whom were poor, indigenous Indians or descendants of former African slaves. Within ten years all the Latin American countries I named here had become democracies, and The Carter Center had observed early elections in Panama, Nicaragua, Peru, Haiti, and Paraguay.

COORDINATING FOREIGN POLICY

I had a diverse group of key advisers in the White House, State Department, Department of Defense, and the CIA, and I wanted to be sure that we were all working harmoniously on the same agenda. There were never any serious congressional obstacles to most decisions I made on foreign policy, but I saw the need to avoid misunderstandings and potential conflicts among my National Security team by assembling them on a regular basis. I began having breakfast meetings each Friday when I was in Washington with Vice President Mondale, Secretary of Defense Brown, Secretary of State Vance, National Security Adviser Brzezinski, Hamilton Jordan, and sometimes Jody Powell and CIA Director Stansfield Turner. We covered an agenda open to all of us in advance. Brzezinski took notes, recorded our common decisions, and during the following week consulted with Brown and Vance to assure that my decisions were implemented. If cabinet officers could not attend, their deputies were sometimes included. This procedure worked very well for us and helped ensure that we were working as a team and addressing issues in the same way. This is an inevitable challenge for American leaders, because there are influential people in every department who want to shape policy that affects the rest of the world, and sometimes this desired unity is not achieved.

FEMA

After having to address several natural disasters, I realized that there were a multitude of federal agencies responsible for dealing with the emergencies in local communities, and no effective way to coordinate their efforts. In June 1978 I sent a reorganization plan to Congress to bring together the key groups that provided weather information, federal housing assistance, crime control, insurance, and many other federal, state, and local services. About a year later this process was completed by my Executive Order, with a guarantee from me that the new Federal Emergency Management Agency would have a director who was competent and experienced, and would have complete control over the disaster area, and that the agency would be adequately funded. The new agency would also have the authority to coordinate efforts of our military services, including National Guard units if necessary. Except for a failure following Hurricane Katrina in 2005 along the Gulf Coast, when none of these guarantees were honored, FEMA has performed superbly as envisioned.

CHAPTER SEVEN:
PROBLEMS STILL PENDING

Some of the major issues I had to address while in the White House have continued to confront my successors, because I failed in my efforts to resolve them, because later presidents had different priorities or yielded to political pressures that I resisted, or because circumstances have changed with the passage of time.

DRUGS

The key issue of illicit drugs is still hotly debated. During the first year and a half of my administration, Dr. Peter Bourne served as my White House adviser on health issues and director of the Office of Drug Abuse Policy. I considered him my drug czar, after he had filled a similar position for me in Georgia, and he helped me make my first and most definitive analysis of the complicated subject. One option was and is to reduce drug supply at the source with action by military forces and by spraying coca or marijuana plants or poppies with herbicide, combined with imprisonment of those who possess or use narcotics. Another choice is to offer alternative farming income to producers of coca and poppies, emphasize the dangers of drug use, and provide treatment for drug users who become addicted. Peter and I were strong supporters of the latter approach, and in August 1977 I called for decriminalization (not legalization) of marijuana and treatment options for addicts as an alternative to prison. My statement was well received, but my successors have taken the opposite approach. Our government has spent many billions of dollars since then in a counterproductive effort to reduce international trade in narcotics. Military action against producers and aerial poisoning of crops have often resulted in drug wars, enhanced production of narcotics, and increased demand for them. Punishment of drug users is emphasized, instead of treatment for addicts. Strong moves have evolved in Europe and Latin America to correct this mistake, but the U.S. government is a major obstacle to reform.

A sad corollary has been that the number of incarcerated people in our country has skyrocketed. The proportion of imprisoned Americans was about the same in 1980 as in 1940 (about one in one thousand), but since then the number has increased more than sixfold. Since the Anti–Drug Abuse Act was passed in 1986, our penal population has increased from around 300,000 to more than 2 million, and in just five years the imprisonment of African-American women in state prisons for drug offenses increased by 828 percent! Combining drug policy with a much more punitive attitude toward law violators, America now has a higher percentage of our citizens in prison than any other country, with only feeble efforts being made to concentrate on preparing inmates for successful return to a normal role in society. There are more than 3,200 Americans imprisoned for life who have never committed any crime of violence.

INTELLIGENCE AGENCIES

As president I was concerned about how fragmented the various intelligence agencies were. We could count at least nine, and it seemed that there was very little communication or coordination among them or across the inherent barriers between the departments of State, Defense, and Commerce, and the CIA. I wanted to bring in the most forceful and competent leader I could find and get him and the Congress to cooperate on putting all the agencies under one coordinator. I chose Admiral Stansfield Turner, who was my most outstanding classmate at the Naval Academy. He had been a good athlete, the top commander of the brigade of midshipmen, and later a Rhodes Scholar, captain of a cruiser, and president of the Naval War College. I consulted with Secretary of Defense Harold Brown, and he regretted losing Stan from the top military leadership but agreed that he would be an outstanding CIA director.

When I made one of my visits to CIA headquarters, I asked the heads of all other existing intelligence agencies to attend the meeting. The director of intelligence in the Defense Department said that they welcomed Stan as their "titular" head, and I replied that he would have *full* authority over all the agencies and would report directly to me. As predicted, we had tremendous opposition from the agencies concerned and especially from congressional committees that had "claimed" responsibility for the various agencies, but we accomplished our consolidation objective. Stan joined National Security Adviser Zbig Brzezinski and Fritz Mondale regularly in our high-level discussions.

Although sometimes neglectful of diplomatic niceties, Stan accomplished the goals I set for him with skill and political courage. Unfortunately, the intelligence agencies again have become much more fragmented, isolated, and competitive with each other and have resisted every effort for streamlining and coordination. According to an exhaustive *Washington Post* investigation published in 2010, there are more than three thousand government organizations and private companies in about ten thousand locations working on homeland security and intelligence, with an estimated 854,000 people holding top secret clearance! And this largely uncoordinated array is still growing.

Another challenge was to balance the need for intelligence about foreign threats to our security and the Fourth Amendment guarantees of the privacy of American citizens. I was concerned before becoming president by the revelations of the Frank Church Senate committee in 1975 and 1976 that President Richard Nixon and other top government officials were spying illegally on Americans and that the CIA had been involved in plots to assassinate foreign leaders, including Patrice Lumumba of

Congo, Rafael Trujillo of the Dominican Republic, the Diem brothers of Vietnam, and Fidel Castro of Cuba.

During my presidential campaign, I had promised to bring an end to the abuse of citizen privacy in the name of national security. The Foreign Intelligence Surveillance Act (FISA) was proposed with great fanfare on May 18, 1977. We supported it through debates in Congress for a year and a half, and I signed it into law on October 25, 1978. Its main purpose was to protect the privacy of American citizens, requiring probable cause that a target was engaged in spying or other clandestine activities, to be determined by a specially constituted court composed of seven federal district judges, each from a different circuit and selected by the chief justice.

This strict limit on privacy violation remained in force until President George W. Bush began violating and then advocating amending the law to permit increasingly intrusive wiretapping with minimal judicial oversight. In effect, it is now permissible to collect information about every phone call made, every letter posted, and every e-mail exchanged between American citizens. The law restricts the disclosure of the content of some of these exchanges unless the FISA court approves, but news reports reveal that during the past ten years these judges rarely if ever decline a request submitted by the intelligence agencies. The senior judge can issue approvals or directives without informing the other ten judges.

A *New York Times* article by Eric Lichtblau on July 6, 2013, reports: "The court has taken on a much more expansive role by regularly assessing broad constitutional questions and establishing important judicial precedents, with almost no public scrutiny, according to current and former officials familiar with the court's classified decisions. The eleven-member Foreign Intelligence Surveillance Court, known as the FISA court, was once mostly focused on approving case-by-case wiretapping orders. But since major changes in legislation and greater judicial oversight of intelligence operations were instituted six years ago, it has quietly become almost a parallel Supreme Court."

I doubt that even the few remaining legal restraints are always honored. I assume that all my communications are monitored by government agencies. When I want to send a private message, perhaps to foreign leaders through their embassies in Washington, I use a personal envoy or type a letter and send it through the U.S. Postal Service. I learned recently that postal clerks make photographs of envelopes and send them to the National Security Agency. There has been a dramatic and largely unnecessary intrusion into personal privacy, more than in Western European countries. Congressional oversight is minimal, with any member having access to the secret legislation being sworn never to reveal it or discuss it with news media or other members. This is just one of many violations of the Universal Declaration of Human Rights and the Geneva Conventions that have occurred since the tragic 9/11 attack of 2001. Others have included lifetime incarceration without trial; torture at Guantánamo, in U.S. prisons in Afghanistan, or in "dark sites" in foreign countries; and assassination by drone attacks, even of American citizens.

SPECIAL INTERESTS

Surprising to me, it was people with whom I felt most friendly and whom I attempted to help who caused the most trouble, no matter what we accomplished. I had more women in my cabinet and at other high levels than any predecessor, and appointed more female federal judges than all previous presidents combined. I approved an extension of time for consideration of the Equal Rights Amendment (ERA), and Rosalynn and I made hundreds of phone calls to doubtful state legislators to support the ERA. It had one simple provision: "Equality of rights under the law shall not be denied or abridged by the United States or by any state on account of sex." It was defeated by opposition from women, led by Phyllis Schlafly, who maintained that creating equality for women would restrict the laws that protected them. She began her many speeches by thanking her husband for giving her permission to speak. Despite our best efforts, leaders of women's organizations were the most demanding and unappreciative. In 1979 the president of the National Organization for Women threatened to chain herself to the fence around the White House. I believe the issue was my disagreement about abortion rights.

Fritz Mondale and I also did everything possible to improve the status of working people, but union leaders were never satisfied. There was a serious nationwide coal strike early in my term, and I resolved it by taking a balanced approach rather than endorsing all the coal workers' demands. These are two of many diary entries on other labor disputes:

"4/77 Had a luncheon with labor leaders. I thought they were excessively rude and abusive. . . . I'm not sure that I'll meet with any more of them in a group like this. Might let Fritz handle it."

"4/78 I met later with George Meany and gave him hell because in almost every instance when we've supported the AFL-CIO agenda successfully, he's taken all the credit for success. He spends half his time kicking me and the Democratic Congress in the teeth, and repeatedly comes back for help on additional programs."

We had a harmonious relationship after Lane Kirkland became president of the AFL-CIO, and I had overwhelming endorsements from labor unions in my 1980 campaign. I understand better now that the leaders of almost all organizations are expected to pocket what they have achieved, take as much credit as possible for progress, and then demand everything left on their always-expanding agendas.

There has been a dramatic change since I left office in the political influence of special interest groups, primarily because of the massive infusion of money into political campaigns. The tragic ruling of the U.S. Supreme Court in *Citizens United v. Federal Election Commission* in 2010 removed restrictions on campaign contributions by corporations, labor unions, and other associations. When I ran for president against Gerald Ford in 1976 and Ronald Reagan in 1980, we financed our general election campaigns from public funds derived from individual taxpayers who allotted one dollar each from their income tax payments — without any private contributions. The amount spent was about $26 million.

Having abandoned public financing, in 2012 each of the major candidates, Barack Obama and Mitt Romney, spent more than $1 billion. Much of the funding came from super-PACs that enjoyed their new privileges under the *Citizens United* ruling. United Press International reported in January 2015 that the Koch brothers and their associates will contribute $889 million to Republican presidential hopefuls and other candidates who share their conservative-libertarian views. This amount is almost as much as the entire budget of either major political party, and may increase before election time. Democratic candidates will attempt to match these funds.

It is not yet possible to assess the influence that this "legal bribery" has as government officials make decisions about taxation, government regulation, and other privileges and restraints.

EVANGELICALS

Many politically moderate Christians, including me, consider ourselves to be evangelicals, but the term has become increasingly equated with the religious right or the Moral Majority. Neither Jerry Ford nor I appealed directly to religious groups during the 1976 campaign, except that I continued my appearances at a number of African-American churches. It was estimated that Ford received about 55 percent of the votes from "evangelical" Christians, but we attributed this to his being better known than I among religious leaders.

It may be hard to believe now, but until my third year in office, I had never heard of the "religious right." In early 1979 I asked Bob Maddox, a Baptist minister from Georgia, to join our staff and act as liaison with the many religious groups that were demanding my attention on federal aid to religious schools and prohibition of prayer in public schools. In January 1980 he arranged a breakfast meeting for me with about a dozen prominent evangelical leaders from around the nation. The group included critics, such as Jerry Falwell. They asked me questions, including many about my own religious background. The meeting was interesting and relatively uneventful, but a few weeks later we heard that Falwell was making critical remarks about me and had contrived a conversation that never occurred. Maddox had recorded our meeting, and he shared the transcript with several religious magazines to show that Falwell was untruthful. I understand that this was when Falwell was promoting the Moral Majority, which was founded in 1979.

Several Democratic candidates had been defeated in the 1978 mid-term elections where the abortion issue was important, and subsequently conservative Christians collectively decided to adopt this as an important campaign topic and combine it with the tax-exempt status of "segregation academies" and religious colleges, especially Bob Jones University and Falwell's Lynchburg Christian Academy. They aligned themselves almost completely with the Republican Party as the 1980 election approached. The religious right supported Ronald Reagan, despite his previous incompatibility with their basic principles. For instance, Reagan had never been affiliated with any particular Christian group and had supported a law as governor that was more permissive of unlimited abortions than any other in the United States, while I had done everything possible to minimize abortions, except for cases when the mother's health was endangered or when the pregnancy resulted from rape or incest. Now, however, I refused to support a constitutional amendment to prevent any abortions, while my opponent endorsed the entire agenda of the religious right. In addition, they hammered away at my normalizing relations with "Red China," failing to attack Iran militarily, letting Panama have the canal, and refusing to endorse unlimited prayer in public schools or tax exemptions for religious colleges. The melding of the religious right with the Republican Party has been permanent since then.

WATER PROJECTS

Perhaps the most persistent altercation I had with the Congress involved water projects. All over America young members of Congress would propose damming up a free-flowing river in their districts and the Army Corps of Engineers would supposedly assess the benefits and costs. By one means or another, the exaggerated benefits would always seem to exceed the minimized expenditures. As the congressmen gained seniority, their projects would rise on the priority list and eventually be approved automatically as a courtesy from their peers, with all funding coming from the federal government. Many of our wild rivers and streams are dammed unnecessarily. The Corps of Engineers was complicit in this ongoing scheme because this process had become one of the prime reasons for their popularity with appropriations committees.

As reported in the lead story in *Reader's Digest* in August 1974, I was deeply involved in this issue as governor, when I learned firsthand how precious a federally funded dam could be to a senior congressman, and what a waste of funds many of them were by the time they were approved. I vetoed a congressionally approved plan to build a dam on the Flint River and eventually prevailed after a highly publicized political and legal altercation. As president, I decided to give close scrutiny to each proposed project and to veto those where costs would actually exceed benefits.

This decision caused a continuing furor, and every possible pressure was exerted by committee chairmen, prominent Americans, and my own staff members to change my policy, but I persisted. There is no doubt that it cost me some friends in Congress, but I had strong support from environmentalists, and most members in Congress finally agreed with me, tightening the criteria and requiring some state and local financial contribution to the cost of approved projects.

ECONOMIC COMPETITION, JAPAN AND CHINA

While I was in office our most serious economic competition was with Japan. The manufacture of most clothing and shoes had already moved to Asia and other regions where labor was less expensive. We were now contending for the manufacture of more advanced items, such as televisions and radios, automobiles, tires, steel, and other finished metal products. There were corporate accusations back and forth about improper trade practices, and our friendly diplomatic relationships were endangered. I talked this over with Prime Minister Takeo Fukuda, and he and I agreed to establish a panel of "wise men" to advise us. Each of us chose three distinguished scholars or former diplomats who were familiar with both countries, and they began meeting regularly in Tokyo, Washington, or Hawaii. They addressed the difficult issues in private and gave us confidential recommendations on how they might be resolved most successfully. By the time Masayoshi Ohira became prime minister, we rarely had troubles between us. I believe it would be a good idea for a similar small group of knowledgeable leaders to be formed to address some of the disputes that now threaten the friendly relations between China and the United States created when Deng Xiaoping and I established diplomatic relations in 1979.

CUBA

I wanted to do something about Cuba, because our economic embargo hurt their citizens and strengthened the Communist regime of Fidel Castro, and because restraints on American travel to Cuba were a deprivation of our own citizens' basic rights. A month after becoming president, I wrote:

"My inclination is to alleviate tension around the world, including disharmonies between our country and those with whom we have no official diplomatic relationships, like China, North Korea, Vietnam, Cambodia, Laos, Cuba, and I'll be moving in this direction. I think the country's ready for it, although in some instances like Cuba it's going to be quite controversial to do so. If I get an equivalent response from these countries, then I would be glad to meet them more than halfway."

In March 1977, journalist Bill Moyers gave me a report on his extensive discussion with Castro, who wanted to end our trade embargo without conceding anything. I wanted Cuba to release several thousand political prisoners, reduce deployment of troops in Ethiopia and other African nations, and refrain from interfering in the internal affairs of countries in this hemisphere. Although Castro was unwilling to go that far, we did make some progress. We removed travel restrictions on U.S. citizens, signed a fisheries agreement and a maritime agreement, and each of us established "interest sections" in the other's capital. (The U.S. interest section in Havana has continued and expanded. In 2011 I spoke to about three hundred American diplomats and Cuban employees in the same building that had housed our embassy before diplomatic relations were broken in 1961.) Unfortunately, Cuban involvement in Africa prevented further improvement of relations. Because of White House staff member Robert Pastor's persistence and later travels to Cuba, I was able to induce

Castro to release 3,600 political prisoners in 1978. Representatives of our Justice Department screened them, and we brought about one thousand of the acceptable ones to America. There was no real change in this situation until the Soviets invaded Afghanistan, in December 1979. After that, Castro sent word to me that he wanted to have substantive talks, and I sent Bob Pastor and Peter Tarnoff from the State Department to Havana. My diary, on January 18, 1980, outlined how, during an eleven-hour discussion, Castro "described without any equivocation his problems with the Soviet Union, his loss of leadership position in the NAM [nonaligned movement] because of his subservience to the Soviets; his desire to pull out of Ethiopia now and Angola later; his involvement in the revolutionary movements in Central America but his aversion to sending weapons or military capability to the Caribbean countries; and so forth. He's very deeply hurt by our embargo and wants better relations with us, but can't abandon the Soviets, who have supported his revolution unequivocally."

Whatever Castro's inclinations, he prevented better relations with the United States when from April to October 1980 he enabled what became known as the Mariel

Boatlift. This included numerous criminals among legitimate refugees coming to our shores. Further progress was stymied by Cuba's additional troop deployments to Ethiopia and continued promotion of communism in some countries in this hemisphere.

I have no doubt that the best way to encourage democracy and human rights in Cuba is for the United States to restore a policy of free travel to and from the island, lift the economic embargo, and let Cubans see the advantages of a free society. President Obama's decision in December 2014 to reestablish diplomatic relations is a long-overdue step in the right direction, but the right to make other decisions concerning Cuba was transferred from the White House to the Congress when President Clinton signed the Helms-Burton bill into law in March 1996.

ECONOMIC EMBARGOES

The imposition of sanctions or embargoes on unsavory regimes is most often ineffective and can be counterproductive. In Cuba, where the news media are controlled by the government, many people are convinced that their economic plight is caused by America and that they are defended by the actions of their Communist leaders, who are strengthened in power. I have visited the homes of both Castro brothers and some of the top officials, and it is obvious to me that their living conditions have not suffered. Many Cuban families are deprived of good income, certain foods, cell phones, access to the Internet, and basic freedoms, but they have access to good education and health care and live in a tropical environment where the soil is productive and many houses are surrounded by fruit trees. In addition, Cubans receive about $2.5 billion annually in remittances from their friends and relatives in the United States.

The situation in the Democratic People's Republic of Korea is more tragic. The U.S. embargo, imposed on North Korea sixty-five years ago, at the beginning of the Korean War, is being strictly implemented, with every effort being made to restrict and damage the economy as much as possible. During my visits to Pyongyang I have had long talks with government officials and surprisingly outspoken women's groups who emphasized the plight of people who were starving. When I checked with the UN World Food Program, they estimated that at least 600 grams of cereal per day was needed for a "survival ration," and that the daily food distribution in North Korea had at times been as low as 128 grams. Congressional staffers who visited the country in 1998 reported "a range of 300,000 to 800,000 dying each year from starvation." The Carter Center arranged for North Korean agriculture leaders to go to Mexico in 2002 to help them increase production of their indigenous crops, and the U.S. contribution of grain rose to 589,000 tons after I went to North Korea in 1994 and relations improved between our two countries with an agreement under President Clinton. However, U.S. food aid was drastically reduced under President George W. Bush and terminated completely by President Obama in 2010.

I visited the State Department at that time and was told that the North Korean government would not permit any supervision of food deliveries, which was the main problem. In April 2011 I returned to North Korea, accompanied by former president Martti Ahtisaari of Finland, former president Mary Robinson of Ireland, and former prime minister of Norway Gro Brundtland, who was a physician and had been director of the World Health Organization. We stopped first in Beijing for briefings from World Food Program officials, who said there were no restraints on monitoring food deliveries to families. They followed us to Pyongyang and accompanied us to rural areas where food was being distributed. The government sent an official guarantee that all such food deliveries could be monitored by America and other donors. I reported to Washington that one-third of children in North Korea were malnourished and stunted in their growth and that daily food intake was between 700 and 1,400 calories, compared to a normal American's of 2,000 to 2,500, but our government took no action.

There is no excuse for oppression by a dictatorial regime, but it is likely that the degree of harsh treatment is dependent on the dissatisfaction of the citizens. Hungry people are more inclined to demand relief from their plight, and more likely to be imprisoned or executed. As in Cuba, the political elite in North Korea do not suffer, and the leaders' all-pervasive propaganda places blame on the United States, not themselves.

The primary objective of dictators is to stay in office, and we help them achieve this goal by punishing their already suffering subjects and letting the oppressors claim to be saviors. When nonmilitary pressure on a government is considered necessary, economic sanctions should be focused on travel, foreign bank accounts, and other special privileges of government officials who make decisions, not on destroying the economy that determines the living conditions of oppressed people.

NONPROLIFERATION

An urgent challenge for me as president was to establish a clear national policy on the handling of nuclear materials and how to set an example. I consulted with Admiral Rickover, Secretaries Harold Brown and Jim Schlesinger, and other experts.

In April 1977, I announced that we were terminating our prospects for reprocessing spent nuclear fuels, shifting from a heavy dependence on plutonium as an energy source, and attempting to cooperate closely with other nations to achieve the same goals. I had adverse feedback especially from France, Germany, and Japan, who were enjoying the economic benefits of trading technology and nuclear fuel to other countries.

The Nonproliferation Treaty of 1970 had been adopted by all nations except Israel, India, and Pakistan (North Korea withdrew in 2003, and the new nation of South Sudan has not acted). A key provision was that the major powers make every effort to reduce our arsenals and lead the way to prevent the spread of nuclear materials or equipment, even without close supervision by the International Atomic Energy Agency. I rejected intense pressure from Pakistan and India to provide assistance to them, and my immediate successors maintained this policy. However, the two countries were helped with fuel and technology by Canada, Great Britain, China, and others, and they developed atomic weapons in the late 1980s. President George W. Bush signed an agreement in 2008 to provide India with nuclear fuel and technology despite Indian leaders' refusal to comply with the Nonproliferation Treaty, and President Obama has confirmed and expanded this agreement.

NO MORE VOTERS

One of my biggest disappointments was the reluctance of both Democratic and Republican legislators to expand the ability of our citizens to vote. As governor, I had sponsored a law that authorized all high school principals to be deputy voter registrars, and I had a contest each year to see which schools registered more upcoming eighteen-year-olds. At the national level, when I proposed this or other moves toward more universal registration, there was a persistent opposition that I didn't understand. House Speaker Tip O'Neill finally explained to me that few incumbent congressmen wanted the voters' lists expanded because they were satisfied with those who had put them in office.

More intense efforts by Republicans to restrict registration of students, minorities, and elderly voters by imposing identification requirements have been (unsuccessfully) criticized and legally challenged, especially in the South after the voting rights legislation was weakened by Congress in 2013. The conservative Supreme Court has refused to take action to guarantee the right of Americans to vote, or to end the gerrymandering of congressional districts to favor whichever political party dominates a state government.

THE KOREAS

Progress on the Korean Peninsula was frustrated by reluctance among both the Koreas and some of my own military leaders. As a submariner during the Korean War, I had felt frustrated when it ended with an arbitrary line drawn between North and South Korea plus merely a cease-fire and not a permanent peace treaty. When I was president, South Korea was still governed by a dictator, General Park Chung-hee, but was making notable economic progress with massive assistance from the United States and other nations. Communist dictator Kim Il Sung ruled the North with an iron hand, and this region was isolated and suffering from strict economic sanctions, with many people starving. Both leaders paid lip service to reunification. We had about thirty thousand American troops in South Korea, and these and the Korean forces were commanded by an American general. With Secretary Harold Brown and other advisers, we decided it was time to begin reducing our military presence. The South was affluent and technologically capable of defending itself. The American major general John Singlaub made a public statement in Seoul condemning the plan, and I summoned him to the White House. I described that meeting in my diary:

"5/21/77 I met with Major General Singlaub about his statement that if we withdrew troops from South Korea a war would result. He denied making the statement. He said he was just quoting from Korean officials. Then he said that the reporter was not given authority to quote him. I don't think he was telling the truth, but I felt sorry for him. He emphasized over and over that he was not disloyal, that he'd meant no insubordination. So instead of reprimanding him I just told him that we would transfer him out of Korea."

Amazingly, the next Defense Department intelligence estimate of North Korea's military capability was abruptly twice as great as ever before! I was deeply skeptical, but the assessment was shared with congressional leaders and I had no way to disprove it. I decided to back down on my decision to withdraw U.S. troops but to remove nuclear weapons. Under President George W. Bush a reduced number of military bases were concentrated farther south, but about the same number of American troops are still there. North Korea has retained its army strength and now has a threatening arsenal of nuclear weapons. There were six-power talks under President George W. Bush involving the United States, North and South Korea, Japan, China, and Russia designed to promote peace and restrict development of nuclear arsenals, but these have not been continued by President Obama.

NUCLEAR QUESTIONS, AND RICKOVER

I was delighted when Admiral Rickover and I established a close friendship from the beginning of my presidency. He told me that he would never mention to me anything that related to budget allocations or priorities for any ship in the nuclear navy. He insisted that I throw the switch that started operation of a prototype "breeder reactor" at Shippingport, Pennsylvania. It operated for five years, generated about twenty-five megawatts of power and, as planned, produced more fissile material than it consumed.

Secretary Schlesinger, Admiral Rickover, and I decided that it was not necessary to launch a program of producing electric power from large breeder reactors, although I realized that the technology might be needed in the distant future, when uranium became scarce and the advantage of "breeding" fuel would be more important. There was a strong move in the Congress to continue the effort, initiated under President Nixon, to build a full-scale model alongside the Clinch River in Tennessee. Originally estimated to cost $400 million, the projected price for completion had increased eightfold by the time I made my

With Admiral Rickover alongside the USS Los Angeles, *May 27, 1977.*

decision to cancel the project. Although I was familiar with its prospective use of liquid sodium as a cooling agent from my submarine days and believed the design to be safe, I was concerned about the by-product from breeder reactors being massive quantities of plutonium that could be used by us or others for nuclear explosives. A group of senators, led by those from the region, were successful in appropriating enough money to maintain a caretaker staff, and President Reagan attempted to restart the project. By that time the Congress had adopted my position and finally withheld all funding for breeder reactors in 1983.

In May 1977 Rosalynn and I flew down to Cape Canaveral and spent the day with Rickover on the nuclear submarine USS *Los Angeles.* He and the captain put the new ship through extreme maneuvers, and he pointed out that all the U.S. atomic-powered ships would stretch for more than ten miles if lined up stem to stern and that there had never been a nuclear incident that caused any damage or injured a person. I was surprised when I asked him how he would react to a total elimination of nuclear weapons — and nuclear power production — from the earth. He said it would be one of the greatest things that could happen.

THREE MILE ISLAND

Despite the financial loss and frightful scare of the Three Mile Island nuclear accident in March 1979, there were no injuries. I was informed immediately and sent highly qualified people to the island to monitor and control the situation. Luckily, I was familiar with the technology and could understand the briefings and make reasonable decisions. The coolant system had failed because of human error, and the reactor core melted, causing the overheating of cooling water and a buildup of high-pressure steam in the reactor container. Radioactive gases were within the steam that had to be released into the atmosphere to reduce pressure. All this was done under carefully controlled conditions, but I advised the governor to remove some children and pregnant women from the vicinity. Although the governor and scientific experts explained the facts, *The Washington Post* and a few other news media presented the situation as horrific, a threat to the lives and safety of millions of people. I called the *Post* executives to correct their mistake, but they were undeterred in their crusade to frighten as many people as possible. Rosalynn and I decided to go to the site personally; there we received a briefing and then went into the plant's control room adjacent to the reactor, with the highest possible live media coverage. This calmed most of the public fear.

Pressure in the reactor was soon returned

to normal levels, and I appointed a panel of experts, on which Admiral Rickover helped, to put in place some safety measures patterned after those he maintained in navy ships. The Nuclear Regulatory Agency made them mandatory for all power companies that operated reactors in America. This was the worst nuclear accident in U.S. history, and the financial costs were substantial. I had seen the damaged reactor at Chalk River, Canada, and now this incident in Pennsylvania — with no injury to people — but I remain convinced of the efficacy of nuclear power generation, especially as an alternative to the extremely threatening prospect of global warming caused by excessive consumption of coal, oil, and other fossil fuels. There will have to be an emphasis on simplicity and safety of design and highly trained personnel to operate the reactors.

SPACE

The primary project of NASA during my presidency was to develop four space shuttles, the most complex aircraft ever built. The first one, *Columbia,* was delivered to its launch site at Kennedy Space Center in March 1979 and launched in April 1981. Later, two of the shuttles were lost in flight, the *Challenger* in 1986 and *Columbia* in 2003.

I was especially interested in *Voyager 1,* a space probe that was launched in September 1977. On March 5, 1979, my science adviser and other space experts joined a group of us at the White House movie theater to view closed-circuit television photographs as *Voyager 1* approached Jupiter and its moons. I still followed its travels as it made close observations of Saturn and then photographed the solar system from outside the farthest planetary orbit. As I write this, in 2014, *Voyager 1* is in interstellar space, now more than 12 billion miles from earth. This is farther than any other man-made object and is beyond the influence of the sun's gravity. *Voyager 1* is still sending back radio signals in answer to NASA queries, and the round-trip for radio waves, at the speed of light, requires thirty-six hours. The spacecraft is expected to be in contact until about 2025, when its power plant is likely to fail.

I am not in favor of the most costly space projects, such as sending astronauts to Mars, to the moon again, or to other heavenly bodies. Unmanned vehicles with scientific instruments and robotic probes can accomplish the same goals, and many others beyond the reach of humans.

I am often asked about the UFO I sighted in the late 1960s. I was district governor of fifty-six Lions Clubs in Southwest Georgia, and one of my duties was to visit each club during the year. I was standing outside a school lunchroom in Leary with about two dozen men, waiting for our evening meeting, when we saw a light in the western sky, larger than Venus. It grew closer and larger, reaching about half the apparent diameter of a full moon. It stopped, changed color, and then disappeared back toward the west, soundlessly. We all saw the strange light and discussed its appearance and possible explanation at our meeting that night. On the way back to Plains I dictated on my small tape recorder what I remembered.

Later, in public office, I was asked if I had ever seen a UFO, and I responded with that brief account. I have never thought there was any extraterrestrial involvement but surmised that it was some kind of military balloon or other device from nearby Fort Benning, a major military base. This disclaimer has not dampened the intense interest that some people have in the prospect of interstellar travelers having been seen by one of America's presidents. It was, indeed, a UFO — an *unidentified* flying object.

CLAIRVOYANT

There was another experience I have never been able to explain. One morning I had a report from the CIA that a small twin-engine plane had gone down somewhere in Zaire, and that it contained some important secret documents. We were searching for the crash site using satellite photography and some other surreptitious high-altitude overflights, but with no success. With some hesitancy, a CIA agent in California recommended the services of a clairvoyant woman, who was then consulted. She wrote down a latitude and longitude, which proved to be accurate, and several days later I was shown a photograph of the plane, totally destroyed and in a remote area. Without notifying Zaire's President Mobutu, we sent in a small team that recovered the documents and the bodies of the plane's occupants.

ENERGY

The most far-reaching and controversial domestic issue I addressed as president was a comprehensive energy policy. Overdependence on foreign oil had plagued our nation for many years, with resulting boycotts, long lines at fuel pumps, and little effort being made to address the basic problems. Prices for oil and natural gas were pegged at a very low rate, which encouraged excess consumption and discouraged domestic production and competition among producers. There were few substantive efforts, or reasons, to improve energy efficiency in homes, transportation, machinery, or household appliances, or to promote cleaner-burning coal or increase the use of power coming from the sun through wood, wind, or photovoltaic cells. My announced goal was to derive at least 20 percent of our total energy from renewable sources by the year 2000. We introduced legislation to address all these issues and were remarkably successful. In spite of worldwide inflation and economic restraints resulting from a shortage of oil supplies in 1980 from Iran and Iraq during their war, a broad array of job opportunities were created from new energy technology. Because of this and public works projects, there were more jobs created each year I was in office than under any other president since World War II.

As a symbolic gesture, I installed thirty-six solar panels at the White House, but they were removed by President Reagan. We have acquired one to be displayed in our presidential museum, and on a recent visit to the largest panel manufacturer in China, I found one displayed in their factory entrance.

Our only major failures resulted from the political necessity to leave options for future administrations to ease the efficiency standards in some important areas, and the oil and automobile industries have been successful in approving the continued production of gas-guzzling trucks and cars and encouraging unlimited use of fossil fuels.

Since then, some countries, but not the United States, have made notable progress in increasing the portion of electricity produced by nonfossil energy: Canada, 64 percent; Spain, 42 percent; Germany and Mexico, 25 percent; China, 18 percent; France and the United Kingdom, 15 percent; the United States, 10 percent. Most of our new energy conservation laws, however, have remained intact, including requirements for home insulation, efficiency of motors and large household appliances, and some government-sponsored efforts to find new sources of energy in the United States that have resulted in a major increase in production and use of natural gas.

I decided that 95 percent of the offshore areas in Alaska would be open for oil exploration, but we left intact a prohibition against drilling for oil in the Arctic National Wildlife Refuge. Unfortunately, I failed to include the area in the permanently protected system of national parks or wilderness areas, never dreaming that Reagan and other Republican presidents would make all-out efforts to persuade Congress to reverse my decision. On several occasions during the past thirty years I have worked with environmental groups to convince key members of the House and Senate to prevent this action. The threat to open this pristine area to oil drilling still exists.

THREAT OF NUCLEAR WAR

Shortly before being inaugurated, I was given a detailed briefing (and for the first time I included the vice president) on what I had to understand concerning a nuclear threat and possible responses. Most Soviet long-range missiles were located in silos, and we had the ability to detect their launch almost immediately. Their flight to Washington would take less than thirty minutes and could not be intercepted, and that was all the time I would have to decide how to respond. Our arsenal was equally formidable, with missiles that could be launched from silos, airplanes, or submarines. The multiple warheads from one submarine could destroy every Soviet city with a population of 100,000 or more. Each side had more than fifteen thousand nuclear weapons in its arsenal, and we both knew that nuclear war would be a global catastrophe. This was a scenario that was constantly on my mind. I wanted to maintain peace and to reduce the world's nuclear weaponry as near to zero as possible.

During these confrontational times, I was always acutely sensitive to the attitude of Soviet leaders and tried to understand them as well as possible. Zbig Brzezinski made a droll comment that under Lenin the Soviet Union was like a religious revival, under Stalin like a prison, under Khrushchev like a circus, and under Brezhnev like the U.S. Post Office Department. We knew that even our bureaucratic postal officials sometimes made bad decisions. I would often sit by the globe in the Oval Office, turn it to Moscow, and try to imagine myself in President Brezhnev's shoes. I knew that he sometimes felt isolated, under duress, and may have been paranoid, and I was careful never to do or say anything that might precipitate a resort to nuclear weapons.

With the threat of a nuclear exchange ever-present, I had to develop plans for my own status during this possible brief period of destruction, and to decide how best to preserve what would be left of America. Working closely and privately with the vice president, national security adviser, and secretary of defense, I decided that I would continue my duties as president and the vice president and a small group of other officials would go quickly to a safer place, from which communications and command could be exercised after the disaster. This would probably be in an airplane already specially equipped for this purpose, and we conducted drills several times to practice this procedure. A substantial portion of the nuclear arsenals survive today, unfortunately and unnecessarily still in a state of readiness for launching.

ABORTION

One of the most frequent questions I've had to answer has been, What was the greatest conflict between my religious beliefs and my public duties? The answer has always been "Abortion." I took an oath to uphold the laws of the United States, as interpreted by the Supreme Court. The *Roe v. Wade* ruling of 1973 was that during the first trimester of a pregnancy the decision to abort must be left to the mother and her physician. As a Christian, I have never believed that Jesus Christ would approve abortions unless the life of the mother was endangered or the pregnancy was caused by rape or incest. As president, I had to uphold the law, but I still did everything possible to minimize the number of abortions.

Studies show clearly that fewer abortions result after family planning education or a prospective mother's assurance that she and the baby will be economically viable, or that a beneficial adoption will be possible. I encouraged the availability of sex education and contraceptives and initiated special financial and food assistance for indigent women and their babies, which is known as the WIC (Women, Infants, and Children) program. We tried to make the procedure for adoption as convenient and natural as possible, with minimum embarrassment for the birth and foster mothers.

In the United States in 2011 there were 13.9 abortions per 1,000 women aged fifteen to forty-four. In some Latin American nations all abortions are legally outlawed and little financial assistance is available. The Latin American and

Caribbean region has the highest regional rate of unsafe abortions in the world, at 31 per 1,000 women.

1980 ELECTION

The 1980 election was dominated by the hostages in Iran. During the primaries I remained at the White House whenever possible but went into key states as much as necessary to meet the Democratic challenge from Senator Kennedy. My popularity seemed to vary according to the latest news about the hostages, but eventually I carried thirty-six states and Kennedy, ten, with the other states sending unpledged delegates to the convention. On the stage, when I became the Democratic nominee, Kennedy ostentatiously refused to grasp my hand, and his high level of bitterness prevailed between then and the general election. Ronald Reagan was nominated by the Republicans, defeating George H. W. Bush in forty-four of the forty-eight states that had pledged delegates. I gave my kickoff speech at Warm Springs in Georgia, where Franklin Roosevelt had been treated for polio and died in 1945. I was somewhat disconcerted when Reagan made his introductory speech in Philadelphia, Mississippi, which was well known as the place where three civil rights workers were murdered by Ku Klux Klan members and buried in a dam. His key statement, at least to Southerners, was "I believe in states' rights." Although I had swept the region in 1976, Georgia was the only Southern state I won in 1980, along with just five other states. Once again my poll results fluctuated with the likelihood of American hostages being released, and they dropped during the last week before Election Day. The ultimate irony was that this was the anniversary of the hostages having been taken. Reagan received 50.8 percent of the votes, I got 41 percent, and the independent candidate John Anderson received 6.6 percent, including a substantial number from Democrats who were Kennedy supporters. I accepted the disappointing results with relative equanimity, but Rosalynn was especially grieved and angry. My own feelings were helped by trying to think of some positive things with which to reassure her.

I had wonderful legislative successes during my "lame duck" months before leaving office, getting final congressional approval for the Alaska Lands legislation, major components of my energy package, and the Superfund bill, which prescribed cleanup procedures and funding for toxic waste sites.

One of the happiest moments of my life came just after I was no longer president, when I was informed by my military aide that the plane carrying all our hostages had taken off from the Tehran airport after sitting there loaded and ready since early that morning. Although books have been written about the question, I have never known what caused the Ayatollah to delay granting their freedom until I was out of office.

REFLECTIONS

My time as president was very gratifying to me and my family, and I learned a lot about our country, including its strengths and weaknesses, its aspirations and achievements, and the threats to realizing its inherent greatness. I tried to honor one of my campaign pledges, to make our government "as good and honest and competent as the American people," and to understand this challenge I paused on occasion to read the U.S. Constitution, and also the Universal Declaration of Human Rights, a simpler but more complete description of the goals to which we were committed.

My two basic objectives were to protect our nation's security and interests peacefully and to enhance human rights here and abroad, and these goals were achieved. I faced some unanticipated challenges, especially the Iranian revolution, the taking of our hostages, the Iran-Iraq war, which caused the price of petroleum and worldwide inflation to skyrocket, and the Soviet invasion of Afghanistan. With very few exceptions, I was able to maintain good relations with other peoples around the world. Many of these relationships have deteriorated in recent years.

I was fortunate not to have to ask for special favors from individual supporters or organizations, so I was not bound when elected to appoint particular people to judgeships or diplomatic posts. Headed by Florida's former governor Reubin Askew, a blue-ribbon committee screened aspirants for each post and gave me a list of five whom they considered to be most qualified. I customarily made my choice from these.

There were many political disputes, some caused by my willingness to enter them voluntarily and others because of mistakes I made. I decided to resolve the long-pending problems of allocating large areas of land in Alaska, concluding a Panama Canal treaty, normalizing diplomatic relations with China, developing a comprehensive energy policy, promoting democracy in Latin America, deregulating major industries, and bringing peace between Israel and Egypt. All of these were controversial. I had gratifying success in working with the Congress but was not able to deal harmoniously with the news media. A serious political mistake was not being more attentive to the Democratic Party, both in preparing it for the 1980 election and in avoiding the schism between my supporters and those of Senator Ted Kennedy. I should have made a better effort to maintain the cooperation that he and I enjoyed during my early months in the White House.

Being governor and president were life-changing experiences. Rosalynn and I had to expand our involvement in the lives of many people, and we developed knowledge and personal relationships that provided a foundation for the many gratifying and enjoyable projects of The Carter Center during the next thirty-five years.

Chapter Eight: Back Home

In Plains

Our agricultural supply business and farms were flourishing when I was elected president, and I placed them in a blind trust while I was in office, not permitting my trustee even to give me annual reports. When I was preparing to leave the White House I learned that, because of inept management and three years of severe drought, we had accumulated a very large debt, with no business assets to be used for payment. I was afraid we might lose our farmland and even endanger ownership of our home, but fortunately Archer Daniels Midland Company decided to enter the peanut business and bought Carter's Warehouse for almost as much as we owed. We retained the farmland on which peanuts, cotton, soybeans, grain, and pine trees still grow. I phased out my duties as an active farmer and have relied on partners or renters who have modern equipment for planting, cultivating, and harvesting the fields. We still enjoy caring for the timberland, while consulting with an expert forester.

One decision I made before leaving Washington was to write a memoir of my presidential years. I examined the voluminous diary notes I had dictated in the Oval Office and found that they comprised twenty-one volumes and more than a million words. I spent my first year reading them and writing about the most significant events. The resulting book, *Keeping Faith,* was a best seller.

When we came home I had no idea what I would do with the rest of my life. I was fifty-six years old, one of the younger survivors of the White House. After we unloaded our belongings in the garage, our first task was to add more storage space in our home. Rosalynn and I decided to put a floor in our large attic, which proved to be quite a challenge because the roof trusses and joists were made of rough lumber and had to be smoothed and leveled as a preliminary step. This kept us busy for the first few weeks, before I bought a word processor and began to write my presidential memoir. It was a far cry from

Home in Plains, Christmas, *oil on canvas, painted September 2011.*

modern computers, but better than my small portable typewriter.

EMORY UNIVERSITY

I had several offers to assume an academic role, either to become president of a university or to teach, and I finally accepted an offer from Emory University to become a "distinguished professor." I was guaranteed complete freedom of expression and would not have obligations to teach specific students for a semester and deal with their grading. My duty was to lecture to large and small numbers of students, on subjects to be decided between me and the professors and deans. My Emory duties include lecturing in different schools and departments each month during the academic year, including history, political science, environmental studies, theology, African-American studies, business, medicine, nursing, and law. My first session each September is a town hall meeting with several thousand students, where I answer their unpredictable questions. So far, I have not avoided answering a question because it might be politically or personally sensitive, and I follow the same policy in lectures to smaller groups. I have enjoyed this freedom in my academic role but sometimes create a brief flurry in the news media when I comment frankly on decisions made by public officials in America or other countries.

Rosalynn and I spend at least a week each month in Atlanta, where I work on the affairs of The Carter Center, meet with foreign leaders, enjoy supper one night with about twenty-five family members in the area, have extended discussions with a few Emory professors and deans on mutual interests, and Rosalynn and I have breakfast with the university's president and spouse and the CEO of The Carter Center.

PANCREATIC CANCER

My father had been fifty-nine years old when he died with pancreatic cancer, and my doctors at Emory University became concerned when, in 1983, my sister Ruth, fifty-four, died from the same cause and five years later my brother, Billy, fifty-one, suffered the same fate. The National Institutes of Health began to check all members of our family regularly, and my last remaining sibling, Gloria, sixty-four, was diagnosed with pancreatic cancer and died in 1990. There was no record of another American family having lost four members to this disease, and since that time I have had regular X-rays, CAT scans, or blood analyses, with hope of early detection if I develop the same symptoms. By the time it is detected, cancer of the pancreas has often metastasized to other vital organs and is usually fatal within a few months. A worldwide search has revealed a few other families like ours, and it is most likely that a genetic defect is involved, possibly triggered by smoking cigarettes. Being the only nonsmoker in my family may have been what led to my longer life.

My most challenging obligation was to raise about $25 million in private contributions to build a presidential library. As a defeated Democratic candidate with no prospect of returning to public office and few wealthy friends or supporters, I found this task difficult and time-consuming. I finally decided to begin construction using architectural plans we had approved and go into debt for the amount still to be raised. I was not interested in just building a museum or storing my White House records and memorabilia; I wanted a place where we could work.

I awoke one night after a few hours of sleep, called Rosalynn, and said, "I know what we can do for the future. We can create a place in Atlanta near our presidential library and museum and invite people to come there like Anwar Sadat and Menachem Begin came to Camp David. I can offer my services as a mediator to help prevent or resolve conflicts, either within or between nations. If they prefer, I can go to their country." This was the birth of The Carter Center. We expanded my concept of our Center by including conferences on important issues in which I had been involved as president, including peace in the Middle East, international security and arms control, business and the environment, education, and global health. Working with Emory, we established The Carter Center legally in 1982, and during the next five years I spent much of my time raising funds from private donors to pay for the presidential library, with adjoining buildings to house the work of the Center. Emory provided me with an office on the top floor of their library, and I began to make more specific plans with the help of Dr. Steven Hochman, who for the next year or so was my only assistant.

We adopted a few basic principles: Our Center would be nonpartisan; we would be as innovative as possible, not duplicating or competing with other organizations that were addressing issues successfully; we would not be afraid of possible failure if our goals were worthwhile; and we would operate always with a balanced budget. The Carter Center expanded its operations into eighty nations, including the promotion of peace, human rights, democracy and freedom, and better health care. We now have an annual cash budget of about $100 million with an equal amount of in-kind contributions of medicines and other supplies that are distributed in our health programs, primarily in Africa and Latin America. Our normal staff of 180 is sometimes supplemented with several hundred trained experts on our payroll plus thousands of unpaid volunteers whom we train to work on our projects in targeted countries. We have adhered to the original principles and met our goals during the past three decades, and I am still performing my duties at Emory University.

HEALTH CARE

The most unanticipated development has been that global health has become our largest commitment, now encompassing a majority of our employees and expenditures. We concentrate on malaria plus five "neglected tropical diseases" that are no longer known in the moderately developed world but still afflict hundreds of millions of people in Africa and Latin America: onchocerciasis (river blindness), schistosomiasis, lymphatic filariasis (elephantiasis), trachoma, and dracunculiasis (guinea worm).

To initiate a project in the early years, I would go first to a country and meet with the president, prime minister, and ministers of health, transportation, education, and agriculture. I would inform them about our

We expanded my concept of The Carter Center by including conferences on important issues in which I had been involved as president, including peace in the Middle East, international security and arms control, business and the environment, education, and global health.

plans, outline what was expected of them, and we would conclude a "memorandum of understanding" that included a clear description of our mutual responsibilities. Our health programs are now known and respected throughout Africa and in the regions of Latin America and the Caribbean where we work. At Emory University, whenever I meet with groups of international students, I find that I am thanked for our contributions to health in the students' home countries. We give the local people as much credit for accomplishments as possible. I spend a good amount of my time at celebrations, honoring the achievements of dedicated local health staff and volunteers. Our Carter Center staff plus those we train go into the most remote villages in jungle and desert areas to explain our goals, recruit volunteers, and train them and a few paid supervisors. Then we deliver donated medicines, water filtration cloths, and insecticide-treated bed nets and make sure that people know how these materials are to be properly used. We are treating about 35 million people every year. Over half of these are now for river blindness, and so far we have been able to eliminate this disease in four indigenous countries in Latin America and to demonstrate in Uganda and Sudan that the same goal can be reached in Africa. In 1986 there were an estimated 3.5 million cases of guinea worm in about 26,000 villages in twenty countries. In the entire world we had fewer than 130 cases in 2014. We are looking forward to having this disease be the second in history eradicated from all nations. (The last case of smallpox was in 1977.)

We are responsible for about a third of the world's surgeries to correct trachoma, the major cause of blindness except for cataracts, and have assisted in the construction of more than 3 million latrines to reduce the population of flies that transmit the disease. We have helped to install two bed nets in each home in Ethiopia and Nigeria where malaria exists. The nets are treated with an insecticide that kills mosquitoes on contact. These insects are the carriers for both malaria and lymphatic filariasis. One of our newest projects is to eliminate the two diseases from the Caribbean island of Hispaniola, and the governments of Haiti and the Dominican Republic, not always compatible, are cooperating fully on reaching this goal.

Our Center's unique International Task Force for Disease Eradication has assumed the continuing responsibility of analyzing every human illness to determine which ones might possibly be eliminated from a particular region or country or eradicated from the entire world.

AGRICULTURE

In 1985 Nobel Laureate Norman Borlaug, Japanese philanthropist Ryoichi Sasakawa, and I met in Geneva, Switzerland, and decided to organize Global 2000, an agricultural program designed to increase production of food grains in several places in Africa. We began our project in Ghana, Sudan, Zambia, and Zimbabwe, and expanded it to fourteen African nations, eventually teaching 8 million African families how to double or triple their production of maize (corn), wheat, rice, sorghum, and millet. With Japanese funding, Dr. Borlaug's knowledge of agronomy, and our help with organization and implementation, we taught them how to use the best seed, plant in contoured rows to minimize erosion, use necessary fertilizer, control weeds, harvest at the right time, and store and market crops properly. We usually began with forty farmers in a country as demonstrators and expanded in three years to about sixteen thousand. In Ethiopia the number of farms using our simple but effective farming practices reached several hundred thousand as Prime Minister Meles Zenawi financed the expansion with his government's funds. After I met with national leaders to conclude agreements on how we would share responsibilities, I would travel with Borlaug to monitor compliance with our instructions.

On one visit to Addis Ababa, I was sleeping in a Western-style hotel and was wakened by intense itching of my left knee. I went into the bathroom and saw two small perforations, rubbed on some ointment, then returned to bed and went back to sleep. The next day Dr. Borlaug and I went about 150 miles south to visit some farm plots, spent the night there, and when we returned to Addis my knee was swollen. I went to the U.S. embassy, and the medical doctor gave me some antibiotic pills to take. When my entire leg then swelled to almost twice its normal size, he put me to bed with an IV. The following morning he decided that my life was threatened, and he and the Secret Service agents arranged for me to be flown to a U.S. military hospital in Wiesbaden, Germany. The doctors there increased the strength of the medication, identified the probable species of spider from the puncture marks, and sent me back to Atlanta. By that time my body was covered with a rash, and I stayed in Emory University Hospital for five days while a team of doctors tried various treatments to reduce the swelling and intense itching. I recovered slowly but still have an aggravating rash that has to be treated regularly with prescribed salves and creams. Dermatologists say that the problem is permanent but manageable.

PEACE

Although The Carter Center and I have engaged in conflict resolution efforts with the United Nations and the United States, we more often have addressed threatening situations where we were on our own. These choices are not always popular, because they put us in contact with unsavory people or groups. They have included Maoists in Nepal, the Communist dictator Mengistu Haile Mariam in Ethiopia, Mobutu Sese Seko in Zaire (now the Democratic Republic of Congo), Radovan Karadžić in Bosnia and Slobodan Milošević in Serbia, Kim Il Sung and his successors in North Korea, the Castro brothers in Cuba, Omar al-Bashir in Sudan, and leaders of Hamas in Gaza and other places. In every case we keep American leaders informed about our plans and the results of our efforts.

I have addressed numerous threats to peace on behalf of The Carter Center. As examples, let me describe some that occurred in 1994. For three years, President Kim Il Sung of North Korea requested that I come to Pyongyang to help resolve some of the antagonism between him and the

Rosalynn and I received the honor of wearing traditional garb during a visit to Tingoli village, northern Ghana, in 2007.

government of the United States, but I had an initial aversion, derived from the Korean War, to accepting his request. I was eventually convinced that my services might be helpful, but my normal requests to the White House for approval of a visit to North Korea were rejected.

There was a crisis in the spring of 1994. North Korea disavowed its commitment to the Nonproliferation Treaty, expelled international inspectors from their nuclear facility, and began processing spent uranium rods into plutonium. The U.S. government refused to talk to the North Koreans and went to the UN Security Council to secure a condemnatory resolution. Some Chinese friends told me that North Korea would attack South Korea if their government was branded an international outlaw and their worshiped leader a criminal. Having developed a strategy that I was convinced would defuse the crisis, I decided that I needed to go. When President Bill Clinton rejected another request to approve my visit to Pyongyang, I wrote him to say that I was going despite his disapproval. However, Vice President Al Gore intercepted my message and convinced me to modify the wording. He then sent the message to Clinton, who was in Europe, and he gave his approval. My one caveat to Kim Il Sung was that we not be routed through Beijing but enter North Korea directly from South Korea. He responded that even the secretary-general of the UN came through China, but he finally relented. Rosalynn and I were the first persons in forty-three years to travel directly from Seoul across the Demilitarized Zone and on to Pyongyang.

With my knowledge of nuclear engineering, I was able to discuss the issues competently. We found Kim Il Sung to be congenial and surprisingly familiar with all the topics. During a long boat ride from Pyongyang to the sea, we reached agreement on about a dozen important subjects, including the nuclear problem and the return of international inspectors, summit talks with South Korea, withdrawal of troops from proximity to the DMZ, and recovery of the remains of buried Americans.

I reported these agreements to the White House. Kim Il Sung died soon after I was there, and I received a message from his son Kim Jong Il that he would honor his father's commitments. Official talks in Geneva resulted in approval by both sides of what we had negotiated, and Secretary of State Madeleine Albright visited Pyongyang in October 2000, to strengthen the mutual commitments. The U.S.–North Korea agreement was disavowed in 2002 by President George W. Bush, who branded

North Korea an "evil empire," and since that time Kim Il Sung's successors have expanded their development of nuclear weapons and long-range missiles. The United States now avoids almost all contact with North Korea, and strict economic sanctions are still imposed on the often starving people.

Later in 1994 an emergency developed in Haiti. The elected leader, Jean-Bertrand Aristide, had been forced into exile in 1991. He was replaced by General Raoul Cédras, and both leaders had asked me to serve as mediator. I was very knowledgeable about Haiti and had a longtime personal relationship with both men. For years President Bush and then President Clinton had wanted to try other means for returning Aristide to power, but none of these had worked. By September 1994, President Clinton had decided to assemble thirty thousand American military personnel as an invading force. I, meanwhile, had asked former senator Sam Nunn of Georgia and General Colin Powell to join me in a peace effort, and we had conveyed our proposal to President Clinton. He approved our plan to go to Haiti and make a final effort at negotiation before sending in the military.

In Port-au-Prince we negotiated for two

days with the assembled generals and found Cédras reluctant to accept any of my proposals. I called Rosalynn to tell her of our failure, and she said, "I have been informed that Cédras's wife, Yannick, is extremely influential. Why not talk to her?" I took her suggestion, and the general's wife was indeed the key to his improved attitude. We knew Cédras as a competent and admirable leader. He had been Haiti's universally respected military commander who maintained security while Rosalynn and I headed Carter Center observers who had monitored Aristide's previous election, and he had saved Aristide from an assassination attempt when he was deposed.

After long and intense negotiations, Cédras was finally ready to accept our proposals, prepared to stand alongside the American general and welcome U.S. troops if their arrival was peaceful and if the Haitian military personnel were treated with respect. I agreed to find an acceptable place in another country for him and his family to live. At this moment of apparent agreement, one of his subordinates, Brigadier General Philippe Biamby, rushed in and announced that President Clinton had launched fifty-two airplanes from U.S. military bases loaded with paratroopers, headed to invade Haiti. Biamby had received this report from a Haitian who worked at Fort Bragg in North Carolina. At this time there were thousands of angry demonstrators surrounding the building in which we were meeting.

Both negotiating teams rushed out a back door and drove to the office of the president, Emile Jonassaint, an elderly retired chief justice. General Powell got on a phone line and finally connected to the White House while Cédras and I presented our written agreement to the president. After reading it, he said, "I understand and agree, but it will have to be translated into French before I sign it." This was done rapidly, and he and I signed the document. By this time the American planes were halfway to Haiti, but Clinton ordered them to return to their base and the crisis was resolved. As agreed, General Cédras and his family moved to Panama. Aristide returned to Haiti, proved a disastrous leader, and was again forced into exile in Africa, this time by pressure from Washington.

My last duty as a mediator that year involved the Bosnia-Herzegovina conflict with Serbia, after its declaration of independence from Serbian-controlled Yugoslavia. I was initially contacted by Radovan Karadžić, who expressed a desire to resolve differences peacefully between the Bosnian Serbs, which he led, and the Bosnian Muslims and Croats, the two other major ethnic groups. He made a series of commitments about peace, human rights, and a comprehensive cease-fire if I would agree to come to Sarajevo. I informed President Clinton and UN Secretary-General Boutros Boutros-Ghali and got their approval for the mission. I arranged for Karadžić to repeat all his commitments on CNN. Serbian president Slobodan Milošević asked that I meet with him during my visit, and I agreed. My goals were to orchestrate a cease-fire with guarantees of human rights and clear demarcation of geographical control, and to discuss some key constitutional issues.

On December 18 I met first in Zagreb with Croatian President Franjo Tudjman, who supported the mission, and then proceeded to the Sarajevo airport, wearing and sitting on flak jackets because snipers had been firing from both sides. I was grateful for Karadžić's promise to refrain from attacks during my visit. I had a long talk with Alija Izetbegović, the president of Bosnia and Herzegovina, who was seeking independence from Serbia and whose small territory was surrounded on three sides by Serbian forces. He supported my mission but limited any cease-fire to three months. I awoke early the next day, wrote out my most hopeful proposals, and then Rosalynn and I made a drive of almost two hours to reach Pale, a distance of only nine miles through a beautiful mountain area, site of ski racing competitions in the 1984 Winter Olympics. It seemed that there was a military checkpoint around every curve in the road. Karadžić met us, accompanied by the top leaders of the Serbs, including General Ratko Mladić, army chief of staff, and they gave me an official welcome witnessed by a large news media contingency. In our private negotiations with Karadžić, he insisted on a twelve-month cease-fire, and I finally got him down to four months in an attempt to accommodate Izetbegović. I agreed to request a lifting of economic sanctions against Serbia from the United States and UN but could not promise any positive results.

I witnessed the signing of my document by Karadžić and Mladić. Its basic terms were cessation of hostilities on December 27, 1994, UN forces to be stationed along the line of confrontation for four months or for a longer period if mutually agreed, both parties to negotiate a comprehensive peace agreement, unrestricted movement of relief convoys, unimpeded use of the airport at Sarajevo, and the protection of human rights. The White House was pleased with the draft agreement but stipulated that Izetbegović would have to approve. When I called Sarajevo to tell him that all his demands had been realized, he refused to talk to me.

We drove back to Sarajevo and discussed the issues with Vice President Ejup Ganić, and the next morning we returned to Pale with a few minor amendments. After some intense arguments with his subordinates, Karadžić agreed to a final statement, which now had the cumulative approval of Izetbegović, Karadžić, Mladić, the United States, and the UN. We returned to Sarajevo and boarded our plane, shielded from ground fire by a large UN truck. The previous plane had taken four bullets through its left side. We took off with our flak jackets on, but I also wrapped an extra one around my hard disk and its documents and copies of the signed documents.

After proceeding through Zagreb to Belgrade, we met with Serbian President Slobodan Milošević, who, like everyone I met, had first to recite a history of the region. I was thankful that he began with World War I instead of the twelfth century. I showed him a copy of the agreement, and he approved, but he was vituperative in his condemnation of Karadžić, his competitor for Serbian leadership. I asked him repeatedly what it would take for them to be reconciled, and he finally said that if the parliament voted for the "Carter Plan," this would be adequate.

The cease-fire went into effect the following week and prevailed for four months, but it was not extended. Conflict erupted again, and the international community supported Bosnia-Herzegovina and condemned Serbia. War crimes were committed by both sides, most terribly by the Serbs, and NATO dispatched sixty thousand peacekeepers and launched more than 3,300 bombing sorties against Serbian forces, mostly with American planes. Another more permanent cease-fire was signed in Dayton, Ohio, in December 1995, approved by Milošević, Izetbegović, and Tudjman. After Milošević conceded defeat, war crimes charges were leveled by the International Criminal Court against him, Karadžić, and Mladić. Milošević was arrested in 2001, and the trial continued for five years, until his death in 2006. Karadžić was arrested in 2008 and

Mladić in 2011, and both are still on trial for war crimes. I have often pondered what might have happened if the basic terms of the 1994 cease-fire agreement had been fully supported by the international community.

PEACE FOR ISRAEL

A preeminent foreign policy goal of my life since I became president has been to bring peace to Israel, which of necessity means peace for the Palestinians and other immediate neighbors. This also became a key commitment of The Carter Center, which maintains full-time offices in Jerusalem, Ramallah, and Gaza and has monitored the three Palestinian elections. The first was held in 1996, when Yasir Arafat was elected president and members of the Palestine National Authority were chosen. After Arafat's death, Mahmoud Abbas was elected in 2005 to replace him as president, and then in January 2006 there was another election to choose new members of the parliament. Fatah, the Abbas party, and Israel did not want the election to proceed because candidates of Hamas were predicted to win up to 35 percent of parliamentary seats. However, the United States insisted that the already overdue election take place. The problem with Hamas was that it had not subscribed to the terms of the Oslo Agreement, which provided the basis for the Palestinian Authority.

It was an honest election, and Hamas did much better than expected, winning 74 of the 132 seats. The elected candidates included doctors, lawyers, educators, business executives, and previous holders of local office. I carried a request from Hamas to President Abbas to remain in office and to appoint Fatah members to some of the choice cabinet seats. While willing to remain in office, Abbas resisted the option of including Hamas in a unity government. I returned home to Plains, changed clothes, and flew back to London to attend a meeting of the International Quartet, comprising the United States, United Nations, European Union, and Russia. They allowed me to make a brief appeal to support the election results and then voted without debate to nullify them by making demands that Hamas would not accept. Nevertheless, in March a Hamas-nominated cabinet was accepted by President Abbas, and during the summer there was movement toward a unity government. Israel arrested eight Hamas cabinet members and twenty members of parliament who lived in the

West Bank and East Jerusalem, and a number of these officials were imprisoned for several years.

I wrote a book that analyzed the situation in the Occupied Territories and spelled out a workable plan for a comprehensive peace in the area, compatible with long-standing official policies of the United States and the United Nations. *Palestine Peace Not Apartheid* made it clear that without a "two-state" agreement with the Palestinians, Israel would inevitably become committed to a one-state solution. This was a prospect that Israeli prime ministers had described as potentially catastrophic. With Israelis controlling the area from the Jordan River to the Mediterranean Sea, they would either have to give Palestinians equal voting rights and ultimately relinquish Jewish control of government affairs or treat non-Jews as secondary citizens, without equal rights. My book was condemned by the pro-Israel lobby, AIPAC (American Israel Public Affairs Committee), and a number of prominent political leaders, primarily because of its title, in which I was careful not to mention Israel. Within a few days of its publication, I received 6,100 letters, a strong majority supporting my position, with many writers identifying themselves as

Jewish. Despite my attempts at book signings and other public events to reiterate my lifelong support for Israel and its security, this altercation has been very painful to me. A full-length film, *Jimmy Carter: Man from Plains,* was made of the book tour, directed by Jonathan Demme.

The political fallout has persisted. When the 2008 Democratic Convention was held to nominate Barack Obama, I planned to attend and make a speech, as is customary for former presidents. I was contacted by his aides, who told me that neither Bill Clinton nor I would speak, but we were requested to make twenty-minute documentary films to be shown to the delegates, each film designed to be of most help to the current candidate. They wanted me to go to New Orleans and the Gulf Coast, where Rosalynn and I had visited five times to build Habitat houses in the aftermath of Hurricane Katrina, and demonstrate how Republican leaders had failed to respond properly to the disaster. I spent a day in the area to carry out this assignment, but when we arrived at the convention in Denver, I was told that the film length would be only four minutes and I was requested not to speak, even to greet the delegates. (Clinton and his wife, Hillary, played major roles in the convention.) Obama's top aide, David Axelrod, explained that he didn't want to endanger his Jewish support. Unfortunately, this "estrangement" has persisted through his time in office, but our Center has continued our efforts to support U.S. and international policy and to encourage the Middle East peace process in every way possible.

The Carter Center monitored the parliamentary and presidential elections in Egypt from 2010 to 2012 following the overthrow of President Hosni Mubarak. I was there to head our group of observers. In my meetings with candidate and then president Mohamed Morsi, I urged him to honor all the terms of the Egypt-Israeli peace treaty that I had negotiated in 1979, which has been carefully observed by both nations. He complied with this commitment while in office.

When Rosalynn and I went to Washington in January 2013 to attend President Obama's inauguration, John Kerry and his wife, Teresa, came to our hotel room and spent two hours that morning talking about his goals as the prospective secretary of state. He informed us that he would make an all-out effort to conclude a peace agreement between Israel and the Palestinians, and that President Obama would be visiting the Holy Land early in his new term. Secretary Kerry has done his best to reach this goal. There was hope for some months that the United States would present a definitive plan, based on international law and long-standing policies of our country, and let this public proposal be considered by the disputants and the international community. With full involvement of President Obama, it would be difficult for either the Palestinian or the Israeli leaders to reject this all-out effort. Without overt assistance from the White House and direct involvement by the president, these hopes have not been realized. The crucial relationships among Israel, the Palestinians, and the United States have deteriorated, and the Palestinians are now making efforts to refer the dispute to the United Nations.

MONITORING ELECTIONS

In my mediation of civil conflicts, I soon learned that antagonistic military leaders would refuse to negotiate even through an intermediary, and I decided to rely on the premise of "political self-delusion" that motivates almost all candidates, who believe they will be chosen. I began to propose an honest election, monitored by The Carter

Center, and to encourage both adversaries to convince themselves that they would be the winning candidate. Following this strategy, we began to monitor elections in Latin America and soon were being asked to work in other countries around the world. Our role is to help nations to develop democratic societies by empowering their citizens. We also are a leader in improving election standards. Our normal routine is to send from four to six long-term observers into a country for an extended period in advance of the election, to learn everything possible about the country's history, geography, government, and politics, and to become acquainted with political parties, candidates, and issues. They assess the registration of voters and the integrity and competence of the central election commission. Several days before the election, we send between forty and eighty short-term observers, and they receive a crash course from the long-term observers and are dispersed to key voting areas in pairs, each with an automobile and driver, an interpreter if needed, and a radio or mobile phone. We visit as many polling sites as possible, and the observer teams make reports to me, Rosalynn, or our other leaders, who remain in the capital city.

The Carter Center has developed a handheld electronic tablet similar to a Kindle that permits each observer to make immediate reports on the situation at each site. We call the device ELMO (*el*ection *mo*nitor). After we consolidate and assess information from all observers, we make an announcement about whether the election process has been fair and free, accurately representing the will of the people who voted. The Tunisia presidential election in December 2014 was the ninety-ninth we have observed, and we normally complete three or four of these assignments each year.

ROSALYNN'S AGENDA

Rosalynn has been a full partner with me in establishing and governing The Carter Center, joining me as an observer of troubled elections, negotiating peace agreements, and making final decisions concerning our other projects. In addition, she has proceeded with her own agenda. She has maintained a commitment to mental health for more than forty-five years, including a superb program at The Carter Center after our time in the White House. In addition to annual meetings of representatives from all facets of mental health, Rosalynn recruits and educates leading journalists from

America and foreign countries so they can report accurately on the subject. One recent project has been to train 144 psychiatric nurses in Liberia, where there was only one psychiatrist to serve people who have mental problems after decades of intense civil warfare. Rosalynn works to immunize young children throughout America and founded the Rosalynn Carter Institute at Georgia Southwestern State University to promote the status of caregivers. As she points out, "Everyone will be involved as a caregiver, either being one in the past, present, or future, or benefiting eventually from their services."

HABITAT FOR HUMANITY

Our work with Habitat for Humanity has been difficult, unpredictable, exciting, and gratifying. For thirty-one years, Rosalynn and I have led groups of volunteers for a full week of hard work, building and renovating homes for poor families who have never had a decent place to live. The families are required to pay full price for the houses over a period of twenty years, with no interest charges, and payments are invariably less than rental charges in the same general neighborhoods. The families are also expected to put in several hundred

Installing siding on a new home during the 2014 Jimmy & Rosalynn Carter Work Project.

hours of labor on their own or neighbors' homes. This has given us an opportunity to work with these ambitious and hardworking people, and to understand their plight and respect them as equals.

Habitat leaders and I approve the site location and basic design of the homes about a year in advance, and we attempt to simplify the proposed plans. Our normal project includes about one hundred houses, and the goal is to complete construction within five days, beginning on a Monday with just the foundation in place. We adjust the size of the work crews to make this schedule possible, and they range from twelve to thirty-five people, depending on the size of the homes and the type of construction. Our general policy is to alternate our annual work projects between the United States and foreign countries, and we have completed projects in many American states and in Hungary, South Africa, three cities in Mexico, South Korea, Canada, the Philippines, Haiti, China, Vietnam, Laos, Thailand, Cambodia, and South Korea (including in the Demilitarized Zone). In 2015 we plan to build one hundred homes in Pokhara, Nepal.

LIFE AS AN AUTHOR

After writing *Why Not the Best?* in 1974–75 for use in my presidential campaign, and *Keeping Faith: Memoirs of a President* in 1981–82 to explain aspects of my presidency, I found that I enjoyed writing. My books have sold well and provided a much-needed source of income for my family. An ancillary benefit that I didn't anticipate has been a unique opportunity to present my political views and describe our work at The Carter Center. Talk shows and interviews on television, radio, and in newspapers have provided much greater opportunities than my teaching at Emory University or making occasional public speeches.

My next major effort, in 1985, was *The Blood of Abraham,* which was based on my extensive travel in the Middle East, where I met with key leaders, took careful notes of their personal opinions about the prospect of a comprehensive peace, and compiled this information from Israel, Egypt, Lebanon, Jordan, Syria, Saudi Arabia, and the Palestinians.

We had a major consultation at The Carter Center in 1984, which we called Closing the Gap. This analyzed the difference between what medical experts and individuals knew how to do and what they actually achieved. Afterward, Rosalynn and I decided to coauthor a book, *Everything to Gain,* focusing on personal health, and how the major determining factor was often a person's own habits and success or failure in adopting universally accepted health information. Writing this book together evolved into the worst threat we ever experienced to our marriage. We divided the chapters between us, and each was to write the text and submit it to the other for editing. I write very rapidly, and Rosalynn treated my chapters as rough drafts. She writes slowly and carefully, and considers the resulting sentences as though they have come down from Mount Sinai, carved into stone. It is painful for her to see them modified in any way. Another difference was that we didn't always remember events in the same way or treat them with equal importance. We had constant arguments and could communicate with each other only through harsh e-mails. When we decided to cancel the project and return the publisher's advance payment, our editor came to Plains and proposed that he divide the controversial paragraphs between us — as unilateral authors without the other's input. In the book, each of these paragraphs is identified by a "J" or an "R," and our marriage survived.

My next book, in 1988, was a labor of love. *An Outdoor Journal* was about my experiences with nature, beginning with my boyhood and extending from our farm to trout streams and mountains in Alaska, Argentina, Japan, and Nepal. *Turning Point,* in 1992, described my first political venture, when an election was stolen from me by a dishonest official who stuffed the ballot box, voted dead people, and browbeat other local officials. That same year, Dutton requested that I write a book, which could be used as a textbook, about the causes of conflicts and techniques used to resolve them. I used some of my own experiences to illustrate the points I made in *Talking Peace: A Vision for the Next Generation.*

Soon after I left the White House I met Miller Williams and some other poets from Arkansas, and they encouraged me to prepare some of my poems for publication. I did this over a period of several years, and *Always a Reckoning* was published in 1995. My poetry advisers were tough critics of my submitted lines, but our agreement precluded their making specific suggestions of a word or phrase. Both the publisher and I have been surprised at the book's success.

My daughter, Amy, was enrolled in the Memphis College of Art in 1994, and one of her assignments was to illustrate a story for children. As a submarine officer with small boys at home, I had developed adventures of an imaginary sea monster called Little Baby Snoogle-Fleejer, which I recounted to them after returning from cruises at sea. I wrote one of the stories as a text, and Amy painted thirteen scenes in the book.

I was teaching Bible lessons every Sunday in my local church and decided to describe my religious beliefs and experiences in two books, *Living Faith* and *Sources of Strength,* which were published in 1996 and 1997.

By 1998 I was approaching my seventy-fifth birthday, and, considering how enjoyable and gratifying my experiences had been since my "retirement" from politics, I decided to write a book entitled *The Virtues of Aging.* Some jokesters commented that it would be the shortest book ever written. Describing how much unprecedented freedom we have to undertake new projects after we no longer have to meet a regular work schedule, the book has been quite popular.

I completed another book in 2001 that concentrated on how we celebrated Christmas over the years of my life, after having groups of black and white older people come to our home to share their own memories in *Christmas in Plains.*

I decided to write a book just about my boyhood on a farm, with almost all our neighbors being African-American, and was delighted when it was a finalist for a Pulitzer Prize in 2002. *An Hour Before Daylight* has aroused more written and verbal comments than any of my other books, primarily from people who had the same kind of early life as children of farmers, whether in America or in other countries.

I received the Nobel Peace Prize in 2002 and shared my acceptance speech with

Simon & Schuster in advance, so they were able to publish the small book at the same time as the award. Because of the subject and the relatively low price, this book has sold more copies than any others I have written.

I had always been concerned about the lack of history texts or historical novels that presented a balanced and accurate account of major military actions during the Revolutionary War. Knowing of my own ancestors' histories, I did extensive research for seven years, using personal accounts of participants in the American and British military forces. This was in pre-Google years, and I sometimes had dozens of library books on my shelf at a time. Readers of *The Hornet's Nest* from around the world have let me know how they have been surprised and pleased at this view from the South-land, where almost all the major battles were fought.

Many people asked if Rosalynn and I worked all the time or if we ever had time for fun and relaxation, so I wrote *Sharing Good Times* in 2004. I described the many things we have taken up together for the first time at a relatively advanced age, including downhill skiing, mountain climb-ing, bird watching, and fly-fishing in many countries.

I was especially concerned about some of the policies of our government and wanted an opportunity to discuss them publicly, so I wrote *Our Endangered Values* in 2005 to express my views on unnecessary wars, derogation of women and girls, excessive incarceration and the death penalty, unwarranted intrusion on citizens' privacy, the rise of fundamentalism in government, and the intrusion of religion and excessive money into politics. It was critical of some federal government policies and disturbing violations of the Universal Declaration of Human Rights, the Geneva principles concerning warfare, and other international standards that we claim to honor.

Palestine Peace Not Apartheid, published in 2006, has been my most controversial book, not because of its content but because of its title. The next year I finished writing a book about the work we had done at The Carter Center entitled *Beyond the White House.* In 2008, I wrote a book about my mother, who was a registered nurse, a dedicated political activist, and a Peace Corps volunteer in India at the age of seventy. She never observed the principle of white supremacy when I was growing up in the Deep South, which helped shape my commitment to the protection of human rights.

We Can Have Peace in the Holy Land, which proposed a specific plan for peace between Israel and its neighbors, was published in 2009.

I compiled a fairly complete volume of highly personal comments from the day-to-day diary I kept while serving as president. Entitled *White House Diary,* and published in 2010, it included many observations that had been too sensitive or personal to include in *Keeping Faith* several decades earlier.

By 2011 I had taught more than six hundred Bible lessons, which had been recorded in audio and video form and stored in a refrigerated space in my presidential library. I selected 366 of them, and an editor from Zondervan summarized each of the recordings. I edited them down to page-length versions for *Through the Year with Jimmy Carter* with a religious statement for each day. I also provided about two hundred comments to be included throughout a New International Version of the scriptures entitled *NIV Lessons from Life Bible: Personal Reflections with Jimmy Carter,* published in 2012.

My most recent book, *A Call to Action: Women, Religion, Violence, and Power*

(2014), is, I think, the most important. We have held two Human Rights Defenders Forums on the subject at The Carter Center, and a third will take place before this book is released. In my book I described in some detail the horrendous abuse of women and girls that is occurring in almost every nation and made twenty-three recommendations of action that can be taken to alleviate this abuse.

Writing and promoting the sale of these books has given me an opportunity to study a wide range of subjects in great detail, to analyze what I have learned, and to present my views to the general public in America and many foreign countries. This has also provided my best opportunities for interviews with the media, and to answer questions from students and others who hear my presentations. As I write this, in November 2014, I have made recent speeches to overflow crowds at the Kennedy Presidential Library, in San Diego to ten thousand members of the American Academy of Religion, to a larger assembly sponsored by the Islamic Society of North America in Denver, and to students and faculty at Harvard Divinity School, Yale, and Princeton. All the universities are dealing with alleged excessive sexual assaults on campus, with relative impunity to the rapists. I have summarized *A Call to Action,* answered questions from the audience, and then signed copies of the book.

Most of my family's income since leaving the White House has come from the books I have written. Although my time in Plains is limited because of active involvement in the affairs of The Carter Center, Emory University, and Habitat for Humanity, I try to take full advantage of my days at home. I visit our farms regularly, consult with our forester and the farmers who grow the row crops, and take care of routine matters around our house. I teach Bible lessons every Sunday I am at home, and Rosalynn and I are active in the affairs of the local community. On a relatively free day, I get up quite early in the morning and spend as many hours as possible writing on the computer. When I get tired of composing paragraphs and looking at the screen, I walk a few steps out to my workshop to design and build furniture or to paint pictures.

WOODWORKING AND PAINTING

I found a nice wood shop at Camp David, which I used a lot on the weekends, mostly to make small items as presents for friends and members of my family. Many people knew about this interest, and my going-away present from the White House staff and cabinet members was an order to Sears, Roebuck for all the power tools needed to build furniture. Since we no longer owned an automobile, I installed the equipment in our former garage, and during the past thirty-five years I have updated the lathes, jointers, drill presses, planers, and various saws as needed. I also have a complete set of hand tools, and have enjoyed shopping for them in foreign countries, especially Japan.

I restricted my travels during our first year at home, other than to a transition office in Atlanta, where our presidential library and The Carter Center were being planned. Our house and lot had deteriorated badly during our four years in Washington, and this gave us a lot to do. We acquired a half interest in twenty-one acres in the North Georgia mountains and had a small log cabin built alongside Turniptown Creek. I designed and built all the beds, chairs, tables, storage cabinets, and smaller fixtures needed to furnish our "second home." I made stools and dining room chairs out of green wood, using Colonial-era techniques that required only hand tools and did not include nails, screws, or glue to hold the pieces together. I

The woodworking and artwork have been personal pleasures for me, and I expect that an expanding part of my life will be devoted to them as I grow older and have fewer activities away from home.

built four ladder–back hickory chairs that were auctioned at Sotheby's in October 1983 for $21,000 each to help fund The Carter Center.

This began a long process of my contributing a piece of furniture almost every year to our Center to be sold at auction. During recent years I have donated one of my original paintings, or a copy, for the same purpose. Winning bids have ranged from $50,000 to $1 million. In addition, I have given much of my furniture to my children and grandchildren, with cradles being used several times. I realized many years ago that I do not have any special talent as an artist or craftsman, but with a lot of study and practice I have become fairly proficient. More recently, I have written an explanation of techniques and materials used and my reasons for painting particular subjects, and these texts will accompany about sixty-five of my paintings in a high-quality coffee table book, to be sold at an elevated price with the proceeds going to The Carter Center.

The woodworking and artwork have been personal pleasures for me, and I expect that an expanding part of my life will be devoted to them as I grow older and have fewer activities away from home.

FORMER PRESIDENTS

Richard Nixon and Gerald Ford were the two living presidents when I was elected, and I was determined to treat them with respect, to keep them as thoroughly briefed on current events as possible, and to call on them to help me with challenging issues when bipartisan cooperation would be important. President Nixon was in a state of partial disrepute as a result of the Watergate scandals and his forced resignation from office, and he was maintaining a high degree of family privacy. I admired him for his accomplishments while in office, especially regarding environmental issues and his opening relations with China. I knew President Ford to be a formidable political adversary from our contested campaign, exceptionally knowledgeable about congressional affairs, and a completely honorable and dedicated public servant.

I began giving both of them regular briefings on domestic and international affairs, from either National Security Adviser Brzezinski or one of my other top assistants. They responded by offering to help me on controversial issues and did so throughout my term. This is a diary entry I made on March 24, 1977:

"President Ford came by and our scheduled thirty-minute meeting lasted three times as long. He expressed concerns about deficits, which I share. He also met Dr. Brzezinski and arranged for continuing briefings concerning international affairs."

After about six months, Nixon sent me word that the briefings were excessive and asked that they be provided only when he requested more information on specific subjects. President Ford relished the visits, and he and I had an agreement that he would spend some time with me in the Oval Office whenever he was near Washington.

Anwar Sadat was assassinated in October 1981 by militant terrorists, and President Reagan and Vice President George H. W. Bush decided not to attend the funeral. Instead, we three former presidents were given this honor, and we traveled to Cairo

Ronald Reagan Library Dedication, November 4, 1991, at Simi Valley, California. Lady Bird Johnson, the Carters, the Fords, the Nixons, the Reagans, and the Bushes.

on a government plane. Nixon stayed in the region, and Ford and I returned together. We shared a small compartment and spent most of the trip in an increasingly personal conversation. Somewhat to our surprise, we formed an intimate friendship that extended to our wives and children. I remember that when we assembled at the White House in 2000 to celebrate its two-hundredth year as the president's home, the historians commented that the relationship between Jerry Ford and Jimmy Carter was closer than any other presidents, at least in recent history, who had served there. During the summer of 2006 I received a regular call from Jerry, and after an exchange of good wishes he said he had a special favor to ask of me. I agreed in advance. He asked if I would give the eulogy at his funeral. After stammering for a few moments, I responded that I would do so if he would make me the same commitment. A few months later, I was grieved but honored to fulfill my promise.

Unfortunately, my relationship with President Ronald Reagan was strained, and on several early trips abroad during his administration I learned that the U.S. ambassadors had been instructed not to give me any assistance or even to acknowledge my presence. This happened in Turkey, Argentina, and several African nations. My early requests to the president for briefings on key issues were declined or ignored, and when I threatened to call a press conference on the subject, I received a briefing that was largely extracted from current news reports. However, I got along well with Reagan's five national security advisers and with Secretary of State George Shultz. Especially on my frequent visits to the Middle East region, I would be requested to deliver messages or questions to leaders and was often invited to come to the State Department to make a personal report on my observations.

My best and most enjoyable experience with presidents was with George H. W. Bush and his secretary of state, James Baker. Throughout their term in office, they used the resources of our Center as fully as possible, encouraged our involvement in politically sensitive areas, and even sent a plane to bring me directly to the White House for a report after some of my foreign visits.

President Bill Clinton never initiated any request for cooperation with The Carter Center, but he responded to some of my proposals. I appreciated these opportunities for us to help alleviate international tension by accepting requests from contending parties to mediate disputes.

After the contested election in 2000, where the Supreme Court prevented the recount of all Florida votes and ruled that George W. Bush was the elected president, we decided to attend the inaugural ceremonies in January. There were few "voluntary" Democrats present, and the Bush family members were gracious to us. The new president Bush asked if there was anything he could do for me, and I made my only request of him: that he attempt to complete the peace agreement between North and South Sudan, on which our Center had been working for many years but which had been blocked by previous White House policies. He agreed, and kept his promise. As I increasingly promoted the concepts of peace and human rights in my books, classroom lectures, public statements, and forums, it was inevitable that some differences on these issues would surface. Once President Bush invited me to the White House for a full report to him and his national security adviser after I visited Cuba.

Because I had been out of office for more than three decades when Barack Obama became president, there were few opportunities for a direct association between

The Carter Center and the White House. During this period I have enjoyed friendly and adequate contacts with Secretaries of State Hillary Clinton and John Kerry. Since we maintain an active role in the Holy Land, this has been especially important to us after Secretary Kerry renewed the U.S. effort to bring peace to the region. An additional reason for a reduced relationship with the White House is that the primary work of The Carter Center has shifted over the years from peace negotiations to controlling and eliminating tropical diseases and monitoring troubled elections.

On most occasions, Rosalynn and I have attended the national Democratic conventions and always the inaugurations of new presidents. In fact, it was on one of these occasions, twelve years after I left office, that I met my first Democratic president: when Bill Clinton was inaugurated.

A FUTURE AMERICA

The United States is facing an inevitable reduction in its relative global influence with the rise in economic and political strength of China, India, Brazil, South Africa, and other nations. My hope is that our leaders will capitalize on our country's most admirable qualities. When people in other nations face a challenge or a problem, it would be good to have them look to Washington for assistance or as a sterling example.

Our government should be known to be opposed to war, dedicated to the resolution of disputes by peaceful means, and, whenever possible, eager to accomplish this goal. We should be seen as the unswerving champion of human rights, both among our own citizens and within the global community. America should be the focal point around which other nations can rally against threats to the quality of our common environment. We should be willing to lead by example in sharing our great wealth with those in need. Our own society should provide equal opportunity for all citizens and assure that they are provided the basic necessities of life.

There would be no sacrifice in exemplifying these traits. Instead, our nation's well-being would be enhanced by restoring the trust, admiration, and friendship that our nation formerly enjoyed among other peoples. At the same time, all Americans could be united in a common commitment to revive and nourish the political and moral values that we have espoused and sought during the past 240 years.

It seems, at least in retrospect, that all the phases of my life have been challenging, but successful and enjoyable. My early childhood on a farm in Archery during the Great Depression, mostly isolated with my own family and my black playmates, was relatively deprived compared to life with modern-day advantages. Still, I have the fondest memories of those days, even without running water or electricity and when I was required to work as hard as anyone. There was a warm and protected feeling, encapsulated with my parents and siblings, and it is hard to remember the discomforts or unpleasant family relationships.

My years in college and the navy were especially gratifying, as Rosalynn and I set up housekeeping and welcomed our growing family. The hardships I shared with my peers were tempered by my enjoyable experiences, and I reached every goal that a young officer could desire. My submarine service was good training in meeting challenges, and an item that appealed to voters when I ran for public office.

As a farmer and businessman for seventeen years, I established a sound financial base for my family, learned how to deal with hundreds of customers, and formed a long overdue partnership with Rosalynn in all the aspects of life.

I have already discussed my years in public office, and I am grateful for having that experience. I am at peace with the accomplishments, regret the unrealized goals, and utilize my former political position to enhance everything we do in our later years.

The life we have now is the best of all. We have an expanding and harmonious family, a rich life in our church and the Plains community, and a diversity of projects at The Carter Center that is adventurous and exciting. Rosalynn and I have visited more than 145 countries, and both of us are as active as we have ever been. We are blessed with good health and look to the future with eagerness and confidence, but are prepared for inevitable adversity when it comes.

ACKNOWLEDGMENTS

I am very grateful to Alice Mayhew and the other editors and designers at Simon & Schuster. This is the twelfth book that they have helped with their beneficial suggestions and questions. For more than thirty-five years, Dr. Steven Hochman has closely examined the texts of my books, to help ensure their accuracy and clarity, and the contributions of my wife, Rosalynn, have been invaluable. My secretary, Lauren Gay, has joined the staff of our presidential library in helping to choose the paintings and photographs that are interspersed throughout the book.

ILLUSTRATION CREDITS

Courtesy of the author and artist, pages 19, 21, 32, 36, 52, 68, 270, 360, 366, 403.

Courtesy of the Jimmy Carter Presidential Library, Carter Family Photo Collection, pages 91, 97, 213.

Courtesy of the United States Navy, page 107.

Courtesy of Charles Rafshoon, page 131.

Courtesy of the Jimmy Carter Presidential Library, pages 145, 205, 341, 406.

Photograph by Louise Gubb, page 372.

Courtesy of Habitat for Humanity International. Photograph by Ezra Millstein, page 391.

ABOUT THE AUTHOR

Jimmy Carter was the thirty-ninth President of the United States, serving from 1977 to 1981. In 1982, he and his wife founded The Carter Center, a nonprofit organization dedicated to improving the lives of people around the world. Carter was awarded the Nobel Peace Prize in 2002. He is the author of over two-dozen books, including *An Hour Before Daylight; Palestine: Peace Not Apartheid* and *Our Endangered Values.* He lives in Plains, Georgia.